Aare Lund

Christmas, 1947.
R.

JOHN BUCHAN
BY HIS WIFE
AND FRIENDS

A

Books by John Buchan

John Buchan.
Bust by Thos. J. Clapperton, F.R.B.S., Sculptor.

JOHN BUCHAN
BY HIS WIFE
AND FRIENDS

With a Preface by
GEORGE M. TREVELYAN, O.M.

HODDER AND STOUGHTON
LIMITED LONDON

FIRST PRINTED 1947

PRINTED IN GREAT BRITAIN FOR
HODDER AND STOUGHTON LIMITED LONDON
BY T. AND A. CONSTABLE LIMITED EDINBURGH

FOREWORD

I SHOULD like to thank my husband's friends who have helped me with this book. I could never have written my part of it had I not been sustained by their co-operation and approval.

Two of the contributors, Catherine Carswell and Professor Roger Merriman, died before the book went to press. It is a lasting regret to me that they cannot see what they wrote in print. But I am glad that they knew of the appreciation and gratitude of myself and my family for what they had written.

I should like to thank Messrs. Constable for allowing me to use the extracts from Mr. Howard Spring's book *In the Meantime*, and also to include extracts from "A Portrait of a Scotsman" by the Right Honourable Walter Elliot, which appeared in his book of re-printed broadcasts called *Long Distance*. My thanks are also due to Dr. Grosvenor of the *National Geographical Magazine* for permission to include extracts from an article which I wrote for that magazine; to the *Scotsman* for permission to use their photograph of Tweedsmuir; to Mr. Spokes for his photograph of my husband's headstone in the churchyard at Elsfield; to Sir Shuldham Redfern for his photograph of the Tweedsmuir Reserve; to Mr. Arthur Turner for his photograph of the Manor at Elsfield; and to the Oxford University Press for their facsimile of a page from one of my husband's manuscripts.

SUSAN TWEEDSMUIR.

CONTENTS

ILLUSTRATIONS

PREFACE

SOME men are great by what they do, others by what they are. The line cannot always be drawn, for in the world of action, personality is a major instrument. And, even in the world of letters, what a man is inspires what he writes. Moreover, personality is in itself a form of achievement, even when confined to a private circle. Conversation can be an art no less than writing books or painting pictures, although it cannot be conveyed to posterity except in the extremely rare case when a Boswell is in attendance.

Nevertheless, in our loose, practical way of talking, we often say of a man that he was greater than his work; of another, that his work was greater than the man. It would be hard to place John Buchan in either of these classes. The man and his work run an even race. And the two seem inseparable. Lord Tweedsmuir made his Governorship an asset to Canada and to the Empire because he was John Buchan, eager to explore every scene, and giving the best of himself to all whom he chanced to meet. His romances are popular because they embody that zest for the adventure of life which was the most characteristic quality of their author. The part he played as Lord High Commissioner to the General Assembly of the Church of Scotland "when he kept court in Holyrood," and his volume on Walter Scott, were two of the best pieces of his work in life, because in that action and in that book he gave expression to the Scottish side of what he was—the loyal, pious and self-disciplined child of the Manse, and the romantic lover of Scottish history and of the Border country, with the large heart and out-of-doors affections of "the Shirra."

Whenever I saw John Buchan, even in later years when illness did what illness could to clog his activity, I always felt ashamed in his presence that I was not more active, that I did not make more of the wonderful and variegated world of nature and of man, of past and of present, that was our common heritage. One's own little fire was feeble beside his sunlike warmth, but it was part of the world which meant so much to him, and his interest in one seemed to add to one's value. How many men and women of all sorts and conditions have come away from seeing John Buchan feeling just like that, going back the stronger to meet the world and wave of men. Mrs. Carswell, a sincere and a skilful writer, has admirably described (p. 154) the effect of an interview with John Buchan.

And her description of his face is the best I know:

The scar from an accident in childhood drew attention to the strikingly noble contours of his head. The long, queer nose, questing and sagacious as a terrier's, was in odd contrast with the lean, scholarly cheeks and with the mouth narrowed as by concentration or the hint of pain subdued. A peculiar countenance, subtle, in no respect trivial.

To this let me add Mr. Rowse's description (p. 175):

That quick, spare, gallant figure, with the grave face and frosty Northern eyes that could yet sparkle with liveliness and good-humour, with his old-fashioned Scots courtesy and birdlike quickness of movement.

This book, by his wife and others, is a supplement, complementary to that noble autobiography, *Memory Hold-the-Door*. I hope that all who look into this volume will read that other, if they have not done so yet. The two books together go far towards depicting the man, the inner growth of his mind and power, and the outer workings of his contact with the world.

There are many beautiful passages in John Buchan's books, particularly many beautiful descriptions of places and landscapes, but I doubt if he ever wrote anything better than his chapter on the Border hills, entitled "The Springs" and printed at the end of *Memory Hold-the-Door*. It was probably the last thing he wrote, so he had by no means exhausted himself as an author. It is too long to quote here; but I believe that in an Introduction to this new volume I can usefully quote two other passages from his autobiography, because they help to the full understanding of the account rendered of him below by others. Given the pious training of the Manse at its best, which also he has fully described, given his wise and excellent father and his wonderful mother, what were the further influences that formed him in his youth? On pp. 23-24 of *Memory Hold-the-Door* he writes:

As I advanced in years I became less interested in those fanciful nooks than in the hills themselves, where the shepherds lived and wrought. I had my first introduction to an old and happy world. I would be out at dawn to "look the hill," delighting in the task, especially if the weather were wild. I attended every clipping, where shepherds came from ten miles round to lend a hand. I helped to drive sheep to the local market and sat, heavily responsible, in a corner of the auction-ring. I became learned in the talk of the trade, and no bad judge of sheep stock. Those Border shepherds, the men of the long stride and the clear eye, were a great race—I have never known a greater. The narrower kinds of fanaticism, which have run riot elsewhere in Scotland, rarely affected the Borders. Their people were "grave livers," in Wordsworth's phrase, God-fearing, decent in all the relations of life, and supreme masters of their craft. They were a fighting stock because of their ancestry, and of a noble independence. As the source of the greatest ballads in any literature they had fire and imagination, and some aptitude for the graces of life. They lacked the dourness of the conventional Scot, having

13

a quick eye for comedy, and, being in themselves wholly secure, they were aristocrats with the fine manners of an aristocracy. By them I was admitted into the secrets of a whole lost world of pastoral. I acquired a reverence and affection for the "plain people," who to Walter Scott and Abraham Lincoln were what mattered most in the world. I learned the soft, kindly, idiomatic Border speech. My old friends, by whose side I used to quarter the hills, are long ago at rest in moorland kirkyards, and my salutation goes to them beyond the hills of death. I have never had better friends, and I have striven to acquire some tincture of their philosophy of life, a creed at once mirthful and grave, stalwart and merciful.

And when he went from Glasgow University to Oxford, what happened to him there? Again he tells us (pp. 86-87) :

During my four years at Oxford I read hard and finished with a considerable stock of miscellaneous knowledge. That mattered little, but the trend which my mind acquired mattered much. Generally speaking, I accepted the brand of idealism which was then fashionable, that derived from Thomas Hill Green, and expounded in my day by F. A. Bradley, and H. H. Joachim. More and more I became sceptical of dogmas, looking upon them as questions rather than answers. Philosophy did not give us solutions, but it taught us to ask the right questions, about which we could cheerfully go on disputing until the dawn put our candles out. The limited outlook of my early youth had broadened. Formerly I had regarded life as a pilgrimage along a strait and steep path on which the pilgrim must keep his eyes fixed. I prided myself on a certain moral austerity, but now I came to realise that there was a good deal of self-interest in that outlook, like the Puritan who saw in his creed not only the road to Heaven but the way to worldly success. I began to be attracted by the environs as well as by the road, and I became more charitable in my judgment of things and men.

I had some of my Gothic corners smoothed away, but I still had a good many angles, and there remained a large spice of the Shorter Catechist in my make-up. Just as my walks were not random contemplative saunters, but attempts to get somewhere, so a worthy life seemed to me to be a series of efforts to conquer intractable matter, to achieve something difficult and perhaps dangerous. Much as I detested Napoleon, I was for him, as against Thackeray in his "Ballad of the Drum":

> "Come fill me one more glass of wine
> And give the silly fools their will."

Even a perverse career of action seemed to me better than a tippling of ale in the shade, for that way lay the cockney suburbanism which was my secret terror. Again, while I was very conscious of man's littleness in face of the eternal, I believed profoundly in his high destiny. Human beings were compounded of both heavenly and hellish elements, with infinite possibilities of sorrow and joy. In consequence I had an acute sense of sin, and a strong hatred of whatever debased human nature. The conception of mankind, current in some quarters, as a herd of guzzling, lecherous little mammals seemed to me the last impiety.

Had I wished it, I could have stayed on and taught philosophy. But at the end of my fourth year I had come to feel that I was not sufficiently devoted to any branch of learning to give up my life to it, either as don or professor. I wanted a stiffer job, one with greater hazards in it, and I was not averse to one which offered bigger material rewards. The supreme advantage of Oxford to me was that it enabled me to discover what talents I had and what I really wanted to do. Horizons had extended and revealed a surprising number of things which woke my curiosity. I wanted to explore the wider stages of life. Besides, I had become attached to the study of law, and under the inspiration of a great scholar, the late A. H. J. Greenidge, had taken a lively interest in the most arid details of the Greek and Roman legal systems.

So I decided that my profession should be the Bar.

But it was not to be the Bar. He was to be administrator, King's representative, publisher, writer of romances, biographer and historian. I am best fitted to appreciate and criticise his performance as biographer and historian. For that reason his historical biographies are for me the greatest of his works. And the analysis of their merits in the fine essay by Mr. Rowse (pp. 174-187 below) fortifies my own opinion of their excellence. In our age, when so much popular interest is taken in history but when so many histories are written only for specialists, men are required who are at once good popular writers and real historical scholars. There are not a few, but among them John Buchan was pre-eminent.

It was the life-work of two great scholars of a previous generation, Gardiner and Firth, to discover the facts of Cromwell's life in relation to the complex pattern of the events with which he strove to deal. But their books were falling out of popular recollection when Buchan, using their work and knowing also the contemporary sources with intimate affection, drew the best of all pictures of Cromwell as a man, setting forth the peculiar and complicated quality of his greatness and its flaws, in a biography which has attained the popularity it deserved. Moreover, Book I of his *Oliver Cromwell* gives the best account I know of the fundamental causes and issues of our great Civil War.

It is remarkable that it was another Scot, Carlyle, who first dug up the statue of the great Englishman from the muck-heap in which his own countrymen had for two centuries kept him buried. With a more catholic sympathy and shrewder understanding of mixed human motives, this latter-day Scot does equal justice to Cromwell, none the less that he is also the lover and biographer of Montrose. All greatness, all excellent achievement and noble failure are grist to John Buchan's mill.

Classical historians have told that his *Augustus* is as scholarly as it is readable and profound, and I can well believe it. But after all, his *Walter Scott* bears the gree. It is not only the best one-volumed book on Scott, but the best one-volumed biography in the language. He was born and bred to write it.

All men, women and children are equally able to judge his romances, measured by their own enjoyment of them. No one needs to be told to enjoy *Prester John*, or the Richard Hannay and the war stories, or to appreciate Dickson McCunn and the Gorbals Die-Hards. Many of these tales were written on a couch of sickness, to supply the common human need of story-telling, in him a born instinct. Their number, their profusion is amazing. Here is God's plenty! All the tales are enriched by a poet's love of the scenes of nature in every land, many by an historian's power of imagining the past. My own favourite, though not the public's, is *The Path of the King*, a prose poem, that only a fine historian could have written, on the wonder and mystery of the past and the sequence of the ages.

Despising literary coteries, though always at hand to help individual men of letters, avoiding the squabbles and narrownesses to which "intellectuals" of all periods are too prone, he claimed no "privilege of genius" to fail in duty to others. Perfect in all the relations of life, as son and brother, husband and father, friend and colleague, in all these capacities and as writer for the public whom he served so well, he had his full measure of reward : he too might have said at the close—

> My heart doth joy that yet in all my life
> I found no man but he was true to me.

GEORGE M. TREVELYAN.

JOHN BUCHAN

CHAPTER I

MY OWN BACKGROUND

I

SINCE the publication of *Memory Hold - the - Door* members of John Buchan's family have received many letters asking to hear more about him.

In writing his autobiography he set out to make a record of a mental and spiritual pilgrimage, and he has made no mention of certain matters which are of interest to the readers of his books.

He has drawn portraits of his friends and his parents, but has said little or nothing about the rest of his family and daily life.

The aim of this book is to fill in some of the gaps, and while in *Memory Hold-the-Door* he paints portraits of his friends, in this book I and some of his friends are painting, or trying to paint, a portrait of the man they knew.

Harold Nicolson has written some brilliant sentences about what he calls "the widow or family biography," showing only too clearly how hard it is for a wife to write with balance and detachment about her husband after his death. In spite of this I am contributing my quota to this book, as there are aspects of my husband's character on which I can throw more light than anyone else and which are of interest to those who want to know more about John Buchan.

My husband's childhood and early youth have been well portrayed in *Memory Hold-the-Door* and also in *Unforgettable, Unforgotten*, by his sister Anna Buchan. I shall therefore not attempt to write any more about them.

All I know about their delightful childhood is hearsay, as I never met John Buchan until his return from South Africa. I can only add to what has been said that I am certain that what they wrote about their childhood is strictly true, for they have as a family the power of extracting the maximum of interest from everything they do. The fact that their means were small never prevented them for a moment from having amusing adventures.

I remember thinking enviously how much more fun and freedom the Buchan family had had in childhood than my sister and myself. We were brought up in an atmosphere of young ladyhood with all the restrictions and taboos of the later Victorian era.

John's fame had reached me before we met. The set of young men of which he was a member came down from Oxford with an awe-inspiring reputation for brilliance. This was matched by another group of young men nearly all killed in the 1914-1918 war. It has been my fate to meet a cross-section of undergraduates at Oxford since 1919. Many of the young men who came to our house have made their mark in the world, but never since then has there been that galaxy of talent contemporaneously at Oxford.

When John was at Oxford, it was in a way a kind of golden age when life held out pleasant and even glittering prizes for young men. Some of my husband's contemporaries were going into prosperous family businesses. But the majority knew that if they were penniless but able, there were many careers open to them.

Oxford life was not clouded by anxiety for the future. If you had good health and even only a reasonable amount of brains you could feel confident of making a living for yourself and of having a varied and interesting life.

This security gave to the undergraduates of those days a power of careless enjoyment never again recaptured after the 1918 war. It gave them time to cultivate friendships and to go in for exuberant "rags" and to start fantastic clubs with elaborate rituals.

There were no telephones or motor-cars to complicate life and to draw Oxford into the stream of the great world. It was something set apart and to be savoured and enjoyed, which the young men did to the full. They also worked surprisingly hard (more perhaps in vacation than term time), and took University honours and prizes apparently in their stride.

Eccentricity was encouraged. J. G. Jameson [1] could be found in the evening sitting in a room filled with books, bottles and boxing-gloves, with his fencing-foil bared on the table while he read his Bible. Aubrey Herbert,[2] whose eyesight was none of the best, pursued his progress over the roofs of the colleges, singing Italian love songs while he did so.

It was rumoured that when Johnnie Jameson took his essay to his tutor Hilaire Belloc they shared a bottle of beer or port to remove any dryness from the proceedings.

Boredom seems to have been rare, and bores almost non-existent in that happy world.

My husband began by being too poor to dine in hall, and ended his Oxford career extremely wealthy for an undergraduate, owing to having made money by writing whilst he was there and reading for two publishers.

But strangely enough no one in those days thought of him as a writer. He was marked out for a brilliant career as a lawyer and politician. His writing was thought by his friends to be an achievement for an undergraduate (for in those days youth did not usually rush into print) as well as a useful way of making money.

[1] Till recently Sheriff Jameson.
[2] Son of the fourth Earl of Carnarvon, one of the most romantic figures of his generation: see *Memory Hold-the-Door*, page 55.

With a happy childhood and those enchanted Oxford years behind him, my husband came to London to make his fortune. In a chapter called "London Interlude" he tells of his start at the Bar and of his going to South Africa with Lord Milner.

II

My husband and I came from very divergent backgrounds and I make no apology for giving a sketch of mine. Any reader upon glancing at a line or two of these pages will see that I am writing about my own family, and can take a reader's privilege of skipping this section if it does not hold his interest and attention.

The house where I lived with my mother and sister, No. 30 Upper Grosvenor Street, was a pleasant habitation. (It has now been pulled down to make way for the Grosvenor House Hotel.) When we lived there Upper Grosvenor Street had a great deal of old-fashioned charm, a charm which is now only a faint memory to a few people. Our house was airy and spacious, with two staircases. Our front staircase, which ran up from the hall, was not in daily use and led up to a pleasant drawing-room which held a large piano and was furnished with a nice mixture of eighteenth-century furniture and some of William Morris's plates on shelves against a dark Morris wallpaper. Our back drawing-room had the Morris willow-pattern paper as a background to my mother's really admirable water-colours.

The whole room was a mixture of old and new, not cluttered up, as were many rooms of that date, with too many objects. There were no signed photographs in silver frames, for instance, as my mother abhorred them. The rooms expressed the taste of the later nineteenth century at its best. It had its demerits, but it also had its good points and was at any rate individual, and not, as many modern rooms, the expression of the taste of a hired decorator.

My father, Norman Grosvenor, died in 1898, leaving to my mother and all who knew him a deep and enduring sense of loss. He was a tall man with brown eyes and a short beard who habitually wore old clothes for choice. He was the youngest son of Lord Robert Grosvenor, who became later the first Lord Ebury. My grandmother was Charlotte Arbuthnot Wellesley, a daughter of Lord Cowley and a niece of the Iron Duke. My grandmother was in her seventies when I first remember her. She had a fine character and a delightful charm of face and manner. Even now her sayings come back to me, and I realise how much she shaped my mind and point of view.

My grandmother had a strong face, with the incisive Wellesley nose and clear blue eyes. Like her son, she wore old clothes from choice and she disliked people who wore diamonds in the daytime. She was always a little aloof from her surroundings, seeming to our childish eyes infinitely younger and more charming than her daughters. She used to tell me about Uncle Arthur (the Duke of Wellington), whom she had deeply loved.

A great deal of my childhood was spent at Moor Park where my grandparents lived in Hertfordshire. It was a large Palladian house in a beautiful park, the home of romance and adventure to the group of cousins who romped there. My father was the youngest of a large family. For his mother he had a deep and tender devotion, for his father an affectionate tolerance. His eldest brother [1] was an extremely able man of business, who became Chairman of the Army and Navy Stores

[1] The second Lord Ebury.

23

at a time when the peerage did not enter into business concerns, preferring law or politics. My other two uncles were, after office hours, excellent golfers, skaters and cricketers. It is a strange fact that no one in the next generation could do anything with a ball except drop it (the only exception being Francis Grosvenor, later the fourth Lord Ebury, who played an excellent game of polo).

My father's older sisters, Victoria and Albertine, both had compelling personalities. They were an amusing contrast, as Auntie Sis, so-called, was tall and immensely stout, while Auntie B. was small and exceptionally thin. Auntie Sis was good-humoured and masterful, and Auntie B. unselfish to a point which occasionally drove her relatives to the verge of frenzy.

Both my father's sisters worked unremittingly for the welfare of the community. Auntie Sis's room held a big official-looking writing-table with many pigeon-holes bulging with documents. From there she conducted the affairs of the G.F.S. and other activities. Tommy Grosvenor, my father's second brother, died of pneumonia when he was at the Embassy in St. Petersburg. He married Sophie, daughter of Mr. S. Wells Williams, whom he had met in Peking, where her father was the United States Minister. After his death she came to live with her parents-in-law and was much beloved by them and her nieces. Her clothes and all her appointments were exquisite. She had been strictly brought up in the New England tradition, and she told me that, as a child when she sailed with her mother on a China clipper, she was always running up on deck in the hope of seeing a sea-serpent. She thought she did see one once, but it turned out to be a large twisted tree trunk. However, she was always quickly recalled to their cabin by her mother to finish a fine seam or a piece of cross-stitch.

The whole of the life at Moor Park and at 35 Park Street, my grandparents' town house, was a relic of an earlier and more patriarchal age. For us children it meant fun of all kinds in the shadowy romantic old house and the glades of the park, and the rhododendron-shaded pond in the Pleasure-ground. We enjoyed our friendship with the large staff of servants, whose life appeared to us to be so much more vivid and alluring than that of the elders in our family. The upper servants presided over the stillroom, kitchen, and linen cupboard and laundry, and had lots of favours to distribute in the way of sweets and bits of material for dolls' clothes; while our own family grown-ups pursued uninteresting things like philanthropy and politics, music, which to us meant practising scales on the piano and finger exercises, and drawing, in which they were so expert as to be beyond our efforts with pencils and paints.

After my grandfather's death our life was lived more in London. We thought the metropolis a very dull place after Moor Park. No. 30 Upper Grosvenor Street belonged to the Duke of Westminster, who was my father's first cousin. It stood next door to Grosvenor House, which had two gateways where in the centre of a great deal of scrolled ironwork the family dogs simpered, clasping shields in their paws. Behind the gates was a semi-circular sweep of gravel and a long low house of no special architectural pretensions. We liked the look of the house because it reminded us of houses in the country.

I was an incurably romantic dreamer as a child, and my childhood with its unexciting lessons and long walks in Hyde Park fostered reverie (a shiver of boredom still goes over me when I walk down certain of its paths). But it is only fair to say that, if our lessons and walks were dull, our home had a most stimulating atmosphere.

My father had joined the Grenadier Guards as a young

man, and had enjoyed race meetings and all the gaieties that came his way. However, he came to the conclusion that, as a younger son with a small patrimony, he could not keep up this mode of life, and he entered the Sun Life Insurance Office, where he worked hard and successfully for the rest of his days. He never so far as I know went to another race meeting or ball, and outside office hours devoted himself to music, which was the passion of his life, and my earliest recollections are of hearing him practising scales on his piano through our open nursery door before I went to sleep. His outdoor pursuits were walking and fishing. He went for long tramps over the quiet fields and through woods in the south of England with Leslie Stephen,[1] and a few friends who called themselves the Sunday Tramps, and at other times over moorland hills in the north. But his greatest delight was in fishing, and I have sat for hours as a child reading an Andrew Lang fairy-tale book whilst he fished in the swift waters of the Eden near Naworth Castle, a romantic half-Border keep half-country house where we stayed with Lord Carlisle. Since those days I have sat on many river-banks and in many boats with my husband and sons. It seems to have been my fate to be a companion of anglers.

My father married Caroline Stuart-Wortley, daughter of James Stuart-Wortley,[2] and they settled down in a small house in London, No. 58 Green Street, and they spent part of the year there and part of it at Moor Park. My mother, as I have said, was an artist, and she worked for hours daily in a studio at the top of the house when we moved to 30 Upper Grosvenor Street.

[1] Writer and critic; editor of the *Dictionary of National Biography*.
[2] Right Hon. James Stuart-Wortley, Recorder of London 1850, Solicitor-General 1856. He was third son of the second Baron Wharncliffe.

My father had reacted rather violently from his early environment and the world of great country houses and magnificent parties which he had known as a young man. He became a friend of William Morris and Edward Burne-Jones and found an enormous interest and pleasure in their discussions, which ranged over so many artistic and social fields. He was deeply imbued with a desire to help the labouring classes, and one of his lifelong friends was Charles Booth, who wrote *Life and Labour of the People in London*. It is amusing to think that my father was a complete enigma to many of his relations. He was an agnostic and a Liberal and liked to converse with musicians and artists and radicals. It was all very puzzling and unfashionable, and though his relations invited him to their houses and fell under his charm when they did see him, they thought of him as odd and incomprehensible.

My mother and he were ideally happy, and I owe to them that greatest of all assets, the recollection of a home where there is deep devotion and companionship of the best kind.

My parents gave an occasional dinner-party, but most of my mother's entertaining was done at tea-time in our back drawing-room where, seated on a sofa with a high back, she dispensed tea and sympathetic conversation. In those far-off days many men, and even young men, found the tea hour pleasant and restful. Hubert Howard, whose brilliant career of promise was cut off at Omdurman, his father Lord Carlisle, Sir Alfred Lyall,[1] as well as Hughie Grosvenor who died young, and his brother Bertie Grosvenor, and Sidney Peel,[2] and many others, came and sat talking endlessly (as it seemed to us) to my mother.

[1] Writer and Indian administrator.
[2] Son of the first Lord Peel.

My sister and I cordially detested these visitors. They stayed so long, and even remained to continue their conversation at dinner. We, like most children of that date, were very shy and did not like to venture into company, especially as a liberal amount of ink had distributed itself over our hands after a long day in the schoolroom. We abhorred washing and changing into smart frocks, and becoming presentable members of society. I would relapse into reading, which has always been my escape, and so absorbed did I become in the printed page that I would sit on a staircase with my two plaits of hair sweeping up any dust which was there. Passers-by were driven to shaking me hard before I became aware of them, and I would only then move the necessary inches to let them pass. I was faintly conscious of the clop-clop of the horses drawing hansom cabs in the street, and the voices of people in the house, but these sounds only stirred the edges of my consciousness and I continued to read and re-read my favourite books in a kind of happy trance. I had a small gift for drawing and scribbled a little in secret. My mother encouraged my drawing but was too clear-sighted to overrate my talent for it. She was a good teacher but did not believe in praise. She herself worked steadily, but did not, perhaps, realise that young people have need of the stimulus of encouragement. As for the rest of the family, "Very nice, dear" was their most enthusiastic comment as they laid down one's artistic effort. Sometimes they said, "I think you could do better than that, my child." Neither remark was calculated to inspire me to further effort.

As children we spent a great deal of time with my mother's mother (Mrs. James Stuart-Wortley [1]) at Ripley

[1] My grandmother was *née* Jane Lawley, daughter of the first Lord Wenlock.

House in Surrey; and this house was well called
"rambling," as it started with a large drawing-room, ran
through a hall, twisted itself up a staircase and sped away
down passages with endless little rooms opening out of
them. My grandmother had many lovely and interesting possessions. The family Hoppner of Mrs. Dundas [1]
is now at Wortley Hall. She was that outspoken modern
girl of her day who was nicknamed "Jack" Wortley
(before her marriage), for she was the first woman to
ride, even modestly on a side-saddle, in Rotten Row.
Gone is the ornate and splendid sideboard which Mrs.
Dundas and her husband purchased cheaply on their
honeymoon in Paris from a ruined aristocratic family
just after the French Revolution. Gone are many other
lovely things. I specially regret that I do not possess the
De Wint drawings in a portfolio which I used to look at
on wet afternoons, but my memories of my grandmother
never fail me. She and I had a very real friendship for
each other and we conversed gravely together by the
hour. Old people love to tell stories, and young people
sadly enough do not always want to hear them. But my
grandmother's talk was enthralling. She had been a
great friend of the Sidney Herberts, and Mr. Gladstone had
married her first cousin. She told me often of how Queen
Adelaide used to come and see her aunt Miss Neville
in the morning when her young hostess was ill-prepared
to receive her. Miss Neville had perforce to look after a
bevy of young sisters and brothers as her mother had died.

"Was she lovely?" I asked.

"She had a lovely face," said my grandmother, adding
with sudden severity, "but she had no mother to make her
sit up straight, and she became so round-shouldered as to
be almost hunchbacked."

[1] *Née* Mary Stuart-Wortley, she married in 1813 the Right Hon.
William Dundas, M.P.

I quickly sat up straight. Continual stooping over books and drawing and a weak back had made me round-shouldered. My grandmother held herself even in old age completely erect, my mother's and aunts' backs were irreproachable, and to be round-shouldered was considered in our family nothing short of a crime.

All these and many other tales my grandmother told me. Memory, alas, refuses to hold the door open to them more than a crack so that few can slip through. But I do remember her telling me that two old Miss Nevilles in Napoleonic days on discovering that they were related to Napoleon's mother sent their pedigree up the chimney so that no one should ever know that they were related to Boney—a story which seems now too good to be true.

Apart from her children and grandchildren, my grandmother's passion was for philanthropy and she worked for all sorts of good causes. I remember writing blotted letters in a round hand about emigration and her East End mothers' lying-in home which she dictated to me, when she became too blind to write much herself. Grandmama Stuart-Wortley had a noble and commanding presence. She had not been (my mother said) a good dresser in her youth and middle age, but she evolved a dress for her old age which was as near perfection as possible. On her head she wore a transparent round cap which fitted well down on to her lovely white hair. From it flowed two ample streamers which were fastened by a vast silver brooch on her bosom. She wore alternatively a white or black cashmere shawl, and her dress underneath was black satin with a long voluminous skirt.

In her later years she was one of the features of Ripley High Street in her bath-chair pushed (as her family asserted) by the village idiot, a responsible-looking man who did his job admirably. Although my grandmother had not lived in Ripley for many years before her death, her many kindnesses and her help to everyone there was so much appreciated that the village put up a window in the church to her memory.

As my mother's sister and her brother Charles will come again into this narrative, I will only describe Uncle Archie Stuart-Wortley, my mother's elder brother. He was an artist who had studied under Sir John Millais and painted with the pre-Raphaelite attention to detail without the glow and brilliancy of colour of the pre-Raphaelites. He was, up to a point, a successful portrait-painter, but it has never seemed to me that he had the gift of making his sitters lifelike or interesting. The two exceptions to this are his portraits of the cricketer W. G. Grace, which is a vigorous and imaginative piece of work, now, I believe, in the Pavilion at Lord's, and that of his mother, which hangs on her granddaughter's [1] staircase. I recently saw there a small oil painting of Simonstone, the shooting-box in the Wensleydale hills which once belonged to the Wharncliffes, a place much beloved by us and where we had spent some happy holidays. His painting of the long low house with the fells behind it is an admirable one. One wishes that he had done more work like this.

There was always an atmosphere of excitement in the house at Ripley when Uncle Archie came to stay. He was a brilliant talker and the originator of a great many elaborate practical jokes. He had married a famous beauty—Nellie Bromley—who was the most charming and the least vain of women. We adored her and admired her fashionable clothes, and were awed because she used a delicious scent. She was the easiest person in the world to get on with, and her most frequent saying was "That's right, dear," which banished shyness and produced a pleasant atmosphere. Uncle Archie died after a long

[1] Beatrice Cecil.

illness. His son Jack was the one boy in a cousinhood of brotherless girls, and his company was much sought after by us all.

When my father died at the age of fifty-two, in 1898, the world darkened for us. My mother never got over his loss. We lived on in the same house as before, but much of its spirit and charm had left it.

Soon after he died we went for a spring and summer to Dresden. I cast my mind back many years to its wide streets, picture galleries and Opera House, and I think with an ache of the heart that since I was there as a schoolroom girl there have been two wars with Germany. I remember that my time in Dresden opened new worlds to me, for the Dresden of those days was a place where the art of life was well understood. The opera was admirable, the repertory theatre no less so. Art and literature were recognised as of paramount importance in the life of the community.

We lived in a pension in a charming flat which had spacious rooms and tall windows, opposite the King of Saxony's palace where the sentries presented arms when the royal barouche drove in or out. I studied German and painting, and my sister music and German. We went several evenings a week to the play or the opera, and I got to know the Art Gallery so well that I could have found my way to any picture on its walls. The Opera was always full; it was rare to see anyone in evening dress and umbrellas and goloshes were shed in the cloak-room. The scene was made gay by the brilliant uniforms of the officers, who wore splendid epaulettes.

It was the fashion of the girls in the pension where we lodged with our mother, to have a *schwärm* for an opera-singer. This was strange, as the singers of those days were neither slim nor handsome. I remember that my special *schwärm* was for a tenor with a lovely voice. I still somewhere have a photograph of him, dressed in slightly shabby bearskins with bracelets on his massive arms in the part of Siegfried. He would certainly have got an engagement anywhere on his voice, but I fear not on his looks. My mother's presence kept *schwärmerei* within bounds. She naturally thought it silly.

Looking back, I see now that what was to us a time of excitement and interest must have been for her weeks of dragging loneliness and longing for my father's presence. I too longed for him; but very young people can be distracted from sorrow by new scenes and events.

This German world of quiet pleasures with its love of the things of the mind has gone up in smoke and flames, but I should like to pay my tribute of recollection to the Dresden I remember with its leafy parks, fine buildings, cheerful shops and little homely restaurants, and our sitting-room filled with great branches of lilac through which the sun shone on to the white-tiled stove.

CHAPTER II

OUR FIRST MEETING

AFTER we came back from Dresden my mother had taken up the threads of life again. I started to go into society, and was a frivolous young person with intellectual leanings.

Like many girls of my time, I read seriously for hours each day. It was unthinkable to read a novel in the morning, so I settled down to a history-book or a classic, such as Dante with a crib, and worked my way steadily through it. I also went to a great many lectures and wrote essays. I smile to remember that I went to classes at the Polytechnic and was rewarded by receiving First Class marks for an essay on Dante. I wish I could remember a single word of it now !

My husband and I first met several years after my father's death. We had many mutual friends and one of them brought him to dine at our house.

The polite fashion of the time was for a young man to come and call several days after the dinner-party had taken place. On this particular afternoon my mother was out and I gave the visitor tea. We conversed with difficulty and in an intermittent and stilted manner. This was all the more curious as both of us had usually a great deal to say.

After we became engaged, and in later years, we discussed our first meeting. I found that John thought me haughty, while I thought him conceited and difficult to talk to. Why we should have belied our real characters in this way I cannot imagine.

About this time a story which was circulating in London

was repeated to my mother with sardonic comments by a friend. The President of the Oxford Union (I have forgotten his name) made a speech about Oxford. He enumerated some of the great Oxonians of the past, and added that the Oxford of the late 'nineties was also illustrious. "Had they not got Belloc, Buchan and F. E. Smith?"

All the elders who heard this story retailed it as an instance of the extravagance of youth. Belloc they knew had written some amusing rhymes; Buchan was thought to be a clever and promising young man; but "who on *earth* was F. E. Smith?"[1]

Soon after our first meeting John departed to South Africa on a law case and we did not meet again for about a year. I was very fond of going to balls, but John did not care for dancing, so we seldom saw each other in a ball-room. We met often at dinner-parties, and at Crabbet Park in Sussex where Sir Edward and Lady Ridley welcomed us and other friends. They had leased Crabbet for a term of years. This was a charming and spacious red-brick house, which had a large hall in the centre in which a great deal of our time was spent. There were many pleasant things to do at Crabbet—walks through the woods, lazy hours to be spent in boats on the lake over which the wild duck flighted at night. I remember the long afternoons slipping away as I sat in a punt jammed between tall bulrushes where, completely hidden, one could read undisturbed for hours. I also remember John lying under some trees outside the drawing-room window making notes for a review in the *Spectator* of a book on philosophy. He remarked at intervals "this man really shouldn't write about philosophy when he knows so little about it."

We started by having an amusing friendship discussing

[1] Later The Earl of Birkenhead, Lord High Chancellor of England.

35

life and literature at great length and writing long letters
to each other. We soon found that life had brightened
for us both. He had never really settled down in London
after his time of hard work and high adventure in South
Africa, and I was suffering from a feeling of aimlessness.

We met at the right moment, and when we discovered
that our friendship (which we had imagined to be strictly
platonic) was merging into a deeper feeling we soon
became engaged. Our engagement lasted for a year.
John had decided to accept the offer of Nelson's publishing firm to become one of its partners. He went to
Edinburgh to learn about the manufacturing of books
at Parkside Works. He lived in lodgings, going out to
his family in Peebles at the week-end. It was rather a
lengthy and trying time for me, but we corresponded
daily and I set about collecting the nucleus of a home.
We received innumerable wedding presents, and John's
interest and delight in them was inexhaustible. Young
people in those days with a wide circle of relations and
friends were given far more presents, and of a far better
quality, than those of to-day. "What shall we do with
that?" John would enquire anxiously when we received
the fourth replica of a rather useless silver object.

We went up to Peebles for me to make acquaintance
with my husband's family. Peebles was (and is) a small
town with a cheerful High Street, full of people shopping
and exchanging news outside shops stacked with delicious
cakes and scones; and in those days country people came
in and out in pony-carts and gigs. I was charmed by
Bank House with its polished brass door-handle and its
little hall, and the sitting-room with a glowing fire and
books everywhere. I felt strange and a little alien to my
new family, but we soon found that the same things made
us laugh, and no bond is stronger. I was fascinated by my
mother-in-law's ability, and by the rapidity with which

she worked. I can see her now writing long letters with her pince-nez perched on the end of her nose, or putting a lightning patch on her husband's or sons' underclothes, or making spills out of newspapers.

Her powers of work were amazing. She would get up at five in the morning and tackle the day's tasks from then onwards with a pace and concentration which would have exhausted most strong men. She radiated an incessant activity and had apparently solved the problem of perpetual motion. Her husband and children adored her.

My father-in-law was vaguer about everyday life, though he never forgot to visit anyone in trouble. He preached admirably and managed to impart to all who saw him some of his conviction, that the life of the spirit was the only thing that mattered.

We went up by train to Bamflat to see my mother-in-law's brothers, James and John Masterton, on a stormy wet day. Dear lost place, which I would have loved to call my own. If I shut my eyes I can see the small square house with its back to a hill, looking over a valley. John's uncles were to me three-parts incomprehensible, as they talked the broadest Border Scots at the fullest pitch of their lungs. I remember the groaning tea-table with a spread of eatables which would have foiled the appetite of Gargantua.

There was a tiny garden with gooseberry bushes, and a large farm-steading with a machine for weighing corn where our children were always weighed in after-years. It was a different atmosphere from that of Bank House, reading being mostly restricted to the *British Weekly* and the *Scotsman*, but there was the same atmosphere of hard work and achievement. The uncles were among the best judges of stock in the Borders and owned a princely acreage of land and many farms.

37

They were deeply interested in Broughton Free Church, to which they gave generously, while they would save money by not taking in the *Scotsman* but receiving it a day old from their sister. I must pay my tribute here to this Scottish trait of economy where it touches their personal pleasure and comfort, coupled with a great generosity to any cause or person that they love. I early learned a lesson of thrift and giving from John's family. I have perhaps not always followed their good example, but it has remained in my mind as the ideal way to live.

Where the stories of Scottish parsimony come from I cannot think. I have known Scotland for well over thirty years and have never met with it.

John gave a luncheon-party for me in Edinburgh to meet some of his friends. His mother, Anna and I travelled there from Peebles on one of those cold spring days when the wind nips shrewdly in Princes Street. We lunched in a rather gloomy hotel room, but there was no gloom in the company assembled there. The party consisted of J. G. Jameson, the Alec Maitlands, Ian Nelson and Stair Gillon. They were quite unlike the young men I had met in London. Johnnie Jameson, with his massive head and greying hair (all Jamesons grow grey in youth), his dark blue eyes and charming resonant voice which conveyed sympathy tinged with amusement; Alec Maitland, benevolent and shrewd (with his pretty wife); and Stair Gillon, with his unruly thatch of fair hair, pale blue eyes and incisive features—they had a vigour and force all their own. I felt a little bewildered. Stair's voice was more penetrating than any I had hitherto heard, and he held the table spellbound with his account of the "Bile Beans Case" in which he had been counsel. A gale seemed to be blowing through the room and I instinctively held on to my large hat in order to keep it in

place. Their charm and kindness I can never forget, and
their friendship is still one of the best things in my life.

Our wedding took place at St. George's, Hanover
Square, packed with a large congregation, on July 15th,
1907. I travelled to the church in the Grosvenor family
coach, which swung and rumbled slowly through the
streets. We went for our honeymoon to Tylney Hall in
Hampshire belonging to Sir Lionel and Lady Phillips.
Our feet sank deeply into carpets. I poured out tea
behind the barricade of a magnificent silver tea-service.
The walls were hung with lovely pictures and tapestries.
Our walks were witnessed by more gardeners than is
possible to imagine now. Everything was done for us
with princely generosity and kindness.

We went abroad to a world of delight. First to
Aachensee and Innsbruck, then to Cortina to an inn where
we received certain privileges in the way of food and
service owing to the fact that my uncle, Lord Lovelace,[1]
had used it as a climbing centre and was well known to
the innkeeper. Cortina, with its rose-coloured peaks
and flower-starred meadows, was a place of fantastic
beauty, but I must admit also of terror to me, as urged on
by John I climbed mountains for the first time. Lured
on by him I hoped that I was going to enjoy climbing,
but I proved to have the worst head possible for heights,
and when we got to the top of a precipitous rock and I
saw Cortina lying, as it seemed, beneath my feet, I cried
out in horror. John, however, undaunted optimist that
he was, persuaded me to climb Monte Cristallo, the
highest mountain in the Dolomites. I must have made
things perilous for him and our French guide Pierre Blanc
from the Dauphiné, as I had to be coaxed and pulled up
and down precipices and round difficult corners. "Mettez
vos pieds dans le vide, madame," Pierre Blanc would cry

[1] Second Earl of Lovelace, author of *Astarte*.

39

by way of encouragement. A shudder was my only response.

We went to Venice in August, to an hotel overlooking the Grand Canal. John purchased a map and we walked as it seemed to me a long distance every day. I had thought that in Venice you lazily floated about in gondolas, but I reckoned without his love of topography and keenness for exercise. However, he soon found other vents for his energy. We hired a boat with an orange sail and went to Torcello and discovered the Lido, then a modest place with one or two hotels and little wooden booths where one could buy dried sea-horses and mushroom-like straw hats. We hired bathing dresses, massively striped, and bathed in the sparkling waters of the Adriatic.

The return from a happy honeymoon is always something of an anti-climax, and I wept, I remember, in Paris before returning to ordinary life. We started housekeeping in a house in Edinburgh near Parkside Works, lent us by Tommie and Margaret Nelson. It was enormous, even judged by the standards of yesterday, but we existed happily in a corner of it with two excellent Scots servants. The garden had sweeping green lawns and a view of Arthur's Seat which redeemed the gloom of the heavy carved woodwork and the sombre curtains which almost stood up by themselves from sheer goodness and solidity of material. The drawing-room contained armies of sofas and well-stuffed armchairs, and there were stained-glass windows everywhere and all the panoply of the Victorian era. It was not Tommie and Margaret's taste, as I soon saw when we stayed with them in the West Highlands.

Housekeeping was rather fun, I thought, until we went to London to look for a house, getting more tired and less critical as time went on. We finally took No. 40 Hyde Park Square. I engaged a red-faced Scots cook, the inevitable drunkard of all young households from David Copperfield onwards. She distinguished herself by becoming inebriated (after some rather curious behaviour) the night that our daughter was born, thereby spreading confusion in the house.

At that time John and Arthur Grenfell were raising a fund at the urgent request of Lord Grey, the Governor-General of Canada, to buy a portion of the Heights of Abraham, the site of the battle of Quebec, for a public park. This entailed a great deal of speaking and organising work. John was booked to speak at the Oxford Union on June 5th, 1908. Our daughter was born in the early hours of the morning, but I was getting on well and the doctor said that my husband could safely fulfil his engagement. John had been up all night, and he fell asleep the moment the train left Paddington. He occasionally opened one eye to see his fellow-speaker reading and making notes from a large historical tome. The name of the other speaker was Winston Churchill.

I knew nothing about babies, but our daughter Alice was a delight to me from the first. John was charmed with her, though he was no baby-lover and years later in Canada I was forced to explain (or get our A.D.C. to do so) that the Governor-General, though the father of four children, did not feel that he knew enough about babies for it to be of any use for him to visit the maternity wards in the hospitals, and that this was best left to me. I, on the other hand, have a horror of operating theatres, so he took over the duty of looking at them.

We started the first years of our married life, after the departure of our cook, with three delightful Scots maids. Their Scottish speech remained unimpaired by their contact with Londoners. One of them, asked by a visitor after my health, remarked: "Mrs. Buchan hasn't

been just that awfully well this long time back." They
went to Canada and I lost sight of them. In 1936 the
Women's Organisations in Vancouver gave a splendid
tea-party, where I was presented with a golden spoon by
each group of women. Two charmingly dressed ladies
approached me, and standing quite still they just said,
"We're Janet and Mary." The whole meeting was
held up whilst we asked each other endless questions.
They looked, in spite of their prettier clothes, and the
years that had passed, so much the same, and they always
came to see us on our train when we went to Vancouver.

Our first house was tall and slightly gaunt, with a
steep staircase. Like so many houses of its date, it seemed
to have been designed to give the maximum amount of
work for the minimum of comfort; but it was a pleasant
house when in the summer the front drawing-room was
full of a green light cast by the big trees in the square when
they were in full leaf. A conservatory on the stairs was
my joy and pride, and my first gardening experiments
were made there. Journeys are said to end in lovers'
meetings, and an amateur gardener's efforts usually begin
and end with nasturtiums, and I remember that I took an
unsophisticated delight in their brilliant colours.

John worked hard at Nelson's London office and wrote
articles for the *Spectator*. He worked in an effortless sort
of way, and after office hours was fresh and unfatigued.
He loved making up rhymes about his family and I
remember a slightly unkind one he made up about me.
I was then trying to learn Greek, but got very little
distance with that thorny language. I was also working
at juvenile employment and mildly helping with the
suffrage campaign. The rhyme touched upon the roving
propensities necessitated by my various activities:

> To patronise the poor, with votes to fuss,
> And leave Greek grammars in the casual bus.

(The last line referred to my lifelong inability to keep my possessions intact.)

Looking back to the first years of our married life, they seem to have been amazingly carefree and happy. We had a wide circle of friends and relations who were kind to us. We dined out constantly and gave little dinners ourselves. I remember one when the Philip Snowdens came to meet the Robert Cecils. I was a suffragist of the unmilitant sort, and Mrs. Snowden, a pretty golden-haired woman, was deep in the Votes for Women movement. Philip Snowden was an impressive figure. He had a fine head and clear-cut features, and he talked with vigour and incisiveness. John and Robert Cecil were also supporters of women's suffrage, though not so all our other friends, and bitter arguments raged over tea and dinner tables.

Two wars have now ironed out our personalities so flat that I doubt if we could ever dispute with so much violence about much more major issues.

My husband was a good host. He diffused an atmosphere of vivid interest and got the most out of dull people in the way of conversation. But he had one defect, of which I always reminded him, which was, that he became absorbed in conversation and forgot to turn to his other neighbour at dinner, thereby throwing the whole table conversationally out of gear. He was writing a series of essays which were put together under the name of *Some Eighteenth-Century Byways*.[1] It is still a favourite book of a great many people and contains studies of Lord Mansfield, Lady Louisa Stuart, Theodore Mommsen and others.

At this stage of his life no one thought of him primarily as a writer. "Why do you go on writing?" one of my relations naïvely asked him. "Why do you play the

[1] First published in 1908.

43

piano and do embroidery?" he retorted. "One must have some touch with art."

We moved from 40 Hyde Park Square to a charming little house—13 Bryanston Street (now a block of flats). It was of the period of the Adam brothers. The dining-room and drawing-room floors had sets of three little rooms (which opened out of each other) with garlanded mantelpieces and pretty cornices.

Our eldest son was born in 1911, the year that John was adopted as Conservative candidate for Peebles and Selkirk. The summer before and after his birth we took a farmhouse in the Borders called Harehope. It was an uncompromising grey house standing in the Peeblesshire hills, remote from the bustle of life. John made many speeches and we went to endless village meetings and entertained people to meals. Harehope was set in soft rounded hills, covered with benty grass which was easy and springy to walk on, and the burn yielded big baskets of trout about the size of sardines which made excellent eating. The first year we were at Harehope John and Johnnie Jameson both spoke at a Unionist social in Peebles. They spoke well. Johnnie was racy and amusing, and his speech was full of sly allusions to the Liberal Party. John was more serious, and he gave a logical and closely argued presentation of the Unionist case. The audience listened well and silently, as all Scots audiences do, keeping their ears well open to the finer points in the argument.

The following year we wished to give more attention to Selkirk and we took Broadmeadows Cottage from the Langs. It stood on a shelf above the river Yarrow, which was obscured from view by the thickets which clothed the slopes of the hill. We had a large and clumsy car lent by a cousin of mine, which I nicknamed "Alfred the

Elephant." It had every vice a car could have. One afternoon four of its tyres burst. It consumed vast quantities of petrol, but it did carry us about the very large constituency. We visited endless farms and small cottages and held meetings, at the head of Ettrick, consisting of several shepherds and their dogs. The Langs who lived in Broadmeadows House were the most hospitable and charming of families. Mrs. Lang had that wisdom given to old Scottish ladies. Her house was just what a house should be, full of children and dogs and cheerful talk. I shall always feel a glow of gratitude to Mrs. Lang and her daughter for their kindness, as I well remember the great baskets laden with garden produce which constantly appeared at our door from the big house. These holiday months in Peebles and Selkirk were strenuous, and John's political work necessitated odd meals at odd hours. It is an unrestful thing for a parliamentary candidate and his wife to take a holiday in the constituency they are nursing, as there is never a day when you do not feel that you ought to go off and visit someone. But when we could do so we enjoyed the peace of the valley, where the only sound was that of running water or the distant rattle of the haymaking machine, and where often the only human creature to be seen was a fisherman standing motionless on the banks of a river or stream.

This year a small cloud had appeared on the horizon about John's health. He began to be troubled with indigestion which at first yielded easily to treatment, but the hastily eaten meals before meetings did him no good, and that year a deep sorrow came to us. In 1912 his brother Willie came home on leave from India and fell ill with a lingering and painful illness. Of all the sorrows and tragedies I have seen, this was one of the most poignant. We watched the worsening of his condition and the complete helplessness of the doctors in the face of his mysterious illness, and tried to gather fortitude from his stark courage. He was one of the finest-looking young men I have ever seen, and his outstanding work in the Indian Civil Service was admired and recognised. John had to work hard all through Willie's illness and to make hurried journeys up to Scotland. His face grew more and more drawn by anxiety and fatigue, for he not only felt his personal grief so keenly, but the agony of mind which it caused to his family.

All this had the worst possible effect on his health, and after Willie died at a Glasgow nursing home, John had to have a long spell in bed. The discomfort and pain did go away for months at a time, and we always hoped that it would go for good, but it always returned. The doctors diagnosed it as duodenal trouble. John never let it make any difference to the work he was doing and he went on with business and politics as hard as ever. His speaking was improving all the time, and I quote a paragraph from a Glasgow paper which showed what some of his fellow-countrymen thought of him.

Mr. Buchan's address on Home Rule was one of the most able and convincing delivered in Glasgow for many a day. And it showed him far removed from the hackneyed politician so common in the constituencies. His delivery, if somewhat fast, is exceptionally clear, and his arguments can be followed to their ultimate end without the least difficulty. His manner is polished, but he can introduce an illustration in the Doric in a most effective manner. As one would expect, there is no slipshodness about his diction. Every sentence is clear cut, and seems to fit naturally into its place. What adds to his effectiveness is the evidence that he has thought his subject out for himself and that he has brought his own brains and his own experience to bear upon it.

CHAPTER III

HOLIDAYS

IN the first years of our married life we spent many holidays in Scotland. The West Highlands with their magical panorama of mountains and lakes was first shown to me at Achnacloich, Tommie Nelson's property on Loch Etive. The house stood on a promontory overlooking the loch, it resounded with the cheerful noise of children's voices and there was endless sport, fishing in two lochs and much sailing and boating. Tommie was interested in farming and increasing the yield of crops, and was even trying to grow tobacco, but was, I fear, baffled by a totally unhelpful climate. There was an overflowing kindness in this house. Tommie and Margaret Nelson were very fortunate people. They had excellent health and a vivid power of enjoyment. They both worked hard and played hard, and spent a great deal of time in helping other people.

I began to understand more and more the roots from which John had sprung, from which he derived the romantic and poetic aspects of his character which ran side by side with his common sense and his ability to grasp hard facts. In the Scotland before 1914 there was an awareness of past history which was woven into the daily life of the people. The glens and woods where the clans had marauded and fought were still haunted with memories of violence and tragedy. Memories went back a long way and curious links with the past were not uncommon. For example, a very old great-uncle of the Buchans could remember that his nurse had told him when she herself was an old woman that as a child at Lamancha she had been frightened by the Highlanders on their march to Derby.

We went sometimes to Kirkcudbrightshire in Galloway to stay with Lord and Lady Ardwall near a village with a romantic name of Gatehouse-of-Fleet. In the Highlands the past centuries were part of the atmosphere, but in Galloway you lived as it were right in the eighteenth century, in a sunnier climate where religion, sport and legal argument held the foremost places in conversation. I was learning a lot about Scotland and becoming more and more fascinated by the variety and (to me) strangeness of its life. Lord Ardwall, in spite of his great kindness of heart, was a somewhat alarming host, with his stocky figure, cherry-coloured face, a shock of white hair and flashing dark blue eyes. He roared his remarks to his family and visitors in the voice of a bull. I was very shy and rather bewildered by the unfamiliarity of my surroundings, and I remember being made quite speechless the first evening at dinner when, after carving with neatness and precision what seemed to my town eyes to be a chicken, Lord Ardwall turned to me and said in ringing tones, "Do you think I gave Lady Ardwall too much for this hen?" I looked completely blank, as I did not grasp that the Ardwalls had some strange farming arrangement by which Lady Ardwall managed the poultry, which were then purchased for the consumption of the family.

Ardwall was a charming house, whitewashed under a steep roof rather French than Scottish in design. I remember another of Lord Ardwall's remarks. When showing me the wing he had added to the house he said with satisfaction, "I have built it so that it cannot be altered by man or devil," adding, "By man I mean my descendants, by devils their wives." Inside the house there was comfort and a pleasant shabbiness. Armies of dogs followed Lady Ardwall wherever she went, or lay round her in matted heaps on the floor. Ardwall stood on an estuary, and bushes of every kind, notably fuchsias, flourished in the warm damp climate. The lovely hills and valleys of Kirkcudbrightshire came back and back into my husband's books. He wrote a life of Lord Ardwall, and in it he tells a tale of distinguished service as a lawyer, landowner and farmer. John's description of a Sunday morning at Ardwall shows the charm that it held for him.

The picture of summer mornings at Ardwall comes back to me as I write. The house was always full of dogs, including an apostolic succession of terriers of the Dandy Dinmont persuasion. It was a family taste, for Andy, the eldest son, once turned up to see me in South Africa with a strange hound, called Davidson, as his sole companion. There was Lady Ardwall's cherished Faithful, to whom his lordship, like Shakespeare's liberal shepherds, "gave a grosser name." There was, too, an unholy brute called Blondin, which I believe to have been a new species, for its head was indistinguishable from its tail. At later dates came others, including a wraith-like borzoi, called Cossack, a legacy from Oxford. Nor must I forget Johnnie's dog, Rolf the Ganger, a greyhound of exceptional gentleness and grace. I can see such a morning—latish, for there were sleepy members of the household—Lady Ardwall preoccupied with domestic cares and her canine retinue; a guest or two who, having breakfasted colossally, were straining at the leash for a start; his lordship, in a voluminous grey shooting suit, ploughing his way among dogs and wondering alternately whether his house had not become like the outer precincts of the Heavenly City, sacred to hounds, and what would be the end of sons who did not rise with the lark. Last of all, in a fine stage entrance, comes Johnnie, delicately equipped with dancing-pumps, one boxing-glove, and a fencing-foil, only half awake, and asking sleepily whether it was proposed to put our trust in horses or lift up our eyes to the hills. This for the week-days. On Sabbath there was a different scene. His lordship, splendid in kirk-going clothes, mounted the box-seat of the waggonette and drove a contingent to the Free Church in Gatehouse. At luncheon thereafter he was at his best, for his nature seemed to rebound from the enforced quiet of the service. Usually of a Sabbath afternoon he was agriculturally inclined, and would conduct his guests to view his Galloways, much as the Psalmist walked round the bulwarks of Jerusalem.

Visitors to Ardwall in those days were always in doubt as to which they loved most—the uncompromising wisdom of the laird or the divine innocence of the lady. No happier combination could be found: the one clear, emphatic, crisp as a frosty day; the other elusive and unexpected, full of half-spoken thoughts and quaint imaginings. Lady Ardwall had a profound humour, perhaps the subtler of the two; but she exhaled it like an old-fashioned fragrance, so that, while his lordship's sayings stuck to the memory, hers remained an atmosphere and a background. If he was charitable, she was charity incarnate. He had his prejudices, but hers have yet to be discovered; her gentle sympathy rounded and softened the sharp edges of his common-sense. Both had much in common, as must always happen in a perfect union; but, as must also happen, the one was a complement to the other.

I can only add to this that my visits to Ardwall gave another page to the happy pages of my life. Lady Ardwall was very good to me, and to finish off her portrait I will give one more memory. One Sunday afternoon I saw some children coming into the house and was told by Johnnie that they were his mother's Sunday School class. "I think," he remarked, "that her theology is mostly cakes and milk." This may or may not have been true, but no child could have failed to have been made better by hours spent in Lady Ardwall's company.

Each winter we went up to Edinburgh and my husband did some work at Parkside. We stayed at No. 6 Heriot Row with Alec and Rosalind Maitland. Those who only know the Edinburgh of to-day with the weary pattern of queues for overfull trams or for inferior meals, cannot realise the charm it had many years ago. In August and September her squares and crescents were empty of life. The large houses looked blank and shut up and grass grew between the cobbles in the streets, while the feet of the rare passer-by echoed in the silence. In those days I was surprised and charmed by the attitude of the shop people, who urged their customers to buy the cheapest of their wares and were scandalised at any insistence that the expensive article might be more desirable. There were odd little shops in the back streets which sold such unusual objects as large sea-shells, and others where you could buy sugar mice with cotton tails, much beloved by my children.

The light in Edinburgh on a winter's afternoon is cold and clear and the dignified buildings cast long mauve and grey shadows on the pavements. Those luminous northern twilights showed the rooms in the Maitlands' nobly proportioned house to the best advantage. The portrait of Rosalind Maitland in a black evening cloak by Sir James Guthrie filled up the end wall of the long drawing-room, and D. Y. Cameron's pictures were in a worthy setting.

Since those days the Maitlands have added some world-famous pictures to their collection. The part of Edinburgh in which they live now seems to be neatly divided up by the offices and consulting-rooms of doctors and dentists, and it is refreshing to be able still to enter a house containing a real host and hostess who are surrounded by beautiful and well-chosen objects. In the distant days before 1914 the Edinburgh squares and crescents had families living in them. They had mostly inherited frowning pieces of Victorian furniture, the whole effect was very dark, as the walls had sombre embossed wallpapers on which hung paintings of no great artistic value in heavy gilt frames. Those families had a fine tradition of hospitality, and the talk round their tea and dinner tables was acute and interesting.

At the Maitlands' we met Alec's colleagues at the Scots Bar. Noel Skelton[1] came there as well as Johnnie Jameson and Stair Gillon. When a lot of young men get together conversation is apt to be vigorous, and Rosalind and I sometimes found it hard to make ourselves heard. When, however, we managed to be audible, our remarks were treated with kindness and indulgence. But I noticed that when John said something in his quiet voice the others always fell silent and listened. Though they sometimes disagreed with him, they never disregarded anything he said. He enjoyed those evenings immensely when the talk was fast and furious; it had a way of going back to the shared experiences of their light-hearted Oxford days.

Before the First World War we also had three holidays abroad which stand out clearly in my memory. I shall write of them as their landscapes and atmosphere were reflected in John's books.

The first one was a yachting cruise on the *Rannoch*, which belonged to Gerard Craig Sellar. We joined him at Constantinople after a journey across Europe in the Orient express. His steam yacht was comfortable, in fact luxurious—if something so unstable on the waters of the ocean can ever be luxurious. I had, I don't know why, always imagined that I was a good sailor, but I became distinctly pensive and disinclined for effort when the *Rannoch* gently rose and fell in the swell of the harbour at Constantinople. Gerard had put some white flowers on the table in our sitting-room which gave forth a sweet and overpowering scent. I soon arranged to spend as much time as possible on shore, wandering, shopping and sight-seeing. I was entranced by the pariah dogs and

[1] Later Under-Secretary for Scotland, died 1935.

their puppies at the corners of the streets, and the dark
shop where beautifully clean Turks slapped and manipu-
lated a glutinous substance which somehow became
transformed into Turkish Delight, the little striped red-
and-white tulips sold in the streets, and the bustle and
enchantment of the bazaars.

My husband was taken out to lunch with a Turkish
grandee and listened to nightingales in his garden. Conversation turned on to British politics and one of the party
deplored the lack of political talent amongst our younger
men. "Have you not the Honourable Herbert?"[1] said
the Turk.

We went to Broussa and spent a day being slowly
driven past fields where solid respectable-looking Turks
were working, and where storks stood about idly
meditative. When we left Constantinople and went
through the Dardanelles the sea became extremely rough.
I retreated to bed unhappy and protesting. Gerard
Sellar, the kindest of men, caused the yacht to be anchored
at the mouth of the harbour of Lemnos, and restored to
health we went for a walk, I gathering some purple
gelatinous flowers on the shore in the growing dusk.
I think I may have the distinction of being the first English-
woman to set foot on Lemnos; Lemnos of which we
were to hear so much in the Dardanelles campaign.

We landed at Thermopylae, where the *Rannoch* sailors
collected innumerable small tortoises, and John told me
the story of the Spartans combing their long locks for
death. He was steeped in the classics and every turn of
the landscape brought back some allusion or incident.
His short story "The Lemnian"[2] was written after this
trip. One evening we landed on an island in a group
whose name suggested beauty and fragility, the Petali

[1] See note 2 on page 21.
[2] Included in *The Moon Endureth*.

Islands. We walked up a beach, where there sat a circle of peasants round a fire. They paid no attention to us, though in such a remote island the arrival of a yacht and the landing of strangers might well have stirred their curiosity.

Some way back from the shore, standing in what appeared to be walled gardens, stood a long low house with a mellow red roof. It was shuttered and impenetrable. We stared at it hoping that someone might emerge from it who would tell us who lived there, but no one came, and we had to content ourselves with walking along a carefully made road fringed with bushes which dipped and wound round hills and promontories. We returned to the yacht still burning with curiosity about the history of house and island.

Gerard Craig Sellar was one of the most generous and charming of men. Short and not slim, a little bald and wearing pince-nez, he resembled Mr. Pickwick. He had inherited a large fortune but had a horror of tasteless ostentation. He never married, and lived with his mother in London or at Ardtornish on Morvern in Argyllshire, and being shy much preferred the company of a few intimate friends to any larger gatherings. He enjoyed playing the part of an extremely orthodox and cautious person. "I like to know where I am" was a phrase often on his lips. This never failed to delight John, whose own views of life were so different. At heart Gerard was courageous, and in matters of the sea and sailing bold and adventurous.

Gerard had a neighbour in the Highlands who also possessed a large yacht and had chosen this moment to cruise in the Aegean waters, and John invented an airy structure of fancy about the competition between the yachts' crews and their owners. Gerard did things in style and when we landed anywhere took us for a meal to the best hotel. "I like to know where I am," John murmured as we entered their gilded portals. He wrote a little eclogue called "The Argonauts of Delphi" bringing in the idiosyncrasies of Gerard and the rest of the party, which consisted of ourselves, Gerard's brother-in-law Alec Maitland (whose kindness of heart warred with his delight in pricking conversational bubbles), and Captain "Granny" Gordon, who afterwards distinguished himself in the Mesopotamian campaign and whose simple goodness and charm made everyone love him.

"The Argonauts of Delphi" contained a poem called "Echo of Meleager" which was published in *Poems Scots and English*, and there is much in *The Dancing Floor* of things seen and remembered on that trip.

Our second holiday was to Norway with Tommie Nelson. He had taken part of a small wooden farmhouse and a stretch of the Leardal river. Tommie was different from Gerard. His mind quested after problems which as an employer of labour in his large printing works he felt he ought to try and solve. In those days, before so much was done in the way of social legislation and social services, the thoughtful citizen could make valuable contributions to the welfare of the community. I was up to my neck in various schemes of social work and we three discussed them in the evenings near the stove in the sitting-room of the farm. The days were given up to fishing in the swiftly flowing waters of the Leardal, which ran down through the lovely green valley. It was not a very good season that particular year for fishing, and John and Tommie, who were both past masters in the art, did not catch as many fish as they had expected. Fortunately, however, they both liked fishing for its own sake and not for the size of their catch.

I also fished long and laboriously. I am, I fear, the unworthy type of fisherman who longs to catch something, large or small. I often laid down my rod and gazed at the scenery or talked to the Norwegian ghillie or gathered flowers wondering if I could honourably go back to the farmhouse. My one spectacular effort was to catch the earliest sea-trout ever caught in the Leardal. It took me up and down the bank of the river, and this feat happening to coincide with a horse fair which had brought an unusual number of people to the valley I gained an embarrassing amount of publicity from the plaudits of the crowd on the opposite bank of the river. We, Tommie, John and I, though in our own homes orderly people, decided to be as untidy as possible on our holiday. So we threw letters, newspapers and bills behind the sofa on to the floor. Tommie called it the under-tow, and certainly letters thrown into it became at once submerged. The Norwegian setting of incidents in *The Three Hostages* recalls to me something of those happy weeks.

The other holiday was to Bavaria to the Rosensee, where we stayed in a villa by that small and charming lake with our friends Professor and Mrs. Moritz Bonn. I remember that on our way through Germany we wanted to send a telegram to our hostess. John wrote it out in his tiny spidery handwriting, and the face of the German telegraph clerk became suffused with rage and he literally threw it back at us, thundering "Das ist nicht klar," and I had to copy it out in my larger rounder hand before he would accept it. Moritz Bonn talked brilliantly and with expert knowledge on many subjects. His wife, Thérèse, sturdily British in spite of her un-British surname and Christian name, tall and graceful, full of consuming energy, ran the house with gaiety and competence. We ate exquisite food cooked by one of the two Bavarian girls who did the work of the house with a beaver-like steadiness. They had only one grave fault, which was that they removed our clothes and washed them. Our holiday wardrobes were far from extensive and their standards of cleanliness were very high, and John declared that he constantly found himself with nothing to put on.

He had developed a technique of drawing small pictures, slightly reminiscent of the Bayeux tapestry, where angular but animated figures gesticulated and conveyed the meaning of the picture clearly enough. He did one of these at Rosensee which he called by the simple word "Gewaschen," showing himself in scanty attire looking at a long line from which hung most of his more intimate garments.

The Bavaria of those days had a touch of primitive paganism. I remember that we were there at midsummer (Johannisfeuer), and that the bonfires were lit that night through which the young men and girls jumped and capered. There was something haunted about the whole country, and John described in his autobiography how he and his guide after climbing the Alpspitz were coming down a valley when an unreasoning panic swept over them and they ran for their lives. He rowed a great deal in a boat on the tranquil little Rosensee. It was a real lake of the woods, with pines coming down to the edge of the water. Oxford-fashion, he rowed in shirt-sleeves as the weather was warm. Thérèse Bonn had no objection to his coming into meals like this, but one day a fourteen-year-old German girl came to tea. She took one horrified glance at John, blushed a deep scarlet and nearly upset her cup on to the floor.

This seemed strange because John was dressed with all the respectability of the men of his generation. (Even in the nineteen-thirties, when a near-nudism was fashionable, neither his daughter nor I could ever persuade him to take off his tie or loosen his collar with a view to sunbathing, which I thought might be good for his health.)

I regret to say that this hyper-sensitive German child afterwards went through the divorce court.

CHAPTER IV

EARLY MARRIED LIFE

IN 1910 John had turned his thoughts to writing an adventure story. He set the scene in South Africa, a country for which all his life he retained a deep love and a consuming interest.

He had put much of his enthusiasm for South Africa into *The African Colony*. He had also written *A Lodge in the Wilderness*. In this book a group of people meet in a house on a mountain-side in lovely scenery. The house contains many beautiful objects and has all the amenities of civilisation. The days are spent in sport and other pursuits and in the evening they discuss Imperial problems. He pays a full tribute to the beauty of the landscape and also to the mystery and fascination of old races and beliefs.

His romantic love of South Africa shows itself in *Prester John*, and in the stories "The Green Wildebeest" and "The Grove of Ashtaroth" in the collection of short stories called *The Moon Endureth*; also in the character study of Pieter Penaar in the *Greenmantle* trilogy. *Prester John* was meant to be a boy's adventure story, but it has been read by many people of all ages and both sexes. The scene is laid in Fife at Kirkcaple, easily recognisable as Kirkcaldy, where the Buchans spent part of their childhood in a manse. The hero, David Crawford, is also a minister's son, and a black minister, noted for his preaching powers, comes to stay in the village of Kirkcaple. David surprises him performing heathen rites on the seashore. The story moves swiftly. David becomes a storekeeper in a lonely part of South Africa. From then on we follow breathlessly the doings of John Laputa (ex-minister of the

Gospel), who feels that the mantle of Prester John has fallen upon him, and who is planning to lead the black race against the white. The plot hinges round the possession of Prester John's ruby necklace. There is a scene in a cave with smooth and unclimbable rock-walls on three sides, and on the fourth a huge waterfall. John Buchan never wrote a better or more skilful piece of narrative than the description of David Crawford's escape from the cave, by the mountaineering feat of climbing precariously up the side of the vast sheet of descending water into the light of day.

Prester John has become a school-book, and was also made into a film, and has found its way into a series of broadcasts. I don't think John ever enjoyed writing a book as much as he did *Prester John*. It gave him a welcome relaxation from office and other work. I remember that I had had 'flu and we went to a seaside resort for me to recuperate, and he read me the chapter called "The Drums Beat at Sunset" sitting by the fire in our banal hotel bedroom. I shivered with pleasurable terror as if something elemental and frightening had invaded the room.

Nelson's made a new departure in the publishing world by its cheap reprints called *The Nelson Sevenpennies*. They were compact little red books, well bound and admirably printed. When asked why they were sold for sevenpence instead of sixpence or a shilling, John replied because sevenpence was such a handy sum, as any man could take sixpence out of one pocket and a penny out of the other. Whether all men kept their small change as neatly divided into copper and silver as he did, I don't know. The "Sevenpennies" have stood up manfully to the years. When I was running my Prairie Library scheme in Canada many generous people gave me books, and there were many "Sevenpennies" among them. Their backs were unbroken and their print still beautifully clear and black. This series was an instant success, and later, many were sent to the soldiers in the field, who found them extremely handy to put into their pockets. Nelson's also expanded their business on to the Continent and started a series of French classics which sold well, French publishers being then, apparently, unable to produce cheap editions in this small and durable form.

Then came the German business. Nelson printed books for Uhlstein's, the great German publishing house, and just before August 1914 one of the Uhlstein partners came over to work in Edinburgh and see how things were done there. Parkside Works had most admirable machinery. I loved to go there and see the different machines doing colour-printing for children's books, or doing clever things with stamping the gold "N" on the backs of the "Sevenpennies." John was on very good terms with all his partners, and all the people in the Works, and he specially enjoyed talking to the typesetters, who in Scotland have an individuality all their own.

I also liked to visit his office in Paternoster Row, which is now a handful of dust after bombing. We decided to have a party for all the staff workers there, and we did this till the war came; those excellent suppers remain in my memory as very delightful and happy occasions.

I belonged to a very affectionate and close-knit family, and the members of it took John to their hearts. My mother had been my very special care and responsibility, for she never really recovered from my father's loss, though she always contrived to live an interesting life. She was tall and had an erect carriage. A Victorian oculist had made her wear glasses for an astigmatism at the age of twenty-three, and her blue eyes looked kindly, if sometimes a little austerely, through them at the world.

She had a strong sense of family duty and the ties that should bind members of it together. My sister and I often protested about this; some of our relations bored us, and we should have preferred to fill the house with livelier people who were just friends. But my mother was adamant on this point.

John respected this trait in her. As a Scot he also had a great sense of clan solidarity, but compared to our hordes of relations his own were comparatively few, and he did not really know the whole picture. Between my mother and John there was great friendliness and affection. The difficulties of the mother-in-law and son-in-law relationship have been a joke since the Stone Age, but it can be a happy one, and in this case it was. My mother was both tactful and uninterfering by nature. She always helped us when we needed help, and having suffered from duodenal trouble herself, her advice about John's health was very often to the point.

My mother liked young people very much, and though she could be severe with them when she disapproved of their conduct, she had a natural wisdom where youth was concerned. She liked babies, but did not find these interesting, as many women do, preferring children when they were old enough to be read to or to be told stories, and liking them better still when they were old enough to be persons on their own account.

She had the knack of always having a household who were devoted to her, so she rarely had to do any domestic chores. In return she was a most considerate mistress of a house and saw to it that her staff had a good deal of time to themselves.

In common with the rest of her family she had a very strong sense of public duty, sitting on many committees and attending many meetings. She devoted herself seriously to the problems of emigration to the Dominions and made two trips to Canada to study the conditions for women out there. Her scheme dealt with the more educated type of woman, and some of those sent out by her organisation did extremely well in Canada and took a real share in the life of the Dominion. But her greatest joy was in her painting. She had had a most thorough training in drawing and her water-colours have a cool and pleasant quality. She had been brought up in the days when you drew as carefully and as factually as possible or you abandoned the attempt. She had a horror of slipshod methods and what she described as plausible work. My mother had also a very distinct gift for writing, and before and after our marriage John helped her with this. He found the title of her first book for her, *The Bands of Orion*. She wrote three novels in all, and then stopped abruptly and went back to her painting, although her books had been read and enjoyed and she had been given good reviews. Her novels give an interesting and accurate picture of a world which is past, and I wish she had written more of them.

My mother's only surviving brother, Charles Stuart-Wortley,[1] sat for many years as Conservative Member for the Hallam division of Sheffield. He was twice married, first to Beatrice Trollope, and then to Carrie, daughter of Sir John Millais. I don't think that his heart was ever in politics. He lived in London but his outlook was not urban, and he joyously put on country clothes to go fishing or walking. He was the nicest possible guest, as he arrived armed with gardening-gloves and scissors and only asked to be allowed to prune or weed.

The great interest of his life was music, and both he and his wife were real musicians. Uncle Charlie would always play the piano if one asked him to do so. Aunt Carrie, on the other hand, rarely would do so in case she

[1] Afterwards Lord Stuart of Wortley.

had not practised quite enough and her performance might fall short of the almost unattainable standard she had set herself. Their house, No. 7 Cheyne Walk, was a rendezvous for Sir Edward Elgar, W. S. Gilbert and many other musicians.

John had a complete blind spot where music was concerned, though his ear was so well attuned to the rhythms of poetry and prose. He was, however, an extremely good listener, and when people played he sat still with an attentive expression on his face while his thoughts were far away engaged on some creative enterprise of his own. In the House of Commons he would sit by the hour listening to speeches, and Noel Skelton once asked him why he did so. John replied, because he was interested. "You can't possibly be," retorted Noel. "Well, then, because it's a cheap way of acquiring popularity," said John. "Cheap," scoffed Noel, "it's the most expensive waste of time possible." (It may be noted that Noel was not nearly such a busy man as John, but he much preferred talking to listening.)

My family were not only devoted to John but they attached far more importance than he did to his opinions. When he was not there they questioned me as to what he thought of this political or that literary matter, and I with my head full of the more pedestrian things of daily life frequently gave the wrong answer, to John's endless amusement.

My mother's four sisters played such a large part in our lives that I must mention them here. Her eldest sister, Mary, whom we called Aunt Mamie, married Ralph, Lord Lovelace, who was Byron's grandson. He was a recluse in whom a solitary childhood and youth had bred a distrust of the world and its ways. He had large estates and was in no need to fight the battle of life in the professions or the Services, and his life was passed in study and playing the violin. Aunt Mamie had a strong courageous nature, she was very different from her husband and she must have adapted herself with difficulty to the secluded life he liked to live. Uncle Ralph was a first-class mountaineer; it was sad that he and John never met because John had a great admiration for his exploits.

When *Astarte* [1] was published, John reviewed it for the *Spectator*, and I remember his reading passages from it aloud with exclamations of delight. Uncle Ralph left his widow large responsibilities, and she threw herself into the work of estate management with zest. She had taken a training in an architect's office, and built and improved cottages in the days when landowners knew little about the practical side of such things. She specialised in forthright remarks. Someone was extolling to her the moral virtues of a servant. "I want a cook, not a vestal virgin," Aunt Mamie crisply replied. As children and adolescents we dreaded her criticisms, but we became increasingly fond of her as years went on. John delighted in her sayings and she liked and often consulted him. We spent one Easter with her at Ashley Combe, near Porlock in Somersetshire. The sea was an Italian blue and we felt disinclined for effort. It was pleasure enough to sit on the terrace and just gaze at the view. Aubrey Herbert came to lunch and told us that he had just written to some charitable institution to say that he was unable to send more than a small subscription to their funds, and at the same time to his stockbroker asking him to invest some money that was lying idle. He then had put the letters in the wrong envelopes. I think this story was a fanciful one, but it was delightfully told. Hugh Walpole was also staying there. He was becoming a well-known writer and announced that he intended to settle down and write.

[1] First printed in 1905.

John and he argued a great deal about this, John sustaining that settling down when you were young, only to turn out books, was not productive of the best literature. "You should," he said, "write, but you should enlarge your knowledge of life by working at some other job as well." Hugh did not agree with this, but the war came soon afterwards and he went with an ambulance to Russia and wrote *The Dark Forest* and the course of his life was changed. There was a friendly kindness about Hugh Walpole and a humorous turn to his talk which made him a very pleasant companion. We met him again at Ockham, where my aunt lived, in Surrey. Henry James was also a fellow-guest. Aunt Mamie was very anxious that he should settle down in a small house on the Ockham estate. It was not an especially interesting dwelling and it was sunk in rather dull fields. Henry James praised it in elaborate sentences, but as we started to walk home he said under his breath to Hugh Walpole, "I should call it Suicide Cottage."

The house at Ockham had spaciousness and charm. It was utterly different from Ashley Combe, as it stood in flat country surrounded by woods and fields. The lawn in front of the house was shaded by some splendid cedars. There was a formal garden and a terrace where there were urns at intervals which blossomed with scarlet geraniums. I have seldom been in any spot where there was such a sense of peace. Both Ashley Combe and Ockham had a relaxing climate, though the winds could rush through the wet woods at Ashley and ruffle the lazy sea. Under the cedar trees at Ockham and in the eighteenth-century orangery time seemed to stand still. Aunt Mamie, however, supplied a tonic quality, and the strident screams of her parrots rent the air most of the time.

My mother's second sister, Margaret Talbot, was a

famous Victorian and Edwardian beauty. She was married to Reginald Talbot, whose distinguished good looks matched her own. Aunt Margie was tall and slim; her blue eyes matched in colour with the pale sapphire ear-rings she always wore. She dressed with Parisian elegance, an art which she had acquired in Paris when her husband was Military Attaché there. She was less clever and forthright than her elder sister, but she had a far more sympathetic approach to life, and a childlike innocence of mind which caused her often to make startling remarks showing considerable shrewdness. She was very generous, and if she noticed any deficiency in her nieces' clothes or household furnishings she set about to supply what was missing with unobtrusive kindness. Reginald Talbot had been attached as a very young soldier to General Sheridan's staff in the American Civil War, and John, who was an earnest student of that campaign, plied him with endless questions about this far-off experience. We stayed with the Talbots a great deal in their quiet retreat in the Chiltern Hills, where you could walk through beechwoods and black lambs gambolled in a field in front of the house.

John was on the best of terms with all my family, but his greatest affection was given to the quietest and shyest of my aunts, Blanche Firebrace. She never went out in society and lived within her family circle almost exclusively, though she entertained a few old friends to excellent meals, as she was a good judge of cooking. But if Aunt Blanche did not go out much, she loved to discuss the oddity of human nature, and to probe the motives which caused people to do strange and unlikely things. We brought her all the gossip we could collect, and though she never wanted to meet the people we spoke of in the flesh, it amused her to hear what they were doing. She would have labelled herself the complete Victorian, but she was really more akin to the wise women in the eighteenth century with her shrewd common sense and strictly realistic outlook. Jane Austen and she would have got on very well.

Some sentences in one of Edith Olivier's charming book *Four Victorian Ladies of Wiltshire* has brought back Aunt Blanche so vividly to me that I quote them here :

> Possibly because there was then no organized system for the higher education of women, the women who cared for things of the mind were often more cultured than the women of to-day. Their reading was individual. Their minds became like the old family still-rooms in which could be found rare home-made preserves, curious wines, and essences subtly distilled; instead of resembling the standardized contents of the tins which are now displayed in the windows of multiple shops.

Aunt Katherine, the youngest of my mother's sisters, lived in a whirl of activity. Her husband, General Sir Neville Lyttelton, was Governor of the Royal Hospital at Chelsea and she kept open house for her relations and friends. She had also many outside activities, and one day her Irish butler was pressed by an insistent caller to say where she was at that moment. He threw up his hands, exclaiming dramatically, "How can I say where her Ladyship is? Her Ladyship is everywhere."

Aunt Katherine yielded perhaps too often to the temptation of being amusing about other people. But any wounds she inflicted by the sharpness of her speech were soon healed by the kindness of her actions. She was unsparing in her work of helping people, and she reaped her reward when she was an old woman living in a small flat in Chelsea, incapacitated by disabling illness. Streams of her friends came to see her who owed much to her kindness and help. She arranged the great drawing-room at the Royal Hospital most skilfully, with furniture in harmony with the splendid portraits on the walls and the ornate carvings. On the mantelpiece she placed some severely beautiful white china urns given to her by her lifelong friend Sir Edward Grey, who wrote some of his most charming letters to her, and whom we often met at her house. Lucy Lyttelton, Katherine's eldest daughter, married Charles Masterman, with whom John was to be associated later in the Department of Information during the war of 1914-1918. Charles gave one the impression of immense vitality; he was a brilliant talker, tossing back a long black lock, which fell over his forehead, every few minutes. Lucy had a mass of red-gold hair piled up on her head. She has achieved distinction as a poet and a biographer of her husband.

I have lingered perhaps a little long over my relations, but the cosy family life and the mutually interesting companionship of a clan has been so much shaken by wars, that it is perhaps not out of place to make a short record of it.

My husband's family we saw twice yearly. They visited London in the spring, and we usually stayed with them at least once a year at Peebles or at Gala Lodge at Broughton, which was a paradise for the children. Gala Lodge stands on the side of a hill looking over a wide glen to Ratchel Hill, which always reminds me of a very worn Persian carpet, its stone screes, patches of heather and green slopes making a harmonious pattern.

My husband has painted a portrait of his mother in *Memory Hold-the-Door* but has hardly mentioned his sister Anna or his brother Walter. Between them and John existed a deep devotion. His respect for Anna's opinions on books and life, and Walter's on other matters, notably politics and business, was profound. He consulted Walter constantly on all sorts of matters, and to hear them talking together of their childhood and youth revealed the close-knit companionship of those days.

One activity of Anna's in which he took an affectionate but remote interest was her acting and producing of plays. She had wanted in her youth to become a professional actress, but this was an unheard-of proceeding for a minister's daughter, and she contented herself with doing any amateur acting which came her way.

Whenever I see her act I feel that she is a real loss to the stage. She shows so much sense of the character of any part she undertakes, and so much finish and expertness in her rendering. Walter is also a most talented actor, and my husband, though he seldom could be lured to act, acquitted himself well in any small part he was given to play. Anna and Walter always go to the theatre whenever they can, but plays bored John and he declared that the moment he was settled comfortably into his seat "sleep like an armèd man" came over him. He even asserted that he would far rather go to hear a sermon than go to a play. He rather liked to go and see Shakespeare acted, but he much preferred reading the plays to himself. Someone once came and read him part of a dramatisation of one of his own novels. Sleep again overcame him while he was supposed to be listening. In spite of this, he had a play in his head which never got written.

Anna's pen-name, O. Douglas, is widely known in the Dominions as well as in the British Isles. She has a daily fan mail from all parts of the world. In this war young soldiers have written to her from many battle-fronts to say how happily her books have reminded them of the charm and intimacy of their homes. Her descriptions of the Border country are lovely and her characters are set firmly within the framework of her stories. Her country people with their idiomatic speech and realistic outlook live and breathe. There is an atmosphere of such goodness, friendliness and kindness in Anna's books that it is not surprising that in these difficult days people want to read them. They have helped me through many a dark patch of sorrow and anxiety.

Henry Newbolt said of Anna's writing: "It is like sitting in a delightful room by a warm fire. This doesn't mean that the wind isn't howling outside, but one can enjoy the charm of the room and the fire all the more." I wish she wrote more books, but she has unfortunately too kind a heart, and can never say "no" to anyone, however tiresome, who comes to interrupt her work. Anna and I have seen much joy and sorrow together and our friendship has deepened over the years. She is much sought after as a speaker, which is not surprising, as her speeches and lectures are full of excellent matter excellently presented. As an aunt she is almost a legend. Her power of story-telling and ingenuity in providing treats and amusements, as well as her immense generosity, set her in a class by herself.

Walter succeeded his uncle as Town Clerk and head of the Commercial Bank of Peebles when he was a young man. His outstanding ability would have won him an assured position in any sphere, and his happy temperament and contentment with his surroundings make him delightful to work and live with.

Both Walter and Anna did much mountaineering in their youth, and Walter still walks fast and far. He has written the standard history of Peeblesshire as well as a book on the Duke of Wellington's campaigns, but he does not seem inclined to write anything more. He possesses an excellent library and reads many books, and his conversation is a blend of humour, wisdom and kindliness which charms all those who are lucky enough to meet him. Many people would like to know Walter better and to see more of him, but he is too busy a man to have time for this, and, when he is not at a meeting, Anna and he spend their evenings quietly reading after their long day's work. Peebles is indeed a fortunate place to have had two such people living there, who not only work so hard for the community, but add so much distinction to the place in which they live.

CHAPTER V

LIFE IN THE FIRST WORLD WAR

IN 1913 we moved from No. 13 Bryanston Street to No. 76 Portland Place. It had all the spaciousness and grace of an eighteenth-century house, with a courtyard at the back where I again tried my hand at gardening, to be defeated by the voracity of the sparrows, who devoured every bit of green stuff that I planted. The house had a charming hall paved with black and white squares of marble, and John's library (the room we used the most), lined with bookshelves, was a pleasant room. Our drawing-room had a lovely ceiling, and Sir Hugh Lane found for us a blue French wallpaper which was put up by an aged paper-hanger who used what looked like a miniature garden-roller to smooth it down on to the walls. We were near the Regent's Park end of Portland Place. Its width gave it an airy freshness, and a glimpse of trees a slightly country feeling. Alice and Johnnie quickly discovered the joys of Regent's Park with its population of grey squirrels who came close to them demanding nuts.

The year 1914 had brought us troubles and anxieties. Alice was in the country staying with my aunt Blanche Firebrace. She developed an earache with a mounting temperature and had to be brought to London to be operated upon hurriedly for a mastoid. John and I clung together in those anxious days when the surgeon feared that a second operation might be necessary. Happily her temperature slowly went down and she recovered.

In July 1914 the doctors decreed that Alice should go to the sea, and about two days before war was declared we went to Broadstairs. John had seen Sir Edward Grey that morning and appreciated the gravity of the European situation. I realised that the man we had so often met at the Royal Hospital and at the Glen in Peeblesshire (who lay back in his chair in the evening while we all listened to Pamela Glenconner reading poetry aloud) was one of the arbiters of the destinies of Europe.

We had some quite nice lodgings at the seaside and should have enjoyed ourselves, as Alice's health improved all the time, but the war precluded all happiness and comfort. We were cheered at first by the length of the resistance at Liége, but I well remember the grim look on John's face when we saw the Fall of Namur on a poster. From then on we were to know little peace or happiness for the next four years.

John was seized by one of his unaccountable pains and had to go to bed.

His mind had been turning for some time towards the writing of detective fiction. He read a few thrillers and said to me one day before the war, "I should like to write a story of this sort and take real pains with it. Most detective story-writers don't take half enough trouble with their characters, and no one cares what becomes of either corpse or murderer."

He must have had the idea of a story in his head before the war began, but if he had not had to go to bed at Broadstairs *The Thirty-Nine Steps* might never have been written. He was corresponding with the War Office about joining up in the Army, but was told that in his present state of health it was useless to think of it, and that he might be used in other ways later on. To distract his mind from the dull bedroom in our lodgings he

started on a book. The Grenfells [1] were also at Broadstairs. They had been lent a villa on the North Foreland :
the tenancy carried with it the privilege of a key to what
our Nannie called the "private beach," a small cove
which was reached by a rickety wooden staircase. How
many steps there were I do not know, but John hit on
the number thirty-nine as one that would be easily
remembered and would catch people's imagination.
The staircase to the private beach has now disappeared
and has been replaced by an imposing steel or iron erection.
When this was done we received a small block of wood in
the shape of a step bearing a minute brass plate with the
words *The Thirty-Ninth Step*. But if the steps have
disappeared the book maintains its early popularity. John
used to read each chapter aloud to me and I waited
breathlessly for the next one. In 1935 a film was made
of it which has caused some controversy and a good deal
of disappointment to those who love the book and who
did not like the introduction of a woman into the story,
and other drastic alterations to the plot. We went to the
film *première* just before we sailed for Canada. John
enjoyed it and did not mind the alterations in the least.
My own opinion is, that it would have been a better film
if the producer had stuck to the original story; but if
one forgets about the book, *The Thirty-Nine Steps* as a
film is a very good piece of entertainment.

When we returned from Broadstairs we let our Portland
Place house and went to live with my mother at 30 Upper
Grosvenor Street. John was ordered a complete rest in
bed and special treatment, and we had a nurse to look
after him who seemed to find us a bewildering but amusing household. My mother's house with our two selves,
our Nannie and two children, was stretched to bursting
point. She was very good to us, and her cook, Mrs.

[1] My first cousin, Hilda Lyttelton, married Arthur Grenfell.

Bird (a lifelong family friend), had a knack of making everything seem easy when really things must have been very difficult.

In the spring of 1915 John acted as *Times* correspondent in France, and that summer the F. S. Olivers proposed a delightful arrangement to us. They suggested that we should live at their house, Checkendon Court in Oxford-shire, and that they and their sons and daughter should come down for the week-ends. Checkendon is a charming old red-brick house on the outskirts of a village, set in a beautiful garden and surrounded by beechwoods, where in those days crafts flourished of all kinds. On a common in the heart of the woods there was a clearing where an old man made chair-legs, carving them out with a knife with great rapidity and precision, and "Chair-leg Common" soon became the children's favourite walk.

The Olivers came for week-ends. Fred was working hard at his business in London, and, in spite of the war strain, conversation was lit up by flashes of wit when John and he got together. I remember asking Fred in a letter if we could have some guests on a certain date, and I still have his reply in which he gave a long list of all the people he hoped I would *not* invite to Checkendon, which it would be libellous even now to publish. It was a dreary and alarming summer from the point of view of war news. One spring day I sat in the sunshine beside a great bank of white lilac in the garden trying to make a very elementary type of gas mask, and heard afterwards how the men who bore the brunt of the first gas attack at Ypres lay gasping their lives away under blossoming trees. John wrote in *Memory Hold-The-Door*: [1]

I was in the Salient during the second battle of Ypres, and the scent of hawthorn and lilac battled with the stink of poison-gas,

[1] *Memory Hold-the-Door*, p. 181.

and bird-song in the coverts heard in the pauses of the great guns, seemed to underline grimly the indifference of nature to human ills. I remember a June morning, too, in the Chilterns, the beauty of which seemed to me only a savage irony.

There was still no rationing, and life in England was fairly normal. I was expecting a baby and spent the summer quietly with the children doing any war jobs that I could find, such as rolling bandages on a strange wooden machine.

The casualty lists went on mounting and the world was shocked by the sinking of the *Lusitania*, which brought loss and unhappiness to many people, including my mother, whose friend Sir Hugh Lane was one of the victims of German ruthlessness. We moved back to 30 Upper Grosvenor Street, and our second son, William, was born on January 10th, 1916. I remember as I came round from the anaesthetic hearing bugles playing martial music in Hyde Park. I little thought that my baby son would be a fighter-pilot in another war.

John was in France, mostly at G.H.Q., in 1916-1917, coming back for short leaves. My only sister, Margaret, married in 1916. She had been working in a hospital in France and met there a charming Australian, Jeremy Peyton-Jones, and they became engaged. Their financial prospects were not brilliant, but we all liked Jeremy from the first. He had so much integrity, gentleness and charm. They were married at St. George's, Hanover Square. It has been my fate to have to help with weddings in two wars. In 1942, when my youngest son, Alastair, married Hope Gilmour, there were no cups or glasses to be bought or hired, and I had to put in hand a large-scale scheme of borrowing from my friends.

I remember no such shortage in 1916, though there were other difficulties. A friend of ours, Constance Lane, was staying with me while John was at G.H.Q. She was tall, fair and blue-eyed, and had great charm and distinction. She was a gifted painter and musician and sang delightfully. In her lighter moments she told admirable cockney stories and preached a sermon in a strong Oxford accent which convulsed her hearers with merriment. She was a great comfort to me in this lonely anxious time of war. Tidiness and punctuality were, perhaps, not her strongest points, and I remember the anxiety I endured on the morning of my sister's wedding when Cooie (as we called her) sat up in bed, a wet and slippery kitchen tray balanced precariously upon her knees, while she wove a myrtle wreath for my sister to wear. I kept on throwing anxious glances at the clock as the time of the wedding drew nearer and nearer. It was finished just in time and I rushed with it to 30 Upper Grosvenor Street. When my sister made her way up the aisle the wreath gave a lovely and appropriate finish to the soft white dress and old lace veil which she was wearing.

I find it hard to recapture the atmosphere of the years of 1914-1918. I sometimes feel as if the two-and-a-half decades between were phantom years and that the two wars are merged into one. There is, perhaps, no very exact parallel to be drawn between this war and the last one, as this war has been so much a war of movement. In the earlier war trenches stretched for hundreds of miles and bloody encounters raged for the possession of a few yards of earth, in which men existed somehow in dugouts, in continuous danger, amidst mud and rats and vermin. They came on leave for a few days at a time to London or the country, bringing cheerfulness into their homes by their gaiety and a sort of unstressed irony which masked their knowledge of how brief was their expectation of life in France or Flanders. It was not the fashion before 1914 to wear black except for family mourning, and as time went on one became conscious of

the sombreness of the crowds in London as the casualty
lists lengthened. We had what would now be called a
"dim out" after dark, and Portland Place was lovely at
night. Paper was pasted over the street lights, which
looked like clusters of pale pink flowers in the dusk, and
our window black-out was sketchier than in this war.
The last war, like all wars, was a long, anxious, frustrating
grind for most civilians, although there were those who
made more money than ever before and managed to
enjoy themselves. There were no clothing coupons, but
stuff deteriorated in quality so much that "I am sure that's
not new" was the highest compliment one could pay to
the wearer of a dress or shoes. There were endless experiments in controlling prices, which generally ended in
the article so controlled vanishing completely from the
market. The Government rationing scheme, when
introduced, worked well, but there were queues everywhere. When the air raids began I remember a woman
in a bus saying "What a life, queues all day, raids all
night." The raids were much milder than in this war.
We used to repair to a rather mouldy wine-cellar, underneath the dining-room, with Alice and Johnnie, who
lay warmly wrapped in the wine-bins, and William who
gurgled cheerfully in his pram. John got early notice of
the raids, so we had usually just arrived in the cellar
when they began. The last time the enemy planes came
to London in 1918 we did not go down to the cellar but
took the children to the drawing-room. Our anti-air-
craft barrage had become stronger, and the noise was
formidable. Finally a bomb fell near us in the gardens
between Portland Place and Regent's Park. The impact
on our house was curiously slight. Johnnie was shaken
off the drawing-room sofa and two miniatures fell out
of their frames. I remember sitting in the gardens next
day and listening to the endless shovelling up of splintered

glass. One evening we had been engaged to dine with Violet Markham but a raid supervened. She telephoned to us to come to her house after it was over. We walked to Gower Street and spent the rest of the evening with her. We saw on the way to her house dim figures bent double hunting in the gutters for pieces of shrapnel as souvenirs.

Housekeeping, of course, became harder all the time. The munition factories and Government offices absorbed a great deal of labour, and running a big house caused me endless worry. John's work at the Ministry of Information necessitated a great deal of entertaining. I had added to my difficulties by having a class of children daily in the house under the able charge of Miss Bernau their teacher. The class increased in popularity, but so did the muddy footprints in the hall, which caused such domestic help as I had to look askance at me. It is strange to think that the boys and girls who came to this class have borne the brunt of another war.

One of the things that also appears strange now is the amount of meals which one gave to one's friends and enjoyed in other people's houses. We all worked very hard, but we certainly had more social life than in this war. I was a V.A.D. on the administrative side, and also went twice a week to an Infant Welfare Centre in Kentish Town. This necessitated endless long rides in buses which were always over-full, and taxi-drivers were then, as now, unkind and rapacious. I helped Lady Wolmer to start a day nursery in Gospel Oak Grove for the children of the surrounding district. John was much taken by the intriguing name of this street, and he built some of the narrative of *The Three Hostages* round it.

John's health worsened all through the war, and he had a very bad time in 1916 when he got an internal cramp one night in a cold and comfortless billet in France. He took some hours to crawl inch by inch to the door to attract the attention of the sentry. When he did so he was taken to a Casualty Clearing Station where he lay in great pain until he was given some morphia. Howard Spring, in his book *In the Meantime*, writes:

"A few bright memories survive from those weary years, and most of them are of persons. Taking it all in all, we were lucky in our officers, though there was a sprinkling of nameless swine. I remember John Buchan, a cavalier if ever there was one, always commanding our respect but never forgetting how to unbend. It is a mystery to me how he got through the days as he did. He was doing his work as an Intelligence officer; he was writing his history of the war; and he was somehow fitting in novels as well. For a little time, at Beauquesne, he was unwell, and a sergeant had to call on him in his billet. He found Buchan lying in bed, unable even then to rest, the pages of *Greenmantle* strewing the blankets. Buchan went home on leave towards the end of that year, and told the sergeant he would like to bring him back a Christmas present. I never knew another officer give an 'other rank' a Christmas present, but this was typical of Buchan's warm human personality. The sergeant had the sense to say flatteringly that he would like an autographed copy of *Greenmantle*, a reply which suggests an aptitude for the diplomatic service rather than the Methodist ministry, which I know he decorates, and I trust adorns."

John was recalled from France in 1917 to take over the job of Director of Information under the War Cabinet. He lived at home in comparative comfort, but his health grew no better and the doctors advised a major operation. It was performed in our house and lasted over two hours, and I endured sickening anxiety while my mother and Hilda Grenfell plied me with cups of tea and tried by their kindness and sympathy to distract my mind. John recovered well and we went down to Checkendon. It was a backward spring and there was little in the way of green shoots to be seen on the trees. Dougie [1] and Claire Malcolm and Anna were with us, and Claire and I managed to find two crocuses in the garden, otherwise there were no flowers anywhere. It was an oasis of rest to us all. We read aloud in the evenings and John slept for most of the day. If he could have continued living a peaceful and placid existence he would have been saved from ill-health for the rest of his life, but when we returned to London he had to take up his work. Red leather boxes poured in on him even while we were at Checkendon filled with official papers.

Sir Roderick Jones writes:

"The restless and dynamic urge which made John Buchan work twice as hard as, and far more swiftly than, the majority of people, is not free from evil. There can be no doubt that he constantly over-tried his body if not his brain. I particularly recall an illness he had when directing the Department of Information. Lockhart Mummery performed on him the operation of short-circuiting about which, and its consequences, in those days little was known. It was a dangerous proceeding and called for care and rest in convalescence. Yet disregarding all prudent advice Buchan insisted upon papers being sent to him from the Department, which he studied, annotated, and fixed judgment upon, and, in general, directed the Department from his bed, when he ought to have been relaxing peacefully and allowing nature to do her healing unimpeded. But his unquenchable spirit and energy drove him forward, then and at many another time, and I cannot help feeling that he paid dearly for it in the end."

[1] Now Sir Dougal Malcolm.

I can heartily endorse what Sir Roderick has said. John's work at the Department of Information was a constant drain on his strength. He often worked for fourteen hours a day, bringing home stacks of papers to read in the evening, and I had to sit helplessly by, and see the good effects of the operation completely done away with.

It is very hard to get any data about the Department of Information in the last war.[1] Nearly all John's colleagues are dead with the happy exception of Stair Gillon (who acted for a time as his private secretary), Lord Macmillan, Sir Eric Maclagan, Harold Baker and one or two others, but I quote from what Lord Macmillan and Sir Roderick Jones have kindly sent me of what they remember.

The latter says:

". . . it was not until the 1914-18 war that John and I worked together and laid the foundations of what became an enduring and delightful friendship. When Mr. Lloyd George, as Prime Minister, entrusted to Buchan the task of creating and operating the Department of Information,

[1] Lord Macmillan writes: "John became Director of Intelligence with Harold Baker and myself as his chief assistants. The Intelligence Department has been described as the 'power house' of the Ministry. Its business was to receive and digest all information necessary for the work of propaganda and to inspire a suitable propaganda policy in the different countries. It translated the policy of the Government into terms of propaganda. It is difficult to recall or to give an adequate account of the day-to-day work of the Intelligence Department. It received much confidential material and collected information from all quarters on movements of opinion abroad. On these it based reports and instructions for the sections engaged in the preparation of articles for the foreign press, publications of various kinds, photographs, films, etc. Much of John's time was spent in gathering information from interviews with diplomatic and other visitors and in arranging for visits of British representatives to foreign countries. He was certainly very busy and I think he enjoyed doing work which often bore resemblance to the performances of some of the characters in his novels. All the time he kept on writing and issuing the instalments of his *History of the War*."

John asked me to assist him in the capacity of Government Cable and Wireless adviser. I was at that time head of Reuter's, having succeeded the late Baron Herbert de Reuter in 1915, and I at once placed myself at John's disposal. In the beginning this meant giving up a few hours in the daytime, and working into the night when my normal tasks at Reuter's were finished. But in a little, as the Department expanded, in response to the stimulating impulse of Buchan's inspiration and energy, my work increased and there came a moment when I had to limit myself at Reuter's to the mornings, nine-thirty until lunch-time, and surrender the rest of the day, generally until midnight, to the Department. I mention this, not to magnify myself in my part in the piece but to indicate how the scope of the Department grew under John Buchan's hand, making ever new demands on its adherents, and to illustrate John's capacity for winning support and co-operation from those about him.

For he was tireless and swift. We others strove to imitate him, perhaps not always with success, but certainly with more effect than if we had had a less sympathetic and vitalising leader. I possess no diary or notes of that period, but I remember that two of John's most devoted and, unlike me, full-time assistants, were Charles Masterman and Geoffrey Butler. Butler did admirable work running our New York office. Charles Masterman was in control at Wellington House, S.W., the headquarters of our pamphlet and mail publicity. Much of this publicity was of a peculiar and literary character, and John attached importance to it. Nevertheless it was briskly criticised by certain journalists who considered pamphlets a waste of money and who pinned their faith to telegraphic intelligence. They did not always recognise that Buchan's faith in telegraphic intelligence was not inferior to theirs. They were apt to think him a 'Highbrow.' They recalled

that he had been a member of Milner's 'kindergarten.'
They overlooked that he had also been a successful *Times*'
correspondent and newspaper contributor; and I can
testify that but for his initiative and support British
telegraphic publicity abroad would not have been encouraged and developed as it was.

The truth is that Buchan believed in employing all
means available to his hand of presenting the British cause
to foreign and neutral countries and to the Empire. He
was liberal-minded and had vision. He had no prejudices
and no leanings towards one instrument or one vehicle
more than to another. He certainly gave every encouragement to Charles Masterman's, and to the other, non-
telegraphic departments. But I do not remember ever
submitting to him a recommendation for telegraphic
expansion, of which I was naturally an ardent protagonist,
which he did not support and, within the limits of official
policy and Treasury indulgence, did not authorise. I feel
bound to place this on record because Buchan was criticised
harshly by friends of mine, conspicuously by Sir Robert
Donald, the powerful editor of the *Daily Chronicle*, for
his conduct of the Department in general and of the
telegraphic and literary publicity. The criticism was
unfair, and I gave John every support I could in resisting
it, a fact which he recalled more than once in later years
with a gratitude which I felt I did not deserve. Robert
Donald must have behaved more destructively than I ever
suspected at No. 10, where he had the ear of the Prime
Minister, for John always alluded to him afterwards with
an unmeasured bitterness wholly foreign to him and
reserved for Donald alone. Towards his fellows generally
Buchan was, in my experience, one of the kindest of
men; to decry others or to harbour enmity was repugnant
to him. By the end of 1917 the operations of the Department of Information had so developed, and underground

challenges were such, that the Prime Minister detached it from the Foreign Office and erected it into a Ministry. Early in 1918 Lord Beaverbrook became Minister of Information. The Ministry was planned on a much more elaborate scale than the Department, which it absorbed, and John Buchan accepted the position of Director of Intelligence. I put my functions as head of Reuter's into commission and became Director of Propaganda. In that capacity my happy association with Buchan continued till the end of the war.

During 1917 and 1918 he and I paid several visits together to Flanders, Haig's headquarters, and to France in discharge of our duties. These breaks in our normal activities were precious, chiefly because in Buchan I found the most delightful of touring companions. He was versatile, vivacious, and gay, and his talk extended over an astonishing range of topics; I cannot recall spending a dull moment in his company during our many long hours of sea passage and of travel by rail and motor, coupled with a fair amount of tramping."

On April 9th, 1917, after John had left for the Foreign Office, I received Anna's telegram saying that their brother Alastair had died of wounds. I got into a taxi in an agony of mind. It was a mild, wet spring day and I remember hoping that the taxi would take a long time to get to its destination, so that I could think of some words which would perhaps soften the blow to John. When I arrived at the Foreign Office I wandered through a maze of dark corridors, and, as John had someone with him, I had to wait to see him.

When I got into his room he sprang up smiling to greet me. All my carefully prepared words deserted me, and I held out the telegram to him simply saying "Alastair." We went home together and found a telegram

there to say that Tommie Nelson had also been killed.
Alastair's death was a deep and enduring grief to both of
us. He was a most charming boy, unselfish, amusing and
intelligent, and, with Tommie Nelson, a great slice of
our life seemed to go for good.

To go back to the Department of Information, my cousin
Lucy Masterman has given an admirable account of her
husband's work there.[1] The vicissitudes of that Department will come as no surprise to those who have watched
the fortunes of the Ministry of Information in this war.
It was violently attacked in the press and received scant
praise or recognition, and yet the value of the work it
did was very great. My husband's contribution had
been an outstanding one and was recognised by all
those who came in contact with him. His mind was a
subtle and ingenious one, and he had a long-range
imagination which enabled him to see the kind of
angle in which to present our case to other countries. He
was always very good in ordinary life at seeing other
people's points of view, and he brought this flair into
his work.

Propaganda is a word which now gives us a sickened
feeling, but it is hard to find a substitute for it. It was
highly necessary that Great Britain should put her case
imaginatively and intelligently to other countries and
to explain to them the greatness of her war effort. As
a nation we have a curious distaste for this, and we are
very bad at explaining just what we are doing. Telling
the truth about ourselves we feel savours a little of boast-
ing. (We must have mentioned the word "propaganda"
a good deal in our family circle, as some years later one
of our children asked me what was the exact significance
of the juxtaposition of the words "pope and gander"!)
John says in his autobiography: "I have some queer

[1] *C. F. G. Masterman*, by Lucy Masterman.

macabre recollections of those years—of meetings with odd people in odd places, of fantastic duties which a romancer would have rejected as beyond probability." [1] This was indeed true. Strange and improbable things happen in wars, but I think that, if John was alive to-day, he would say that the second war surpassed the first one in the fantastic stories that have been told, and are still to tell. Perhaps some day an account of the two Ministries of Information will be written, with comparisons drawn between them. I wonder if those who ran it in this war have had the same exhausting and unending struggle with the Service Departments as to the release of news? John had to contend a great deal with this. His personal popularity and vast acquaintance with many types of people stood him in good stead, but he found this part of the work both trying and exhausting. But it was a job well done and John's work has endured. To mention only one part of it, the pictures he commissioned from various artists are still interesting. He enjoyed this part of the work immensely and made great friends with Sir William Orpen, who afterwards painted a posthumous portrait of his brother Alastair. He met again his friend of early Glasgow days, Sir Muirhead Bone. He always liked meeting people and explaining things to them, and he specially enjoyed his contacts with the United States, and distinguished visitors from there poured through our house.

If John's reward for this work was a consciousness of work well done, it enriched our lives also by the friendships we made in England (as well as America), notably that of Henry Newbolt. Henry was one of the most interesting people I have ever met. He radiated sympathy and kindness and was a delightful talker and letter-writer. He was devoted to John, and John to him. He often

[1] *Memory Hold-the-Door*, p. 171.

spoke to me of John's steadiness through every crisis. During the dark days of the German break-through in 1918, when Haig's despatch containing the words "Our backs are against the wall" had sent a shudder through the nation, Henry described to me the lunch hour at the Athenaeum Club, where busy men were rapidly eating a war-time meal. When John came in all heads turned in his direction and whispers were rife. "How does he look to-day? Does he look more cheerful than yesterday?" Henry always said that John's imperturbable calm did not vary, and that this did a great deal to steady people. When the Armistice came he was so exhausted that he did not even go out to see the celebrations on Armistice night, but went to bed and stayed there for a short time. When he emerged after this brief rest he wound up the Ministry of Information with all speed.

I sustained a great loss in 1918 when in March of that year my cousin, Jack Stuart-Wortley, was reported missing in the German advance.

He was seen going into the regimental headquarters in a last-minute attempt to destroy maps and papers; then the German barrage blotted everything out and he was never heard of again. John was very fond of Jack and painted such a vivid portrait of him that I am including it in this volume.[1]

John also wrote about Francis and Riversdale Grenfell. This book was published in 1920, the profits going to the Invalid Children's Aid Association, a cause which the Grenfell brothers each had at heart. It had not only a big sale in the wide circle of "Rivy's" and Francis's friends, but it was read by many other people who knew nothing of the Grenfells but whose imagination was fired by his account of those two gallant and debonair twins. No one

[1] See Appendix.

who ever knew the Grenfell twins could forget them or cease to lament their loss.

Just after the war John and I wrote a little book together. It was on the lines of his earlier book *A Lodge in the Wilderness*. In it a group of people meet in a Scottish shooting-lodge to discuss post-war problems.

It was published anonymously under the name of *The Island of Sheep* [1] by Cadmus and Harmonia. The names were taken from Matthew Arnold's poem, and why we should have thought of ourselves as "bright and aged snakes" I don't know, except that snakes are detached creatures and we wanted to be as detached as possible.

We had the fun of hearing the book discussed and criticised, for the secret of its authorship was well kept. *The Island of Sheep* had a small circulation, and has now vanished from the shelves of even the mustiest of second-hand book-shops.

I re-read it the other day and was touched by our idealism and faith in the future. The chief gain, so far as I was concerned, was the fun I got out of writing a book with John. He took one's ideas and transmuted them into something so much better. He also corrected the proofs and made all arrangements with the publishers. We both enjoyed our bit of joint authorship very much.

If the tone of *The Island of Sheep* was idealistic and hopeful, it reflected the mood of the moment. After the last war we really believed that there would never be another world conflict.

Years afterwards, in *Memory Hold-the-Door*,[2] John writes in a much sadder strain : "The war had shown that our mastery over physical forces might end in a nightmare, that mankind was becoming like an overgrown child armed with deadly weapons, a child with immense limbs and a tiny head."

[1] He afterwards took this title for a novel.   [2] p. 183.

CHAPTER VI

OUR LIFE AT ELSFIELD

LIFE before the 1914 war had many inequalities and disadvantages, and all those tragedies which attend human beings on this earth. Yet to many people, when they look back, the landscape of those days seemed to be bathed in a rosy glow, and autobiographies are now written by the elderly which are eagerly read by the young, who have known adventure but not security.

The years between the two wars are now spoken of with horror and reprobation by many people, but to us both they were very happy ones. Just after the war ended we decided to leave London. Our youngest son, Alastair, had been born on the 9th of September 1918 and our eldest son, Johnnie, was not a strong child, so we thought that if we could live in the country it would make him and our other children happier and healthier. The weary war years in London had given us both a distaste for town life.

There was not the same housing shortage at the end of the last war that there is now. We were very lucky as we only looked at three houses in all. I had longed to go to the Cotswolds, and had seen in my mind's eye a Tudor farmhouse beside a stream with a group of tall chestnut trees standing close by. This proved to be merely a dream, as John had to go to London daily for his work, so we sought for a house near Oxford, the train service between there and London being in those days admirably fast and efficient, and John had always been held by the spell of Oxford since his undergraduate days.

We looked at the Manor House at Weston-on-the-Green,

and then on a winter's day, when the ground was hard and the grass was sparkling with hoar-frost, saw Weald Manor at Bampton. It was just the house of our dreams, a miniature of a mansion with lovely rooms containing stately mantelpieces. Unfortunately it was too far from London for us to contemplate its purchase. I mention it here because this glimpse of it inspired one of John's short stories, "Full Circle."[1] The house in the story is not exactly Weald, nor do the imaginary people with whom he filled it bear any relation to its past or present owners.

Our friend, Captain G. T. Hutchinson, then Treasurer of Christ Church, told us that his College were buying an agricultural estate and village at Elsfield with the manor house. "It's not a gem of architecture, but it has a lovely view," he said. We went out from Oxford to see it. I was charmed by the older part of the house with its panelled rooms and pretty staircase, and appalled by the ugliness of the addition made about 1875. But I soon saw that the house had possibilities and that the garden, laid out in the eighteenth century by Francis Wise,[2] was beautiful. So we bought it and no shadow of regret for doing so has ever crossed our minds. Even in these days, when its capacious basement and precipitous back-stairs cause me endless difficulties, I still would rather live at Elsfield than anywhere else. I had always loved flowers, but never began to work seriously at gardening till I returned from Canada in 1940. I realise now how spread out the two gardens are, the kitchen garden on the one side being separated by acres of lawn from the other flower garden where we also grow vegetables. "Who laid out this garden, I should like to know?" our one surviving gardener asked me bitterly the other day. When I explained that

[1] Included in *The Runagates' Club*.

[2] Mr. Wise, Radclivian Libraries, "with whom Johnson was much pleased," Boswell.

it had been laid out in the magnificent eighteenth-century days he merely grunted in disapproval.

The view from the windows is a perpetual feast of pleasure in all seasons of the year. The house looks west, and the sunsets, framed by our tall library windows, whether brilliant or spectacular or quiet in tone, are something to look forward to at the end of the day. Our garden wood is called the Crow Wood, where the rooks caw and wheel above a tall grove of beech trees.

The front door opens on the village street and we are on intimate terms with our neighbours. Life in a village is full of excitement, and bubbles like a seething pot with dramas from the cradle to the grave. I have for many years taken an active share in the work of the Oxfordshire Federation of Women's Institutes, and the kindly welcome which I receive in many Oxfordshire villages is a delight to me. John had a great admiration for Women's Institutes, and helped them in every way he could. One of his speeches at our Annual Meeting in Oxford is still remembered by those who heard it. He said that if you had an Institute in your village you could never be surprised by anything that happened. If you met your cook on the stairs dressed as Cleopatra, or looked out of the window and saw a group of Arabs with some camels on the lawn, you just said to yourself, "Well, well, that's one of the activities of the Women's Institute." He was never a feminist, but he believed that women had a great part to play in the life of the nation, and he took up the cudgels for any woman who he thought had done some outstanding work and was not getting her due meed of appreciation.

We took some time getting into Elsfield Manor and we lived in a house on Headington Hill while we settled our furniture into our new house. I remember the delays caused by strikes and all sorts of post-war unrest. Sir

Charles and Lady Oman gave a delightful dinner-party for us at which we were the guests of honour, and I was obliged to go to it in day clothes as our luggage was islanded somewhere between Broughton and Oxford. as a result of a railway strike. The Omans were kindness itself, and their daughter Carola, looking like a lovely Venetian picture in a gold evening dress, made everything pleasant and delightful. Her friendship and her books have been a joy to me ever since. John admired her writing and especially liked her historical novel *Major Grant*, which he read aloud to us on a holiday. I used to go out daily from Headington to Elsfield on golden autumn days when the bright leaves detached themselves from the big chestnut trees and slowly floated to the ground.

We finally moved into Elsfield on the 9th of January 1920, in time for William's fourth birthday. I had always lived in London and I secretly wondered how I should take to a country life, but the children's delight in Elsfield and every form of country pleasure was so great that I was quickly converted. We have a great many old outhouses and a barn where they played endless games and set up a carpentry business with a painted sign which said simply "Buchan Brothers, Limited." At first John was less busy in London and we had some time for walks and for exploring the surrounding country, collecting flowers and watching birds. Besides our glimpses of University life in Oxford we made friends with one or two other Oxford people. There is a curious aristocracy of intellect which is outside the colleges, and we saw something of Mr. Claridge Druce, a botanist of international repute who started as a boy in a chemist's shop, and then owned the business in the High Street that bore his name for a number of years.

I remember that I was dressing for dinner one evening

93

when I received a message to say that Mr. Druce was downstairs and that he urgently wanted to see me. Much surprised, I hastily concluded my toilet and rushed into the library, to find Mr. Druce, his face transfigured with joy, holding out a wilting flower for my inspection, saying, "I couldn't pass your door without telling you that I have found this." It was a specimen of a very rare orchis, not, it must be confessed, a very beautiful object, but he was so pleased at having found it that his enthusiasm communicated itself to me. I asked him where it grew but he refused to tell me, merely saying that it was in this neighbourhood. He made us both promise that if we ever did find rare flowers we should never divulge their whereabouts to anyone, as people were so conscienceless about going to dig up the roots. Our other friend was, Mr. Tickner. He was for many years the porter at the Clarendon Buildings and he was said to be one of the greatest field ornithologists of his time. He spent a spring day at Elsfield finding (to us) invisible birds' nests with a sort of wizardry which took one's breath away. Our eldest son has a natural flair for bird life, and to him the country round Elsfield was a paradise.

We sent our three sons to the Dragon School in Oxford, which has a strong individual tradition. Johnnie and William were weekly boarders and Alastair a day boy. John was asked to go and speak to the boys at one of their delightful Sunday services. The prayers are read by the boys most beautifully and with great reverence. Johnnie was rather perturbed at the idea of his father speaking at his school. "How shall I know if they like my talk or if they're bored?" John asked. "If they're bored they will drop their hymnbooks on the floor," was the reply. As no hymnbook dropped, we concluded that the talk had been a success. Another time Mr. Lynam [1] asked

[1] Headmaster of the Dragon School.

John if he would come and tell the boys some stories on a Sunday evening. He did so, holding them spellbound for more than an hour. I believe that several parents afterwards telephoned to ask Mr. Lynam if he really thought that telling exciting stories to boys just before their bedtime was a good idea.

Our three boys went to Eton to three different houses. I went there to see them much more often than John because he was so much more busy than myself, but we spent Saturdays or Sunday afternoons there sometimes together, and enjoyed that delightful freedom by which at Eton parents go to their sons' house by the back door, with the coals and other domestic necessities. We also enjoyed going up to the boys' rooms, and our freedom to have tea there and to read aloud and to indulge in endless conversation. We had many delightful Fourths of June; sometimes we had lovely weather but mostly it was wet and cold. In spite of the feeling of sheer exhaustion as the day went on, and a suspicion that one's tired feet belonged to someone else, they were very happy days. Eton amused and fascinated us both with its ancient taboos and traditions, and we were lucky as Cyril Alington, the Headmaster, married to a cousin of mine, welcomed us yearly for a week-end. Their drawing-room, with its beautiful Chinese paper and dignified and appropriate furniture, was always full of people. Hester Alington moved amongst her guests and children talking to everyone, making us all happy by her laughter and her individual and amusing turn of phrase. She was never ruffled or put out by anything, and her family, distinguished as much for their good looks as for their talents, laughed with her and helped her. To have known the Alingtons and their home life at the Cloisters is a memory to treasure all one's life. I am glad to think that our boys shared that experience with us, although as

Lower boys they were sometimes a little intimidated by meeting members of Pop at the Alingtons'. There was rather an attractive wool-shop in the High Street at Eton. I overheard an older boy asking Johnnie rather condescendingly, "Can you ever get your mother past the wool-shop? I can't ever get mine." I suppressed my laughter as I had a vision of a somewhat undignified scuffle between mother and son.

Three years after the war Roderick Jones [1] offered John the position of Deputy Chairman of Reuter's. Roderick writes:

"It was a whole-time job, designed, amongst other things, to enable me, which it did, to leave England on prolonged tours, including two journeys round the world, upon which I embarked to inspect not only the main territorial centres of the Reuter organisation, but also the isolated outposts.

Our close association at Reuter's was to me, and I believe to Buchan, most satisfying and pleasant. It continued for several years, and on no single occasion were we ever at cross-purposes with each other. In approaching a question we did not necessarily start with the same point of view. But we invariably ended in agreement, after thrashing the subject out.

And here let me mention an almost comic incident illustrative of Buchan's tolerance. He occupied a room next to mine. We had a communicating door. This propinquity obviously had working advantages, but at first it carried a serious drawback. John smoked the most unpleasant cigarettes. I frowned on office smoking. This was well known to the staff, who deferred most considerately to my implied wishes. How ironic and exasperating, then, that I should have to endure by the

1 Chairman of Reuter's.

hour, on my very doorstep, the reek of John's mephitic nicotine.

I stood it for a time; at length I could stomach it no longer. Either John must betake himself to a remote corner of the house or he must abandon cigarettes in office hours. One morning, at the end of my tether, I indicated that the Deputy Chairman's cigarettes were an abomination and had become insupportable. 'My dear Roderick,' came the swift reply, 'only one thing to be done—I drop smoking anywhere in your neighbourhood. Why in the world did you not speak sooner?' With anyone less understanding than Buchan the incident might have produced at least a temporary awkwardness. But over a long period of years I found him to be a lovable character with a gift for friendship, certainly not free from foibles (who is?) but inspired by devotion and loyalty to men or causes and charged with perseverance and a power of work quite out of the ordinary.

Of this power of work I had constant evidence. Reuter's connections and activities, especially in foreign countries, are, on the administrative and executive side, bewildering to a stranger. But their complications soon ceased to baffle John Buchan; very soon he was as familiar with them as some of our veteran managers. I made a practice of passing on to him administrative documents and data which had to be reduced to a handier form for purposes of consideration and decision. He would produce an epitome of the kind needed, for a recital of the facts, arguments and conclusions, in half the time that some of my senior and long-trained assistants would have taken. I suppose his early career as a barrister had something to do with this. But in the main his mental capacity chiefly was responsible.

It was at the beginning of 1923 that I persuaded John to become a working member of the Reuter Executive, as Deputy Chairman, instead of being merely a director and attending rather cut-and-dried monthly board meetings. In the summer of that year I started off on the first of my journeys round the world, designed to fortify by personal inspection and experience my theoretical knowledge of the Reuter men representing us in foreign countries and in different parts of the Empire.

Throughout this journey, which occupied nearly ten months, John wrote me regularly and fully. His letters were both interesting and illuminating, and bore testimony not only to his growing attachment to Reuter's, but also to his quick apprehension of its sometimes mystifying ramifications. There were lighter touches also, as when, after stalking in the Highlands, he informed me that he had developed 'a painful affliction of the skin of the face which Dr. Johnson believed to be congenital to Scotsmen.' 'I am not allowed to shave, and my appearance soon will be a cross between that of Abraham and Lazarus!' . . . It was about this time that John began to acquire a deeper knowledge, as he wrote me, of the Canada over which, twelve years later, he was to reign as Governor-General— he was studying Lord Minto's papers in preparation for a biography which he subsequently produced of that statesman.

I am not a prolific writer, specially when travelling, and apparently it was not until the end of September that John received my first letter since my leaving England. He began his routine budget by intimating that: ' "The First Epistle General of St. Roderick to the Reuterians" was greatly appreciated. You give a most vivid and delightful account of your journey, and I am very glad to know that, as they say in Scotland, your hosts are so much "taken up with you." ' Meanwhile, ever since August, he had been having a miserable time with the facial infection contracted in the Highlands. To quote his own words,

it was 'hideous and most painful and I have been thinking
with great sympathy of Sir John Falstaff.' However, a
drastic course of treatment cured him, and by mid-
October, shorn of the beard that he had been forced to
grow, he and his wife were able to spend a long week-
end at Chatsworth which the Duke and Duchess of
Devonshire had arranged for the Dominion Prime
Ministers who were attending the Imperial Conference
of that year. 'There is a good chance of trouble in home
politics,' he here remarked, 'owing to the determination
of a section of the Conservatives, with the assistance of
the Empire delegates, to press not only for Preference
but also Protection at the Conference.' There is a footnote. 'I am greatly saddened this week by Aubrey
Herbert's death. The most delightful and brilliant
survivor from the days of chivalry. I do not know if you
knew him, but we have been intimate friends ever since
the days when we used to go tandem-driving together at
Oxford, and, as he was almost blind, have the most
awful thrills. Perhaps his death has been merciful, for
if he had lived he might have been totally blind. He
was the most extraordinary combination of tenderness
and gentleness, with the most insane gallantry, that I have
ever known—a sort of survivor from the Crusading times.
I drew Sandy in *Greenmantle* from him.'"

CHAPTER VII

SOME OF OUR FRIENDS

I WAS very insistent that John should have holidays in these years, and we went to the Island of Mull, first to Ardura and then to Ben More Lodge near Salen.

Ardura was a charming little house perched on the side of a hill, full of nice furniture and books. Our two small boys fished incessantly in long black mackintoshes, bringing back quantities of eels which they found hard to dispose of, as no one really wanted them. John and Johnnie did more ambitious fishing and took long walks. Ben More was a Victorian Scottish shooting-box, grim and forbidding from the outside, and the loch was often hidden from us by a heavy curtain of rain, but it was cosy inside and we were very happy there. We spent many hours watching seals and picking up shells on the shores of Loch na Keal, an arm of the sea surrounded by hills. I confess with shame that I was a rather easily worried mother and the proximity of the deep loch caused me constant anxiety. I stood on the shore looking wildly at Alastair, who, having borrowed a wooden tea-chest from the kitchen, pushed it into the loch, got into it and sank very quickly. I was, however, gently rebuked by him next day when I proposed to accompany him to the water's edge. "Please don't follow me about," he said, "it is so disheartening."

The Island of Mull has a special quality about it. Rain falls there continuously, but the sun does sometimes shine, and the mountains have white threads running down their sides from burns in spate, and the wet rocks glisten in the sunshine.

We went to Iona on a day when the seas round the island were a translucent jade-green. We did some exploring and had tea. We were being taken back to the mainland by a sailing-boat at a special turn of the tide, but we were delayed as our dog, Spider, had struck up a friendship with some rather mongrel animals and was only rounded up after a long search. Then some ladies who were staying on Iona found out that Anna was there, and, being admirers of her books, brought bunches of heather for her to the quayside. All this took time and the two fishermen in the boat looked sternly at us when we embarked, and hushed Alastair severely when he started to talk and ask questions.

Each year we went to stay with Gerard Craig Sellar and his mother at Ardtornish near Loch Aline, opposite to Mull. Mrs. Sellar liked to stress the fact that she was a Victorian, but she possessed a charm and beauty which were of no special period, and she had an enormous capacity for laughing at herself, and her sympathy was amazing.

Many people who wished to charm others are clever at simulating sympathy and interest, but Gertrude Sellar listened to what other people had to say with a genuine delight which captivated all who came near her. She always remembered what her friends had told her about their various difficulties, and she made everything seem like an exciting serial story when one continued one's endless narrative; for no one could resist telling her all about their troubles and joys, the more so as she was extremely fastidious and uninquisitive and never wanted to know any more than one wished to tell her.

Ardtornish House is tall and ugly on the outside, but inside was beautifully furnished and full of lovely objects.

The contrast between the ordered comfort of the house and the wild mountain scenery outside was very piquant, and John delighted always in his return in the evening after a hard day's stalking in rough weather to its peaceful charm and pleasant conversation. Life at Ardtornish had a style and form of its own. A member of the younger generation said to me recently, opening her eyes wide, "Is it true that you dressed for dinner every night?" And I replied, "Not only did we do this, but when we returned to the house with muddy boots and shoes we took them off in the hall, rather than soil the beautiful pale green carpet on the stairs." This life can never come again, but I cannot forbear to linger a little on the recollection of its charm. Some of the stalking and fishing is reflected in John's books, and he became noticeably more carefree and happy when we boarded the boat at Oban to take us to Gerard's little kingdom.

As our children grew older we went to Wales for the holidays, as the mechanics of transporting a household there was a much easier task than a mass move to Scotland. We had the good fortune to be able to take Frwdgrech under the Brecon Beacons. It was a rambling house with big stables, and the huntsman would sometimes bring into the courtyard a pack of Welsh hounds whose long pale yellow faces had a comic charm all their own. It was a wonderful riding country and no one seemed to object to us going anywhere that we chose. The Beacons changed colour constantly, with the variations of the weather, and except for the fact that it rained a great deal, it was a perfect place for a holiday. We were as a family more or less philosophical about rain, as the west coast of Scotland and Wales were the places we chose for our holidays.

John, Johnnie and I went one year to Shetland to stay with our old friend Charles Dick, who was minister at a church in Unst, the most northerly island of the British Isles. It is a place set quite apart from the rest of the world. The weather alters every quarter of an hour and the greeting of one islander to another consists of one word, "Showery." The wind blows incessantly and often with great fury, and the cloud effects are lovely as they move rapidly in all sorts of fantastic shapes across the sky.

The miniature Shetland sheep, ponies and collies had a charming habit of always wandering about in threes, and seals played along the shores lifting what Johnnie called "their shiny mackintosh faces" out of the water. He fished in the shallows off the shore in waders for piltocks and flounders, while I watched him from some distance, and was myself watched with candid interest by black-shawled women.

I remember that Charles Dick took us out to tea with two charming and beautifully dressed ladies and I felt a crushing sense of inferiority about my own and Johnnie's clothes. Johnnie had been fishing and I had been sitting in a boat, and we both presented a rather battered appearance. John always remained neat and tidy under all circumstances, and I feel must have wondered why it was necessary for his wife and son to look so much like tramps. One of our hostesses was dressed in a crêpe de Chine frock and the other one in painted chiffon; and they were very kind and overlooked our shortcomings and gave us a wonderful tea with home-made scones and strawberry jam. We enormously admired Charles Dick's mother, who, although over eighty, ran the house with the help of a little wild Shetland girl. Charles Dick was very anxious that John should preach a sermon in his church, and John preached to a congregation of islanders who listened with grave attention.

We embarked at Unst on a fairly calm morning but ran into very heavy seas, and Johnnie and I both succumbed to fearful seasickness, which was not improved by a steward who put his head round the door at intervals asking if we would like to partake of sheep's head. John was an excellent sailor and was completely unaffected by the weather, but Johnnie's and my relief was heartfelt when we felt the granite quays of Aberdeen under our feet.

We went twice to North America before my husband went to Canada officially in 1935. The first time was in 1924. John had refused to go on a lecture tour in the States though he was plied with many financially beguiling offers to do so. He was asked by an agent to give the same lecture many times, and he replied that if he lectured as often as that in quick succession, the large sum that he earned would merely serve to pay his expenses in the lunatic asylum in which he would be forced to spend the rest of his life. When, however, he received an invitation from Milton Academy to give the yearly memorial address for the Milton boys who had been killed in the war, he accepted the invitation and planned a holiday in the States for himself and me. We arranged for Alice to go abroad with my mother and Aunt Blanche, and the boys went to stay with their grandmother, to spend some halcyon weeks at Broughton.

We went first to Canada. We sailed up the St. Lawrence in perfect weather and landed at Quebec. We then went on to stay at Metis with the Robert Refords, then to Montreal and on to Boston, where John's friend and publisher, Ferris Greenslet,[1] welcomed us and we saw something of this delightful city. We ate innumerable and most admirable meals. After years of eating flabby wartime fish the recollection of those savoury dishes of scallops and lobster fill me with nostalgia. Good conversation and good food are my chief recollections of Boston.

Ferris Greenslet had arranged a tour for us in Virginia,

[1] One of the partners in Houghton Mifflin.

as he knew of my husband's passionate interest in the Civil War campaign. We went down to Washington by train and saw Arlington, and John was received by Calvin Coolidge at the White House. On the journey down we slept in the "sections" on the train, and I found some difficulty in dressing in the morning as all my clothes had somehow got lost in the bed. I slept badly and woke late, and was roused by the Negro attendant on the train. My eyes were still sealed by sleep and I cried, "Is that you, darling?' before I realised that it was not John who was trying to wake me.

We were joined at Washington by Samuel Eliot Morison, one of the greatest of American historians, and he and Ferris Greenslet proved to be the most amusing of fellow-travellers. Sam Morison refused to breakfast with us, wherein he had my fullest sympathy, as I have always held that breakfast should be a light and solitary meal. Sam said he nursed what he called a "breakfast grouch," and either went to a café or ate at a different table to us.

John liked a good solid breakfast, and when he awoke in the morning his brain was alert and he was ready for the day's work. I wake with difficulty, my brain working in very low gear at the beginning of the day.

Our journey, which we did in a car, was full of unexpected delights. We visited the Shenandoah valley and Chancellorsville and saw some of the stately Virginian country houses, including Jefferson's house Monticello. We also saw the lovely University of Virginia at Charlottesville. I remember John quoting Falkland's words about "a university in a clearer air" as we looked at the graceful buildings bathed in mellow sunshine under a cloudless blue sky, the leaves of the catalpa trees shining like burnished gold.

We went to stay at Three Hills, Warm Springs, with

the writer Mary Johnston and her sister. John greatly admired her two Civil War novels, *The Long Roll* and *Cease Firing*. He always said that they were the nearest to an epic which any woman had ever written. Mary Johnston had been brought up in the atmosphere of the Civil War, as she was the niece of the Confederate General Johnston, and she told us that in writing her books she sat up late at night drinking cups of black coffee, and that her dreams, when she did get to sleep, were haunted by dead and dying men.

She and her sister had a charming house in which they received selected paying guests. It stood on a shelf overlooking a valley. From the hill behind the house there was a wide and splendid view of the Alleghanies where one saw ranges of peaks stretching away into the far distance. Mary Johnston, brown-eyed and gentle, made us very welcome. Her house was full of books, and the scent of freshly made coffee pervaded it in the morning. The food that she gave us was something to dream of—fried chicken, salads and hot bread, crisp waffles, cakes and fruit (one member of our party suffered torments of indigestion the day we left and had to be given brandy not once but several times).

Ferris Greenslet wrote the following account of this trip : [1]

"In 1924, John and Susan Buchan paid a visit to the States. I drove them around New Hampshire, which reminded them of the Highlands of Scotland. We climbed Chocorua, and John, a member of the Alpine Club, proved a testing companion of the trail. Talking continuously, even on the steepest stretches, he accomplished the ascent in fifty minutes. Muttering 'Non sum qualis eram,' foaming at the mouth but trying to look

[1] John Buchan, by Ferris Greenslet, in the *Atlantic Monthly*, Sept. 1943.

pleasant, I just managed to keep within sound of the one-sided conversation.

We went to Washington, where I sat in the outer office of the White House talking with C. Bascom Slemp while John went in to see President Coolidge. He came out after an hour, twice his allotted time, flushed and smiling. Asked what they had been talking about, he replied, 'Latin poetry.' The President, he said, had shown a surprising knowledge of Virgil and Horace, and had spoken eloquently of what the language and literature of Rome had meant to him all his life.

I enquired rather sceptically, 'Wasn't it you who did most of the talking?'

'No,' he said, 'it was the President himself.'

From Washington, we set out in a large open car for a ten days' tour of the battle-fields of Virginia, where, as Mary Johnston told us later, the trunks of trees are so full of bullets that sawmill accidents are of daily occurrence.

We drove through the fat fields of Maryland to Antietam and Harpers Ferry, and up the valley of the Shenandoah. Equipped with old Confederate battle maps, we followed the marching and counter-marching of Stonewall Jackson's valley campaign. At Port Republic we approached a house marked on the map 'Lewis House,' and found old Miss Lewis sitting on the piazza where she had sat, as a young girl, on a June day in 1862, and seen Wheat's Tigers of Taylor's Louisiana Brigade burst from the woods behind the house to capture a Massachusetts battery on its front.

To my imagination, fed on Brady photographs and the drawings of Frank Leslie's 'own artist in the field,' Valley Pike and the wood roads that climb through the gaps of the Blue Ridge and the Masanuttons were thronged with thin bearded men in shabby grey uniforms. But it was John who told me—told even Sam Morison, who had joined us at Washington—the names of the mountains without looking at the map.

From Staunton we drove to Charlottesville, pausing at 'Miradar' for a glass of the Langhorne sherry; then on to Richmond, and under the expert guidance of Douglas Freeman covered the terrain of the Seven Days, from the Chickahominay to Malvern Hill. There John decided to leave to Freeman the biography of Lee, on the scale of Henderson's *Stonewall Jackson*, that he had long planned to undertake. We visited the great houses along the James—'Westover' and 'Shirley'—and turned north again through Fredericksburg to Washington. John's memory of the trip through the perspective of fifteen years was set down in a paragraph of the eloquent chapter in *Pilgrim's Way* [1] entitled 'My America':

> I came first into the United States by way of Canada, a good way to enter, for English eyes are already habituated to the shagginess of the landscape and can begin to realise its beauties. My first reflection was that no one had told me how lovely the country was. I mean *lovely*, not vast and magnificent. I am not thinking of the Grand Canyon and the Yosemite and the Pacific coast, but of the ordinary rural landscape. There is much of the land which I have not seen, but in the east and the south and the north-west I have collected a gallery of delectable pictures. I think of the farms which are clearings in the Vermont and New Hampshire hills, the flowery summer meadows, the lush cow-pastures with an occasional stump to remind one that it is old forest land, the quiet lakes and the singing streams, the friendly accessible mountains; the little country towns of Massachusetts and Connecticut with their village greens and elms and two-century-old churches and court-houses; the secret glens of the Adirondacks and the mountain-meadows of the Blue Ridge; the long-settled champaign of Maryland and Pennsylvania; Virginian manors more old-England perhaps than anything we have at home; the exquisite links with the past like much of Boston and Charleston and all of Annapolis.

[1] *Memory Hold-the-Door* was published under the name of *Pilgrim's Way* in the United States.

It was during this visit that, for the first time, I heard him make a public speech. I was astonished and charmed when the quiet, swift voice to which I was accustomed deepened its pitch and increased its volume, taking an old cadence of the Kirk of Scotland and an eloquence I had not heard since the brief church-going period of my own youth.

A frequent topic of conversation during the weeks we were together was the part field sports shared might play in international understanding. A little later the manuscript of a new novel, *The Courts of the Morning*, came over from him with a summarising dedication to me in verse :

> The same old tremor of the spring
> Assails the heart of you and me ;
> Nor does the reel less blithely ring
> By Willowemoc than by Dee.

> As bright the Ammonoosuc streams
> Dance through the silent scented woods
> As those which fill my waking dreams
> In Hebridean solitudes.

> Your land, old friend, is one with mine
> Whate'er may hap from time or tide,
> While, with St. Izaak the Divine,
> We worship at the waterside.

In acknowledging it, I quoted Thoreau's fine saying : 'The stars are apexes of what triangles!'"

We went to Philadelphia, where we dined with Edward Newton and saw his collection of books, and then on to New York, and then to Boston to stay with Roger[1] and Dorothea Merriman in that old and pretty house in Brattle Street, Cambridge. Dorothea was vital, gay and endlessly hospitable, and Roger, who had been John's beloved

---

[1] R. B. Merriman, author of the *Life of Thomas Cromwell* and many other books. First head of Eliot House at Harvard, where he was much beloved.

contemporary at Oxford, gave us that special feeling of being fêted that one only has in North America.

It is a very special gift to make your guests feel not only happy, but to spoil them so subtly that they feel they are more interesting and attractive than ever before. One misses it sorely on returning to the bleaker social atmosphere of the British Isles.

Besides Milton Academy we visited several other schools, and Dan Merriman, Roger and Dorothea's son, wrote years afterwards to his father telling him of a walk which he took with John at Groton. In this letter he says :

"You and mother brought Mr. Buchan up on a beautifully clear Sunday, and after lunch he and I went for a walk down to the river, along its bank, and back through the woods by a path that was seldom used. The thing that is indelibly impressed on my mind about that afternoon is Mr. Buchan's knowledge of and interest in everything he saw. No bird, tree, shrub or flower escaped his eye. I thought I knew every detail of the walk ; I loved it and had been over it countless times in all seasons. But I soon found Mr. Buchan asking me about things that I had never noticed before, and more often telling me what they were. His knowledge was incredible, his powers of observation uncanny, and his supply of information about all branches of natural history inexhaustible. If memory serves me right, it was his first visit to this country—yet he knew almost all the things that he saw at once, and made frequent remarks about their counterparts in England, or, still more exciting, their lack of resemblance to anything he had seen before. Above all, his quiet way of teaching the youngster who walked by his side was highly efficient and at the same time completely delightful. It was a lesson I still remember, and it had the greatest effect in showing me what it meant to keep my eyes open."

Roger Merriman has sent me the account of his first
meeting with John at Oxford in a rather different vein :

"I won't dilate too much on the first episode, for it is
a fairly well-known tale and probably you have already
heard it. On the other hand, it was my first and most
dramatic meeting with John, and I shall never forget it
to my dying day. In February, 1898, the Balliol First
Torpid, in which I was number five, rowed head of the
river, but the Balliol parson, Jimmy Palmer, afterwards
Bishop of Bombay, would not let us have a bump supper
on the last night because it was Ash Wednesday. The
result was that we all went out to the club, had an excellent
dinner, and started back via St. Mary's and B.N.C. at
ten o'clock on a glorious moonlight night looking for
more fun. When we reached B.N.C. the gate was open
and we saw all kinds of evidence of celebrations going
on within, for B.N.C. had made six bumps lower down
the river, and had a less squeamish parson than Balliol.
We all filed in uninvited, and were promptly seized upon
by a multitude of genial souls who took us into the Junior
Common Room and ordered us drinks. Almost all the
undergraduates in the Quad were armed with rockets
and Roman candles, and as I was drinking a scotch and
soda with a genial gentleman whom I had never met and
whose name I did not know, one of them came up behind
me and inserted his Roman candle into my trouser-leg.
(I was wearing flannel bags next to the skin, like all good
Oxonians of the time.) Well, the combination of the
Roman candle and perhaps the alcohol which I had
previously absorbed caused me to 'pass out.' When I
came to, I heard loud voices shouting for John Buchan.
'He's the only sober man in B.N.C.!' In a minute a
charming young Scot appeared in front of me, smiling
and rubbing his hands and saying, 'I am exceedingly

sorry this should have occurred. What can I do for you?' And I said, 'I think the best thing would be to take me home.' A cab was accordingly ordered, and I was driven back to Balliol. John wangled his way past the porter despite the fact that it was after eleven, put me to bed, and came round to visit me on the following morning. I shall never forget his kindness. From that moment on I adored him."

Elsfield Manor.

CHAPTER VIII

ELSFIELD, PARLIAMENT AND HOLYROOD

JOHN writes of our early years at Elsfield in *Memory Hold-the-Door* in a chapter called "An Ivory Tower and its Prospect." I had always understood an Ivory Tower to be an abode of complete peace and seclusion from the world, but I can never remember much seclusion in those years. People came and went constantly. At first we had no telephone, but when a local exchange was established we agreed to let one be installed in our house. We did not put our name in the Telephone Directory, but the press and many other people quickly discovered our number, and the telephone rang constantly. Someone always seemed to be demanding that John should write something, or make a speech, or see some group of people or some individual about political or other scheme or schemes. But if we did not have much seclusion we had peace in the house, as John could never otherwise have achieved the daily quota of work he set himself to do. He describes his routine of life thus :

> On most days I went to my office in London, a longish daily journey, but it was worth while getting back late, even in winter, to the smell of wood smoke and the hooting of owls. Later, when I had given up business and entered Parliament, I arranged my life differently. From Monday afternoon until Friday I was in town and concerned exclusively with business and politics. From Friday evening until Monday at noon I was in sanctuary at Elsfield, a minor country gentleman with a taste for letters.[1]

[1] *Memory Hold-the-Door*, p. 193.

There are very few people in this world who have characters that nothing can mar or spoil. Amos Webb belonged to this rare category. When he became our chauffeur we realised that we were indeed fortunate. He had lived a great part of his life at Elsfield and both he and his wife came of good Oxfordshire stock, and he had that profound knowledge of country things which is becoming rarer every day. He drove our car, but that was only part of what he did for us. He knew all about running an estate, and our children's greatest joy was to trot at his heels while he went on his many errands. It was delightful to be driven by Webb, as he knew so much about the whole county, and nearly always when I went to tea at a country house Webb went off to visit a relation in a village or outlying farm, for he belonged to a large family which had many ramifications. Amos Webb went with us to Canada, where he was loved by all who met him, and it gave us a feeling of home to see his delightful smile and to hear his greeting. He had a slight stroke in early February 1940. He returned home before I did, and died in the May of that year.

His grave is next to my husband's in Elsfield churchyard. Both headstones are designed by Sir Herbert Baker and made in his workshops. On Webb's headstone is written: "Amos Webb the friend of Lord Tweedsmuir for twenty years."

We also had the good fortune to have an admirable indoor domestic staff. I must make a special mention of our cook, Mrs. Charlett, who, I am thankful to say, is still with me. She was (and is) one of those rare people whom nothing can surprise, and who, by skilful improvisation, can save the most difficult of domestic situations. My family love her dearly, and as soon as they have greeted me they make straight for the kitchen to talk to her.

To anyone less calm and wise our mode of life would

have been a difficult one to cope with, as people appeared from nowhere asking to see John and bringing him their problems, and friends came to stay for week-ends. On Sundays we sometimes had twenty or more under-graduates to tea.

Through it all Mrs. Charlett maintained a complete and imperturbable calm, and was always ready to surmount any difficulty which might occur. Through the war years she has been a friend to me and my family on whose loyalty and devotion we could always count. We have tried to repay her by affection and trust, but such service as she has given us is beyond repayment.

Soon after we came to Elsfield the children's Nannie, who had bravely faced the war years in London, had to leave us because of ill-health. Mrs. Charlett's daughter Elsie came to be with William and Alastair, and she and I looked after them together. They loved her dearly, her only flaw in their eyes being her avowed preference for little girls. She is now married and has two girls of her own, so the balance has been righted.

Elsie made the nursery a place where calm and order reigned, and the two little boys, with their deceptively angelic expressions, were happy and contented there, although they sometimes rolled together on the floor in violent combat. John liked to go to the top of the house to the nursery, and jokes and laughter overflowed from the room when he did so. The games usually ended in a request for a story, as they had early grasped his merits as an inventor and teller of tales.

The undergraduates who came to Elsfield just after we had settled there were Evelyn Baring and two other young men, Abraham Hewitt from America and Gordon Wesché from Australia, who played for Oxford at Twickenham. Then came David Maxwell Fyfe, John Foster, Roger Makyns, A. L. Rowse, and later Kenneth

Lindsay, Vere Pilkington, Frank Pakenham, Alan Lennox-Boyd, Quintin Hogg, Mary Somerville and Janet Adam Smith, also Christopher Pirie-Gordon and Roberto Weiss and many others. Some, alas, fell in the war, our greatest personal loss being the two delightful Heathcoat-Amory brothers. Patrick was a great friend of Johnnie's. He had a flair for and a great knowledge of politics and John prophesied a brilliant career for him in the House of Commons. He fell at Bir Hakim, leaving a memory of shining intelligence and charm. Gerald was Alastair's greatest friend at Oxford; one of the happiest and most graceful of his contemporaries. He was killed in Normandy one summer morning in 1945.

The young life which poured through Elsfield on Sundays was vivifying and inspiring, if somewhat exhausting. We often had week-end guests who were interesting for the young people to meet and who, in their turn, wanted to know what undergraduates were thinking and doing.

John went into politics in 1927. He could have got into Parliament before but had always hoped to be a University member. I think he felt that his health would never have allowed him to cope with all the rigours of a constituency added to parliamentary duties and other public speaking. When, after Sir Henry Craik's death, he was asked to stand for the Scottish Universities he gladly accepted the invitation. A University member is in a delightful position. His constituents vote by post and no canvassing or speeches are required. He was elected by a large number of votes. The children and I were washing our dog when the telegram came announcing this. We broke off this operation to have a family celebration. Our Shetland pony had foaled that day and we named the foal "Majority." John's association with the Scottish Universities interested and delighted him, and we often paid visits to Aberdeen, St. Andrews, Edinburgh and Glasgow, and I remember a specially charming visit to St. Andrews where we met many University people and heard some brilliant talk. He received an enormous number of letters and occupied himself in furthering all sorts of University and other educational questions. The years he spent in Parliament he enjoyed as much as any that had gone before in his life. He describes it all at some length in *Memory Hold-the-Door*, so I will only say a few words here.

I went to the House of Commons to the Ladies' Gallery to hear John make his maiden speech. He had gone into the House with a considerable reputation as a speaker, and the fact that he was making his first speech in Parliament had been given a very wide publicity by the press. It was very nerve-racking for him, as the House of Commons is a particularly difficult and critical audience. I suffered from no apprehensions that he would not make a good speech, but I was wrought up and excited, and I shivered in the stuffy gloom of the Ladies' Gallery. I felt deeply disappointed as the floor of the House, when John rose to his feet to speak, was almost empty. By the time his speech was finished the benches were full to overflowing. I must have looked rather wan, as an old lady beside me in the Gallery pityingly asked me, not once but several times, why I shivered, and suggested that I should go out and get a cup of tea. John's speech, which was in the debate on the Reform of the House of Lords, was well received and much quoted.

I spent many happy hours in the House of Commons; I always felt my spirits rise when I told the massive policeman at the door I had come to see Mr. Buchan, Scottish Universities. I found the policemen at the House of Commons invariably kind—in fact, my children accused me of pouring any difficulties I had at the moment into their sympathetic ears in the fashion of Mrs. Nickleby.

I went to hear John speak on the Greyhound Racing Bill, which had necessitated a rather difficult change of plans on my part. When I got to the Ladies' Gallery I was told by the policeman that Mr. Buchan had just finished his speech. The policeman gave me his whole attention as I told him of my disappointment. Perhaps listening to sagas by Members' wives is included in the list of duties for the officials of the House of Commons.

During these years we spent a good deal of time in London, living, as far as I was concerned, a rather uneasy kind of double life, as I was very busy with village and county commitments and had constantly to rush back to Oxfordshire for some meeting. We stayed at the Royal Hospital, and the memory of the grace and beauty of the rooms is constantly with me. Aunt Katherine was one of those people, as I have said, who made an interesting life all round her, and we were very happy there though John seemed to get progressively busier.

Alice had emerged as a grown-up person and took her share of the season's gaieties. She never greatly cared for large parties and more enjoyed remaining in a circle of amusing friends. Then she decided that she wished to go to the Royal Academy of Dramatic Art, as the family love of acting was strong in her. Johnnie was at Oxford and spent his Sundays and part of his Oxford vacations with us, combining a family holiday with an adventure like going as a deck-hand in a trawler, or visiting St. Kilda on a scientific expedition, about which he wrote a paper on the St. Kilda wren. One year he and John went off together to the Faroe Islands, which they enjoyed immensely, receiving wonderful hospitality and sport. Some of the landscape and atmosphere of those delightful islands comes into John's novel *The Island of Sheep*.[1]

Altogether we lived a very interesting life, full of

[1] Published in 1936.

activity. John worked harder and harder for the community, and I found the other day in a drawer a small card on which was written, "I have promised my wife not to work so much for other people." I wish he had kept this promise, but, alas, he did not. One of the happiest times in the year for us was April, when John's family came to stay with us. Anna came first for a week, and then my mother-in-law and Walter joined her. When Anna came we gave ourselves up to the pleasure of having her to stay. I prepared a portable desk for her so that she could sit by the fire in the upstairs library, which my husband had built for quiet and retirement at the top of the house. One window looks on to rose-beds and the garden wall, and beyond them to thatched cottages (which were there when Doctor Johnson and Boswell visited Elsfield). Through the two other windows you can see down into the Crow Wood, and to the right a wide view which starts with a downward slope of lawns and fields, then a long line of willows which fringe the Cherwell, which gleams through them like silver when it is in flood. The land rises from the woodlands of Wood Eaton and Blenheim in level ridges to the horizon. Many people have found this room an inspiring one. John wrote many books there, Anna part of her novels and autobiography, Elizabeth Bowen a short story, for Elizabeth and I had a pact that I would go to her house to write, and that she would come here, as it is so much easier to write in someone else's house.

The high-light of Anna's visit was always an expedition to Stratford-on-Avon. I remember driving there on some lovely spring mornings, but more often we went to Stratford on cold windy days when the apple and pear blossom in gardens and orchards were outlined against a steely-grey sky and we were whirled into the theatre by an icy gust of wind. When we returned home we discussed every shade of the performance with John, who was not, as I have said, a playgoer, but warmed with interest at anything which pertained to Shakespeare.

In the spring of 1930 Anna and I spent a few days in London at an hotel. Johnnie had made a bet with some of his Oxford friends that he would walk from there to London in a given time at night. As he passed through Stokenchurch he was stopped by the police. It took some time to convince them that he was not a suspicious character but an undergraduate who was taking a night walk for the fun of the thing. He arrived at our hotel footsore and weary, having failed to complete his journey in quite the required time.

One of the mornings we were in London I received a letter from John saying that the King had appointed him High Commissioner to the Church of Scotland at Holyrood.

It is very hard to write of Holyrood without using every kind of cliché and overworking the word "romantic" beyond all bearing. But the days at Holyrood did hold romance and charm of all kinds.

John wrote of it in *Memory Hold-the-Door* : [1]

> The Lord High Commissioner is the sole subject in Great Britain who on occasion represents His Majesty, and he must therefore conduct himself high and disposedly. Holyroodhouse used to be the last word in shabby discomfort; the High Commissioner had to bring his own plate, linen and other accessories, and bivouac in windy chambers where the rats scampered. Now it is like a well-appointed country house, and I think the west drawing-room, which looks out on Arthur's Seat, one of the pleasantest rooms I have ever entered. The High Commissioner and his wife are for a fortnight Their Graces, and, besides the Purse Bearer, are attended by a lady-in-waiting, by several maids-of-honour, and by four A.D.C.'s. During my two years of office I had as my A.D.C.'s representatives of

[1] p. 232.

ancient Scottish houses—Lord Clydesdale [1] and his brother, Lord Nigel Douglas-Hamilton; [2] Captain Duncan Macrae of Eilean Donan; and my future son-in-law, Captain Brian Fairfax-Lucy (a Cameron of Mamore). They all wore kilts of the old pattern, and made a most impressive bodyguard. I shall not soon forget those dinners in the great gallery of the Palace, where sometimes a hundred sat at table—the lingering spring sunshine competing with the candles, the dark walls covered with the portraits of the Kings of Scotland (daubs two hundred years old, but impressive in the twilight), the toast of the King, followed by the National Anthem, and that of the Church of Scotland, followed by Old Hundred, the four pipers of the Argylls, who strutted round the table and then played a pibroch for my special delectation. On those nights old ghosts came out of secret places.

I was asked by someone if I was nervous of ghosts, to which I replied that the bedroom I had at Holyrood was filled with solid Victorian furniture, the walls were hung with engravings of Queen Victoria on her Highland pony attended by John Brown, and that no one could feel anything but cosy and comfortable there.

But the apartments of Mary Queen of Scots held an enormous fascination for me, and whenever I had a moment free, either morning or evening, I went into her sombre and comfortless bedroom. I gently touched her ornate workbox containing a tangle of silks for her embroidery, and the slender tear-bottle which could not have held many of the tears she must have shed. I would also stand spellbound in the tiny room where she was having supper with Rizzio when he was dragged out and murdered. The sense of the past was all around me and the air weighted with drama. We were allowed some glimpses of Mary's curiously serene and lovely death mask in fragile wax.

I should like to pay a tribute to Lady Kinross, who, as

[1] Now Duke of Hamilton.
[2] Now Earl of Selkirk.

lady-in-waiting, sustained me through all our functions and duties. She never forgot a face or a name, and she always looked and was charming, and if any difficulty arose she dealt with it with infinite skill and grace.

If any words of praise from me would be acceptable to the General Assembly of the Church of Scotland, I should like to pay my tribute to the elevation of mind and spirit shown by this august body. The speeches were eloquent and impressive and filled with an intense spiritual quality, and the problems of the day were discussed with an outstanding ability and vision. When I sat near my husband and heard him speak to the Assembly, and heard their debates, I realised again what a fine thing it is to be a son of the Manse. John enjoyed every moment of our times at Holyrood, and his mother, who had attended General Assemblies for many decades, was a centre of attraction to everyone.

In our first term of office at Holyrood our A.D.C., Brian Fairfax-Lucy, and Alice fell in love and became engaged. They were married at St. Columba's Church in Pont Street in the following July. Of the many kindnesses which Fate has shown me I should like to place high on the list the gift of a delightful son-in-law.

In the dark years of war I have sometimes closed my eyes and remembered those Holyrood days, and heard again faintly coming from a long distance the bugles blowing outside my windows on a May morning.

CHAPTER IX

JOHN BUCHAN BY HIS FRIENDS

NO people were more blessed with friends than ourselves. Some of them have sent me portraits of my husband. The first two are by Scotsmen, Charles Dick and Walter Elliot.

Charles Dick writes from his Shetland Manse near Lerwick. He was John's lifelong friend and acted as his Chaplain during our two terms at Holyrood. He writes of their happy youth; the books they read and the long walks and bicycling expeditions.

"What was John Buchan doing when he was seventeen years of age? The question will be an interesting one to young people who delight in his romances and to others, not so young, who do likewise. A part of the answer is that he, like many other youths, was occupied with ambitious dreams. Apropos of this I recall that on a day of our first winter at Glasgow College he was unexpectedly absent from the lectures. On going to his home in the afternoon to ask the reason, I found him in bed on account of a chill. He told me that the previous night he had had a queer dream: all the world were coming to him to settle their affairs! I was not moved to emulate the patriarch Joseph's jeering brethren. I already held the opinion that I learned later had been expressed earlier by the grandfather to whose memory he dedicated his first collection of essays, that he was going to be 'a very distinguished man.' Nor was the dream inapt for one who was to become the confidant of Prime Ministers and Governor-General of a vast Dominion extending from the Atlantic Ocean to the Pacific.

In his boyhood he had often thought that nothing could be better than the life of a country minister 'in some place where the winters were long and snowy, and a man was forced to spend much of his days and all his evenings in a fire-lit library.' John was a son of the Manse. The son of every manse that is worthy of the name thinks more or less seriously of following his father in the choice of his life's work. The work is upheld as the noblest to which a man can devote his powers. He learns to think of it as a building, not only for Time, but also for Eternity.

John's thoughts, however, were soon turning to a wider, if not a higher, field of influence than a parochial charge. A Professor's Chair in a Scottish University attracted him, probably a Chair of English Literature. Later, I think, his preference would have been for a Chair in Philosophy. He had thoughts also of the editorship of one of the leading monthly magazines. He began to think, too, of Oxford, which, as he said one day, opens the way to everything. It was much later that he set his heart upon some sphere of Imperial service. His introduction to this came about through his journalistic work. On going down from Oxford he joined the staff of the *Spectator*. An article on South African affairs interested Lord Milner, then High Commissioner, who asked Mr. Joseph Chamberlain, at that time Colonial Secretary, to enquire who had written it. The result was that John was invited to go to South Africa as private secretary to the High Commissioner. Meanwhile he was content with the horizon of an Oxford fellowship with, a little beyond it, a Scottish Chair.

The summer of 1893, which followed our first winter at College, was always looked back upon by us as an incomparably delicious time. It was then that we had our first rambles together on bicycle or on foot in the Scottish Borderland. John had an uncle and aunts at Peebles; his maternal grandmother lived at Broughton Green, twelve miles up the valley; my maternal grand-father was a minister at Coldstream, fifteen miles from the mouth of the Tweed. Our relatives allowed us to bring each other to their homes with great freedom, even though we arrived often enough with garments bespattered with the mud of nineteenth-century roads.

There was not, however, much mud flying that summer. My recollection is that that was a summer of very fine weather. I have not consulted records; but my im-pression is confirmed by some of John's letters. About the end of April he mentions 'magnificent weather' and quotes an old shepherd for the reflection that 'there was nae doot but that the millennium had come and that Auld Nick was lockit up.' He refers again in June to 'magnificent weather' with a groan about the consequent very poor fishing. These letters were written from Broughton. In June he says, 'This place is extremely pretty just now.' The extreme prettiness of both upper and lower Tweeddale is one of my outstanding memories of that summer, when, I think, roses must have been having very favourable conditions, the warmth bringing out their fragrance. Aromatic airs, too, from sun-steeped woods that our roads skirted or threaded came drifting across long-settled drystone dykes that were richly clad with lichens and moss. We had the roads very much to ourselves, with no apprehension of being suddenly confronted or overwhelmed by a motor-car. Our cushion-tyred bicycles were the fastest vehicles on the road. The previous summer I had seen a pneumatic-tyred bicycle for the first time in the Lake District. We still preferred, however, to be secure from punctures even if the bicycle had to be heavier. It was in the following year that we came abreast of the times.

Before I ever entered Peeblesshire, what John had told me about it had invested it with much charm. It seemed that no holiday project could be more alluring than to visit him at Broughton, where his people were spending that summer, and then bring him down to Coldstream, my familiar ground. In his letters of April, May and June he tells of his bicycle journeys into the wilds of Upper Tweed and in other directions, when he usually arried a fishing-rod and a book; *The Autobiography of Lord Herbert of Cherbury* and a selection from Browning are mentioned. It was in the spring of this year that he had begun to write about the country with an article called 'Angling in Still Waters' that appeared in *The Gentleman's Magazine*, the shilling monthly that had been begun in 1731 and survived into the twentieth century. Another fishing article, 'Rivuli Montani,' followed. Some early trifles of mine found houseroom in the same periodical, and if the fees that were sent with the Editor's graceful apologies for their not being larger were reckoned in shillings rather than in pounds, we could congratulate each other on being fellow-contributors with such ornaments of eighteenth-century letters as Dr. Samuel Johnson, William Cowper and Sir Joshua Reynolds!

While he was looking forward to the publication of these articles, he was collecting materials for an essay, 'Gentlemen of Leisure,' the subjects of which were the country minister and the tramp. With this he meant to seek one of the blue ribbons of the occasional writer, insertion in *Macmillan's Magazine*. He also proposed an edition of Bacon's *Essays* for the popular 'Scott Library.'

His letters give lists of the books that he has been reading and details of his literary plans and scholastic work, and he repeatedly speaks of my joining him at Broughton.

My visit had to be put off on account of the very serious illness of his younger sister Violet, who died in June at the age of six years and to whose memory he dedicated *John Burnet of Barns*.

The first letter that I ever received from him is dated April 11th, 1893. In the course of it he says: 'I have begun my "Bacon" and am getting on very well. I expect to finish it in a month or so. I find a number of useful books in the manse library. I am afraid my reading lately has been rather desultory. Since I saw you I have read Jerome K. Jerome's *Idle Thoughts of an Idle Fellow*, Conan Doyle's *White Company* and *Study in Scarlet*, and Austin Dobson's *Proverbs in Porcelain* and *At the Sign of the Lyre*. I am very much in love with Austin Dobson. He has some magnificent imitations of the old French poets and Horace. His book *At the Sign of the Lyre* is my *beau idéal* of a book as regards get-up. . . .

'I have spent a very lazy day fly-fishing up Tweed, but principally occupied with lying on my back and reading a French novel, *Tartarin sur les Alpes* by Alphonse Daudet. It is extremely funny—a sort of French *Pickwick Papers*. . . .

'I intend to do all the vacation work in Latin, including the essay "On the Character of the Emperor Tiberius given by Tacitus," and in Greek "Oedipus Tyrannus." What do you think of this as the title of my new essay?— "Gentlemen of Leisure, being some Thoughts on Tramps and Country Parsons."'

It was on the 17th of July that he wrote: 'am delighted to hear that you are coming on Wednesday. I will ride down Tweed leaving Peebles at 5 o'clock p.m. to meet you. Do not cross over to Innerleithen, but keep the road on the *right* bank of the Tweed so that I may not miss you. I cannot say anything of the road before Selkirk, but the road from Selkirk to the Gordon Arms Inn is very beautiful, past Newark and the "Dowie Dens." From the Gordon Arms Inn you will have a very steep two miles to the head of the pass called the "Paddy's Slack"; from there you will have a splendid run all downhill through the valley of the Quair past Traquair, Cardrona and Kailzie into Peebles.'

Mr. William Buchan's [1] home at Peebles is memorable not only for its abounding hospitality. It was a home where good literature was a necessary of daily life, where literary allusions pervaded everyday talk and choice characters of fiction were quoted as if personal acquaintances. There were many shelves of the best of recent books in fiction and general literature. Those were the days when Stanley Weyman's *A Gentleman of France* was having its initial run in volume form after its coming out as a serial in *Longman's Magazine*; when George du Maurier, more famous later through *Trilby*, had just published *Peter Ibbetson*; when 'Q' had brought out his early volumes of romance such as *Troy Town* and *The Splendid Spur*; when Crockett was beginning his Galloway tales; when Anthony Hope, who had published several clever novels, was about to achieve a great popular success with *The Prisoner of Zenda*; when Mrs. Meynell's first volume of essays and Francis Thompson's *Poems* appeared; when Andrew Lang was writing a monthly *causerie* in *Longman's Magazine* and a weekly one in *The London Illustrated News*, and 'Q' was doing likewise in *The Speaker*. We made our first acquaintance with some of these writers at Peebles. Earlier favourites were Lamb and Hazlitt. We had read a good deal of Ruskin, not much of Carlyle, all of Stevenson that had been published—1892 was the year of *Across the Plains*—Walter Pater not yet; it was in the autumn of this year that we first read *The Renaissance*, *Appreciations* and *Imaginary Portraits*. In one of John's

[1] My husband's uncle.

lists *The Intellectual Life* of Philip Gilbert Hamerton is mentioned. He once spoke of this book as having had a great influence upon him. Later, when I referred to this, he somewhat demurred to his own former estimate of its importance for him and said that he owed more to Fichte's work on the Nature of a Scholar.

This summer he was already meditating a romance to be called *John Burnet of Barns*. It was on our first bicycle ride from Peebles to Broughton that he pointed out the house of Barns near the confluence of the Manor Water and the Tweed. The earliest reference to his project that I have found in a letter occurs in October 1893. Writing from Broughton, he says: 'I am very busy collecting notes for my prospective novel, *John Burnet of Barns*, which I intend to write next summer.'

One of our bicycle trails from Broughton was by way of 'the famous Crook Inn, renowned in coaching days and still holding a shadowy place of honour as the only hostel of any pretensions from Peebles to the head of Tweed.' We passed the very small village of Tweedsmuir, from which he was one day to take his title, 'one of the bleakest and most solitary of places' with its church tower 'a landmark for miles,' and arrived about noon on the high moor where the Tweed, the Clyde and the Annan Water all take their rise within a short distance of one another. From that windy moorland height we made the swift descent to the bright, tree-embowered town of Moffat and then trundled along the nearly level two miles to Beattock, where we had a lodging for the night with relatives of John in a house that was formerly a hostelry on the Great North Road.

This journey provided the scenery for 'Sentimental Travelling,' one of the articles reprinted from *Macmillan's Magazine* in *Scholar-Gipsies*. The companion of the writer of the paper had to be, if not a game-keeper, a tramp.

One of our journeys on foot was along the section of the drove road between Broughton and Skirling, a good example of those now mostly deserted routes by which cattle, before the days of railways and to some extent even after railways were made, were driven to and from the great markets. Before I ever saw it, it had a flavour of romance for me, for was it not by the drove road that David Balfour set out on his adventures as he sought the House of Shaws? Later we read of St. Ives 'ascending the side of the mountain by a rude green track.' No doubt when John was writing his book on Sir Walter for publication in 1932 he recalled the track between Broughton and Skirling as he noted that the talk of *The Two Drovers* gives 'an unforgettable picture of the old world of the drove roads.' This is the subject of one of the best of his own early essays.

We also made a bicycle journey to Edinburgh by Romanno Bridge and Leadburn Inn, a sinister-looking landlord of which was commemorated by William Black in *The Strange Adventures of a Phaeton*. We visited the bookshop in Princes Street of Mr. Andrew Elliot, the original publisher of Stevenson's early pamphlet, *The Pentland Rising*. He showed us a copy which he had carefully preserved and some other bibliographical treasures. We had tea with friends of mine in Heriot Row. That first joint descent on Edinburgh in knicker-bockers and cloth caps was recalled in 1933 as we drove from the Palace of Holyroodhouse to St. Giles when John was Lord High Commissioner to the General Assembly of the Church of Scotland for the first time and I was his chaplain.

We went to friends of John living near Mid-Calder in a house that made us think of the House of Shaws, partly because the home to which David Balfour came to dwell with his uncle was in that district and partly because it was a high building and we approached it at dusk.

The next forenoon we rode over the moors amid rain to Carnwath, following the road that was taken by 'Duncan Stewart of Clachamharstan in the Moor of Rannoch,' whose queer experience is told in 'A Journey of Little Profit' in the *Grey Weather* collection of tales, and who expressed his opinion of the way that 'it was most dreary and lonesome with never a house in view, only bogs and grey hillsides and ill-looking waters.' On entering Carnwath we saw a notice-board above the door of 'a decent widow,' who was one day to do for Dickson McCunn in *Huntingtower* what she now did for us. The legend in home-made lettering announced

> Mrs. brockie
>
> tea & coffee

We were rather tired and very hungry and were relieved to find that we could fare adequately on ham and eggs. The above legend was reproduced in facsimile in the early editions of *Huntingtower* nearly thirty years afterwards.

We continued our return journey to Broughton under rain and over mud with great cheerfulness, beguiling the way with a literary project in which we were to collaborate. It was to begin with some sort of dislocation of reality by which we with our bicycles were to be precipitated into the world of *The Monastery*. (Mr. Wells had not yet told the world about the time machine, and Mr. Dunne's *Experiment with Time* was many years distant.) We were to be entertained as distinguished visitors from More Spacious Times by the Lady of Avenel. Cycling conditions would be as bad as possible;

but with less rapid drainage of the hills and more stable conditions for fish-life we should have most glorious sport. John anticipated that the monks of Melrose Abbey would hail us as S. John and S. Josiah of the Wheel. They might thus have provided us with a title for the book. When we came to the Scriptorium, we might make some useful suggestions for widening the scope of the *Chronica de Mailros* and perhaps improving its Latinity. Pen was never put to paper over it, but it gave us a diverting hour or so.

It was now my turn to show John something of the glories of the lower Tweed valley. In upper Tweeddale one is close to the hills—surrounded by them; for large and distant views one must climb the heights. On the other hand, in the great strath called The Merse, beginning about Melrose, the scenery is of a more open, spacious kind.

We rode on our bicycles from Peebles by Innerleithen. Before we reached Yair Bridge, John pointed across the river to Ashiestiel among its trees, where Sir Walter spent his happiest years. Then came the grand part of the valley at Yair, where heavily wooded hillsides slope steeply to the broken torrent.

> Yair,—which hills so closely bind,
> Scarce can the Tweed his passage find,
> Though much he fret, and chafe, and toil,
> Till all his eddying currents boil.

After our evening meal at Selkirk, we strolled down to a bridge spanning a little tributary of the Ettrick Water and sat there smoking cigarettes—I think that they must have been from the first packet that we ever purchased!

The next day we went on by the road that climbs high out of the town and, leaving the Eildon Hills on the left, undulates eastwards towards Kelso, giving meanwhile wide, northerly views across The Merse to a skyline broken by Smailholm Tower standing up like a gigantic hoarding. We remembered what Lockhart tells about the days of Scott's childhood that were spent there. From Kelso we had the easy run down the left bank of the Tweed to Coldstream.

John refers in *Memory Hold-the-Door* to his first setting foot on English soil. 'The thing happened,' he says, 'when I was seventeen, when on a bicycle I crossed the bridge at Coldstream and explored a strip of Northumberland.' John visited many battle-fields in the course of his life, military strategy and tactics being a strong interest with him. Langside was within a mile of his Glasgow home. Philiphaugh, the scene of Montrose's disaster, was probably the next with which he became acquainted. He was now to see Flodden for the first time and had the picture of it in his mind when he referred in his *History of the Great War* to 'the steel circle of the Scots nobles at Flodden.' There were also the strongholds of Norham, Wark, Ford and Etal to be visited. It was on our going to Ford that he noted that the accent of the people's speech was much like what he was accustomed to on our own side of the Border. An old dame who had been a servant in the Castle gave us tea in her cottage and proudly showed us some '*Wadge*wood' ware that in its better days had been used by her employers.

We spent much time on the banks of the Tweed, in the extensive grounds of The Hirsel, and in the garden of the West Manse, where there was a summer-house under a lofty gean tree in which much reading and some writing were done."

Walter Elliot's Portrait of a Scotsman in his book *Long Distance* deals more with John Buchan's later life and his House of Commons days: [1]

[1] Published by Constable.

"John Buchan was a small man with a terrific dent in one side of his forehead—I had almost said 'is,' for he is more alive to-day to many of us, in spite of years of absence, and, at length, his death overseas, than some of those whom we pass every day. That is the way John Buchan comes always to one's mind—as somebody one had very recently met—and the reason of that is, that he was so enormously interested in people—interested, appreciative, receptive. He was interested in you, he liked to know your name, even your nickname, whether he got it right or not. He would stand and face you and discuss endlessly—wedge-nosed, his head forward and to one side, his lips parted, eager to speak, eager to listen. I do not remember that he ever broke off a conversation.

John Buchan wrote as he spoke, and for the same reasons. He liked to meet people; he liked to talk to people; he loved to hear their adventures. When he couldn't meet people he invented them. The most famous group of all his characters—the group that began with *The Thirty-Nine Steps* and *Greenmantle*—came to him only when he was housebound with illness at the beginning of the last war. But he was also a man of affairs; Deputy-Chairman of Reuter's, Director of Nelson's, a figure in the City. Finally—and this is an unusual hobby for a teller of tales—he used to take turns of being a Prince, even a King, or at least a King's spokesman and representative.

We are all familiar, in song or story, with the Prince who goes into the world of Bohemia for adventure, a wandering minstrel. The wandering minstrel who goes into the world of councils and court etiquette as a Prince, for similar reasons, is a less hackneyed figure. This 'castling,' to use a chess metaphor, always fascinated John Buchan. He returned to it again and again. He differed from many men in this; that, enjoying it, his skill grew with experience, and the last of all his adventures in this field was incomparably his most successful—his years as Governor-General in Canada; Lord Tweedsmuir, G.C.M.G.; journeying far and wide in that enormous Dominion, the counsellor of Prime Ministers, guest and host of President Roosevelt, speaking to youth, conferring with age; and doing it all with that fullness and sagacity which so greatly endeared him to those amongst whom he had come.

He began all this in South Africa, to which he was swept away at twenty-five by Lord Milner, from residence in Brick Court in the Temple, studies in the law of income-tax, and an assistant-editorship of the *Spectator*. In a matter of weeks he was jolting through the high plateau of mid-Africa towards his new chief. The Boer War was drawing to a close and the problem was reconstruction. He was to be one of 'Milner's young men'—a group which included Geoffrey Dawson, subsequent editor of *The Times*, and Philip Kerr, afterwards Lord Lothian, Ambassador to the United States of America. They were all very young—Johannesburg, indeed, labelled them the Kindergarten—and with a great chief and a great work they had a wonderful time. They worked well. In the first year after the Peace Treaty, they re-settled nearly a quarter of a million souls on their farms. It meant a lot, in a country where the farmer's definition of overcrowding is 'when you can see upon the skyline your neighbour's chimney-smoke.' But they did more. They laid, for instance, the foundation of a school of agricultural science which has proved of the greatest value—to South African farmers first, and, later, to scientists and farmers throughout the world. Much of the work on nutrition here has been checked up and supported by the studies of the South African workers on the pasture ranges of the high veldt, so far away.

That, however, was technical achievement, and technical achievement was not all that Milner wanted to teach or John Buchan to learn. Milner taught administration; he taught statesmanship; he knew facts, he knew figures, he knew courage. He was a great master for a young man, and it was a great privilege to serve him. And there were other giants in the land in those days: Botha, Smuts, Rhodes. For three years John Buchan served the country and its people. His task was reconciliation—the reconciliation of Boer and Briton—a task which is by no means accomplished to-day. Behind that, he saw an even more stubborn, a much more portentous antagonism, which would have—which will have—to be settled in concord, before any of that work can be considered secure—the reconciliation of black with white.

He came back to London when Milner's group ended. He could not find a place in administration. Law had lost its fascination. He went into business—with the publishing firm of Nelson's. He gave us all the Nelson Sevenpennies. What books! And what a welcome we gave them. But the problems of South Africa lay in his mind, unsolved. Within a year or two he set them out; not in a text-book but, as his fashion was, in a thriller— *Prester John*—since reprinted all over the world. Its real hero is John Laputa, the black man, renewer of the tradition and legend of Ethiopia, and its real tragedy his frustration and death.

Letters, business, administration—each of these aspects of life is a familiar setting for the wandering Scot; and the burr of his Northern tongue is no unaccustomed sound in any of them. The combination of all three, however, is noteworthy. What was the key?

The key was enjoyment. Enjoyment, coupled with an underlying diffidence. Diffidence drove him to try his hand at all these things. It marked him off sharply from another craftsman of letters of his time, also a Scot, whom also we should call a man of the plainstanes, also a great teller of tales—Neil Munro, author of *The New Road*, *John Splendid*, and a galaxy more; an author never properly appreciated out of his own country. But Neil Munro saw no more need to sally out of the West of Scotland than Isaac Newton did to engage in what he called 'controversies with foreigners.' The dent in John's forehead, which I described earlier, came, I believe, from that carriage accident of which he speaks in his auto-biography, which changed him from 'a miserable, headachy little boy.' It turned him, after a year in bed, into that sturdy figure, capable of sixty or even eighty miles afoot within the twenty-four hours, which was the foundation of all his travels, both physical and mental. But the little boy remained—submerged and encrusted, but there for all that. The enormous self-confidence of Neil Munro, who felt absolutely no need of self-justification in any sphere, is a quality more char-acteristic of the English than of the Scots; who are not in their hearts confident that they can 'do it'; and so go about the world subject to the criticism of every mirror, and measuring themselves up to every yard-stick. It makes them train; it makes them hold their heads high; it carries them a long way. But it is justification by works, rather than by faith.

His secret in letters was that immense interest in other people which, paradoxically enough, is the fountain and sparkle of the story-teller. 'Let me tell you a story' is the opening of all the keenest observers from the *Arabian Nights* until to-day. The great poet can look inside his own head and draw from his own experiences what he wants to say; his own terrific inspiration and thought is of necessity his main preoccupation; but the great observer has an equal need of material to record, and of someone with whom he can share it. The Scots run to observers, as the English do to poets—which is why Scots writers so frequently excel in biography, like Boswell's *Life of Johnson* or Lockhart's *Life of Scott.* So the best of his books were his tales—but let there be no apology for that. Story-telling is a part, and no small part, of the art and craft of literature. There is a cult of the formless at present, which would deny any merit to the structure and presentation of a tale. But that is wrong, wrong by all the experience and desire of mortal man.

Story-tellers run in a groove. But John Buchan hoicked himself, time and again, out of his groove and set on new lines. Thus the best books he wrote came at the beginning and at the end of his life. There is an odd parallel between *Treasure Island* at the beginning of Stevenson's literary life and *Weir of Hermiston* at the end, and *Prester John* at the beginning and *Memory Hold-the-Door* and *Sick Heart River* at the end of the long shelf of John Buchan's. The field, long lightly ploughed, has been drained, and trenched, and fertilised, and seeded, and is throwing up a tremendous new crop. The long rest was the rest of recuperation not of exhaustion; there is more yet to be said; out of the magic wallet there is more magic yet to come. The combination of maturity and power is perhaps the most fascinating, as it is certainly the most encouraging, of the spectacles of human endeavour. This combination was coming on John Buchan in the afternoon of his days.

Now, there were three characters in which John Buchan loved to embody himself—three disguises rather, in which he walked the city at night. There was Dickson McCunn, the little Glasgow provision merchant. There was Sir Edward Leithen, the scholarly lawyer. And there was Richard Hannay, the South African mining engineer, hero of *The Thirty-Nine Steps*, of *Greenmantle*, of *The Three Hostages*, and I do not know of how many more.

Leithen, the scholarly lawyer, the bachelor, the dry stick, was his first love and his last. In a lesser-known novel called *The Power House*, a novel of international crime, away back before the war of 1914, set in a London which was still almost the London of Sherlock Holmes, an era of opera and gardenias, where the Russian Embassy was still the gateway to a traveller's land out of a boy's book of adventure. Leithen is his last love when John Buchan began to see death looking over his shoulder when he stood up to the mirror; and sat down to write, with a subject, at last. The subject was the fear of death— *Timor Mortis*—the subject that has preoccupied Scotland ever since the Middle Ages. He had to take that subject. John Buchan, the novelist, knew that there was the Last Story—the end of the road, the finish of the adventure, the last chapter still to be written; and that till a writer has faced his last chapter, till a story-teller can give you the end of the tale, he is not a whole man. And Lord Tweedsmuir, G.C.M.G., the man of affairs, the Governor-General of Canada, felt the shadow of catastrophe lengthening across the Atlantic, even to Canada, even to the States, even to the New World which had seemed so sunlit and so secure. *Timor Mortis*, the fear of death—but what happens if you run away from it? Is there any way to conquer that fear save to go forward and meet it, New World or Old? The answer of his last book is that there is no other way—but that along that way you can meet it—and vanquish it.

John Buchan was also a scholar. He was erudite— his range was tremendous—he would write a Life of Augustus Caesar, of Sir Walter Scott, of Montrose or of Oliver Cromwell, and bring out new facts from old knowledge in each. I remember well him telling me that he was passionately anxious to write the Life of Sir Walter Scott, because only an author-publisher could fully appreciate all the facts about the position of another author-publisher in a tight place—(and certainly it was a new angle, and one at arm's length from that of Scott's son-in-law, Lockhart). But also he liked learning for its own sake—he enjoyed it—he amassed it. Time and again he actually slows up the action of his books by shovelling in masses of learning 'because this is something you ought to know.' That was where lay his real affection for the law—these masses of learning much of which really could be of no practical use to anyone—libraries and libraries of books which only a handful of men would ever master. He had left that world and left it for good—but he always felt, in his own way, a bit of a deserter, and it was under the Sign of the Scholar that he fell in for his final parade.

So he took down Leithen's wig and gown from the hook to explore the last journey.

For all that, learning, even administration, was not his true career. Not the High Commissioner—not the Governor-General—not the author of the great scholarly tomes. Indeed, I would not give the first draft of *Montrose*, with half the length, and none of the footnotes, for all the work and learning enshrined in the avoirdupois of the later volume. The man who could write the chapter on fly-fishing which ends his autobiography—the man who could wrap round his characters a blasting, soaking West Coast wet day, fairing up to an evening of liquid gold, such as you get in *John Macnab*—the man who could gather and set out the poems of Scotland as John Buchan did in *The Northern Muse*—is a man who should be sitting in Parliament, or even governing Dominions, only as part-time.

He could write about the small hidden green valleys of the Border till they closed round you; he could write of journeys, breathless, cross-country, perilous, while your breath came short and your heart hammered on your ribs. He could produce the totally unexpected— the true story-teller's jewel—time after time with no more than a turn of the wrist. However often we read it, we shall always be thrilled by the moment in *The Thirty-Nine Steps* when Dick Hannay, African mining engineer, locked up in Kirkcudbrightshire, identifies the small square slabs in a corner of his cellar as blasting explosive, and realises that he has the professional knowledge and skill to lay a charge just strong enough to blow the wall away and let him free, and no more. There was that gusto about Buchan's work which, when he got going, hurried you along like a high wind. When he got going, I say, for, let's face it, many a time he could not. That is outweighed, and rightly outweighed, by the times when he could and did.

Moreover, here and there, now and again, a queer light, a different power altogether, begins to shine across his page. That is the ballad-maker's strength. And therefore, and so, John Buchan draws in his chair to the table of the great tellers of tales.

His birth and upbringing were Scots of the Scots. He was born a son of the Manse, in Fife, one of the anvils of Scotland, with the North Sea on each side and the mountains at its back. But that was not his true calf country. His ancestry was in the Lowlands and their green inland hills; and here he spent the long years of a child's playtime and a boy's wandering. His father's fathers were lawyers in Edinburgh and in Peebles; his mother's, sheep-farmers, where Clyde and Tweed rise, all alone in the shepherds' hills. That country runs away on the west to the moors of Drumclog and the steep slope

at Bothwell Bridge, hallowed ground of the Covenanters.
On the north it reaches to the outskirts of Edinburgh, in
the high moorlands where Robert Louis Stevenson laid
out the scene of his lawyer-tragedy *Weir of Hermiston*. On
the south it does not stop before the Debateable Land of
its borders, or indeed the Roman Wall; and here is the
home of tellers of tales for generation after generation—
tales and ballads that take no second place to any in the
world. He drew from all these springs.

He left this to go to Glasgow, to go to Oxford, to go
to South Africa, to return to London, to go to France and
Flanders as *Times* correspondent in the last war, to
originate the then Ministry of Information, to return
to London, to enter public life, and at length to go to
Canada—from which he did not return. Meanwhile,
he moved in Scotland as candidate for Peebles and Selkirk,
as member of Parliament for the four Scottish Universities,
as High Commissioner at Holyrood to the General
Assembly, as High Commissioner again, eventually as
Chancellor of the University of Edinburgh; and all the
time he took the run of the country from end to end in
work and in play. I have to leave out the great part that
Oxford and England's town and country played in his
life for I am not making a biography.

But it was from Scotland, really, that he went to
Canada, it was through Scotland he interpreted Canada,
her rivers, her lakes, her cities and plains, her men and
women and their problems of the new times. This led
him to one of the most talked about of his speeches as
Governor-General, when he said, at Montreal, that a
Canadian's first loyalty was not to the British Commonwealth of Nations, but to Canada, and to Canada's King,
and that those who denied this were doing a great dis-
service to the Commonwealth. To a Scot it seems self-
evident, almost a platitude; but it stirred a great deal

142

of interest and emotion in Canada. He wanted to stir interest, to stir questioning. He was by no means complacent about the gigantic Dominion and its future, much as he believed in it. The same problems that he had seen puzzling and disquieting the young people of his own country were evident and insistent in his new sojourning. The title of his last book, his book of Canada, was symbolical in more ways than one—*Sick Heart River*—the valley where men went to be healed of weariness of spirit and were healed, though in a fashion they did not foresee. He thought Canada must find that healing, and might well look for it in great undertakings of her adventurous youth, possibly in that same Far North—those enormous spaces, with their huge deserted rivers flowing into an untravelled sea, a landscape meaningless in its immensity, until quickened and vivified by human ideals and human tasks.

The Russians, with their power of dramatising the work of every day, have publicised their effort in the north under such resounding titles as *Forty Thousand Against the Arctic*. Canada, John felt, was doing much and could do more; but she did not see herself in the part; and here the teller of tales joined hands again with the administrator and renewed again the saying of old Fletcher of Saltoun, 'that if he could make the ballads of a nation he cared not who wrote its laws.'

In John Buchan Britain and America lost a figure they could ill spare, for they lost an interpreter. It was the same loss that we both suffered when we lost Philip Lothian. The great riddle of the years immediately ahead of us is the riddle of the Atlantic; whether we can make the Atlantic into a lake, whose shores will know and understand each other—and be endeared to each other— or whether the New World and the Old are to be separated by a sundering flood. John Buchan always preferred new worlds to old, which is why he turned naturally to Africa,

and away from Asia; and as the new worlds were instinctively aware of this, the new worlds liked him and
trusted him. If one were to seek for a spiritual home for
him it would not be the Tweedsmuir of his title, serene,
content, self-contained, remote; but a house from his
favourite classic, from *Pilgrim's Progress*, the Interpreter's
House, where travellers came and went continually, and
got wise counsel, and heartening; and knowledge, in
addition, of the great perils and the long journeys and the
assaults of the spirit that lay ahead. And John would also
be very proud if he could feel that he had accomplished,
even to a small extent, the further privilege of the Inter-
preter; the foreshadowing of great achievements, which
would reward the adventurer, and a welcome which
awaited him at his journey's end. And this, for many
ordinary people, he did."

I also enclose "J. B.", a note by Lord Baldwin, which
appeared in the Ninth Annual Report of the Pilgrim
Trust:

"One afternoon in the late summer of 1902 I was
turning over a pile of second-hand books on Smith's
bookstall at Paddington. I saw nothing with which I
was familiar, but my hand lingered on a worn copy of a
library book and my eye was attracted by the title *The
Watcher by the Threshold* by John Buchan.

The name of the author was unknown to me, but the
appeal of *The Threshold* was irresistible and a shilling
made it mine. As Browning observed in not dissimilar
circumstances in a square in Florence, 'Mark the Pre-
destination,' and, as I stepped into the train with my new
possession, little could I have dreamed of a future in which
the lives of author and reader would be brought closely
and intimately together, of a friendship of spirit which
became to me at all events an inspiration, stronger to-day

in memory than in life, destined, as I believe, to have no end. And it is of John Buchan that his colleagues of the Pilgrim Trust have asked me to say a few words, of the man we knew, of the loved member of our little brother-hood. As well seek to grasp the rainbow, though the crock of gold was evident to all, in brain as in heart, and in the wealth of friends. In friends indeed, as our Secretary [1] said in speaking in Rhymney of his own life, he was a millionaire. Generous tribute has been paid to him these last weeks, tribute to the novelist, to the historian, to the public man and to the statesman. Our friend was all these, and yet something more, the something so unmistakable, so individual, yet so elusive if you would imprison it in words. Perhaps what drew us together at first was our common outlook on politics, for we both had an abiding faith in the immense possi-bilities of the new democracy, but were under no de-lusions as to the qualities required by both leaders and by the people, if our hopes and our dreams were to be realised. Hence it was that he entered with zest into all our discussions on the political education of the peoples, and from the beginnings of the work done at Ashridge none was more eager than he, none brought a clearer vision, and none gave us more effective help, until he left for Canada. How we were looking forward at Ashridge to his return, as too were we at the Pilgrim Trust! For myself, looking back now through many difficult years, I never failed to find in him complete understanding and sympathy, and his approval of any particular course of action was a greater source of strength than he could ever have known.

What a joy was his conversation! The enthusiasm of a boy, the broad humanity with its comprehension of all classes and kinds of men, the generosity, the knowledge,

[1] Doctor Thomas Jones, O.M.

deep and wide, of our own literature: if I had ever by chance come upon some phrase, some paragraph, some lines, which I felt I must show him, ten to one he would know it, quote the context before you had completed it, tell you where you had found it and give you details of the author's life which had never been published in mortal book.

I doubt if the House of Commons was his real home. I think he enjoyed it: he loved the fellowship and at rare intervals the drama, but I am clear that the public tasks that fell to his lot were more suited to his peculiar gifts and brought him more happiness than he would have found in ordinary political life.

His first experience was as Lord High Commissioner to the General Assembly of the Church of Scotland. I had the pleasure and honour of being his guest for two nights in Edinburgh. He enjoyed the stately ritual which surrounds that great office, but enjoyed it because he was soaked in the traditions amongst which that office had been born. I watched his face closely both in St. Giles' Cathedral and in Holyroodhouse—the face of one who had heard the Word on the hillside. It was fine-drawn, sensitive to every emotion, full of pride in his own country and his own people, and happy that the lot had fallen to him to be the King's representative in his own home. . . ."

The essay in the next chapter has a different atmosphere. Donald Carswell and John had been friends for many years, drawn together by a mutual liking for each other, and a passion for Sir Walter Scott. Catherine Carswell and my husband met only once, although they corresponded a great deal.

When I returned from Canada I asked Catherine to come and stay with me. I consulted her about two projected books: an anthology of John's writings and a book about him to be written by myself and his friends.

She entered into the work with interest and enthusiasm and began at once in helping me with the Anthology.[1] She had a genius for selecting and arranging material and would work late into the night with a mounting pile of slips of typing on one side of her, and of cigarette-ends on the other. She usually forgot to take off the artistically tied orange turban which she wore in the daytime, which, as the evening wore on, she pushed farther and farther off her forehead.

Catherine Carswell never thought much of herself as a writer, often doing cooking and dressmaking when, in the opinion of her family and friends, she should have been plying her pen. She had written a book which John liked very much on Robert Burns, and was, when I first met her, writing her autobiography. She had an amazing knowledge of London and knew well the life of the people in one of the poorer quarters there, and described it with sympathy and wit.

I was always urging her to write about it but she never did so, and, alas, she died in early 1946 after a short illness.

I miss her friendship and collaboration and am so sad to think that she did not see the Anthology or this book in finished form.

[1] *The Clearing House: A Survey of one Man's Mind,* published 1946.

CHAPTER X

JOHN BUCHAN: A PERSPECTIVE

By CATHERINE CARSWELL

IT was not in my experience to meet and talk with John Buchan more than once. I do not count as meetings those few when his words reached me as a member of the public from a platform or high table, though there was a Book Trade Dinner at which he shook hands with my husband and myself among many other guests, and introduced us, in passing, to his wife. He never entered my home, nor I—during his lifetime—his. Our peculiar encounter took place in a London restaurant in the early summer of 1932. It lasted no longer than the luncheon hour of a busy man. I never saw him again.

To produce a portrait by contribution is the object of this book. All the other delineators are knowledgeable for the task. Familiars, colleagues, friends of long standing, they knew "in the round" and under many lights the man portrayed. They are, in addition, severally and notably equipped to deal each with a chosen aspect or feature. They inspire no doubts, require no apology. Where in such a group is the world of a *parvenu*? What can I offer that may justify my presence?

Assuredly it cannot be mere reminiscence. Even if what I have to give in that kind were more illuminating than it is, it would be an impertinence, because very many people could afford better value. Nor in the survey which, upon occasion, can best be made by an outsider. Here again my pretensions are too slender. Besides, this book is not the place for a survey of that sort. Any attempt at useful contribution on my part must be on other grounds.

To make clear what these grounds are—and the purpose deriving from them—some circumstances, unimportant in themselves, must be introduced.

Up to the date of our single meeting, my only approach to personal acquaintance was by way of a few letters exchanged at long intervals, mostly between him and my husband, Donald Carswell—letters cordial but not intimate. They were concerned almost entirely with books. He had a way of writing to any author who drew his attention as a Scot, and he possessed the art of conveying acceptable praise, together with lively difference of opinion, on one side of a small sheet of notepaper. While enjoying and acknowledging such attentions, we regarded them as gracious formalities.

In 1929, when John Buchan was still engaged upon his *Scott* biography, the appearance of my husband's less comprehensive but more controversial study, *Sir Walter*, drew a letter of this kind. Warm appreciation was joined with spirited disagreement on points. This led to a further interchange by post. Never having worshipped at the Waverley shrine (*Ivanhoe*, set as a class-book at school, had engendered a lasting coolness), I was outside the debate. But the name of the great novelist had been much invoked at home, the questions in dispute were familiar, and the cordiality of John Buchan's commendation was the more welcome because it ran counter to most of the press reviews. I felt I must read the new biography when it appeared. Already I had read and admired Buchan's *Montrose*, at that date his only work of biography. His novels and stories I knew only through the immense popularity which made many of their characters and incidents familiar even to non-readers. My tastes in fiction lay in other directions.

I received my first letter from him in 1930. I had written a Life of Robert Burns, and he sent me a page or two of the most genial encouragement.

At this time we were in lower water than usual. My husband, however, had high hopes of a useful, permanent appointment for which he had applied. He seemed in all ways eligible and had good backing. John Buchan, among others, had given his name in recommendation; but, at a late moment, a change in procedure ruled out the appointment of a barrister. It was one of those mishaps that are not less discouraging for being nobody's fault, and it is mentioned here chiefly to indicate the nature and extent of the acquaintance. In 1932, when *Sir Walter Scott* appeared, it was my husband's turn to write a letter of congratulation spiced with difference; this brought a friendly, polemical riposte. Some weeks passed. A further letter arrived. John Buchan wished, he said, to express his lasting appreciation of my husband's book on Scott (he had adopted some of its findings for his own) and his disappointment over the failure of the application. He hoped we should be as happy in accepting as he in sending us a present of forty pounds.

We were surprised, even taken aback. I was even more surprised—after a considerable lapse of time—to have a letter addressed to myself; my second letter, coming more than two years after the first and without explanatory circumstances. He asked me to lunch with him a few days hence.

So brief were his terms that the note read less like an invitation than a polite summons from one duellist to another. I could not help wondering if I was to be arraigned for some unconscious trespass. As no other guest, not even my husband, was mentioned, the meeting was to be without seconds. I was to be in the lounge of a small restaurant in Jermyn Street [1] promptly at one o'clock. My host would be coming from the House of Commons with little time to spare.

I did not flatter myself by thinking that a man of such eminent and multifarious occupations could desire my presence for itself; neither did I see how it might be expected to serve him. I was therefore prepared for disagreeable disclosures or, at best, for suggestions that would be impracticable even if well intentioned. But I was curious. I accepted.

What I could least have foreseen was that this single contact with the man while he lived should lead to a further, incomparably extended acquaintance with him after his life was finished. Yet this has happened. In the summer of 1932 I spoke with him for perhaps an hour. Eleven years later (three years after his death) I found myself seated alone in his library, day after day throughout many weeks, surrounded by the books and other possessions he had been used to have about him.

My employment there, by the desire and with the help of the people who had lived closest to him, was to go through his papers, to arrange them chronologically, and to search out as best I might the pith of his mind in all the words that had been written from first to last by, to and about him. Often while thus engaged I have paused to think how astonished he would have been if, in 1932, anybody had predicted this consequence of our luncheon. He could not have felt more astonishment in the prediction than I in the experience.

The question arises: Why should John Buchan's wife have chosen to confide so privileged a task to hands so unlikely?

[1] I like to think that this was the same "little restaurant in Jermyn Street" at which Scrope and Adam Melfort, of *A Prince of the Captivity*, met and talked. But at the time it had no associations for me.

Partly because, by 1943, the war had deranged younger and absorbed older hands of greater competence. Partly —as I was reminded when I named my disabilities— because I was one of the few left alive and within reach who had shared something of John Buchan's early background. He was my senior by barely four years. I took my first rod-and-line trout-wading in the Tweed. I knew the ways of Glasgow towards the end of the nineteenth century, and the sound that came from its class-rooms and pulpits. If I never heard the Rev. John Buchan preach, I knew those who had done so. A further reason will disclose itself when I return to the order of my narrative.

In any event—as this long parenthesis tries to affirm— I am and remain the outsider. Such value as I may give here must derive from the odd perspective furnished by a trick of time and chance. I have become able to look down a long alley formed by facts and circumstances newly learned, while keeping at the same time in view, with every detail lighted by memory, the stranger who was once my *vis-à-vis*. Does the double impression make him appear no longer a stranger? Or does he appear to be yet more strange (though in a different way) than I thought him at first? I am not sure. I know that the two impressions have come to form a single and a different vision which partakes of both. Tourists who went to the Wiertz Gallery in pre-war Brussels will remember the peepholes through which certain of the pictures could be examined, as it were additionally and with stereoscopic effect. It is only by providing some such *judas*, or extra perspective, that I can hope to serve at all the purpose of this book.

On the morning appointed for our luncheon I was, as I have said, prepared for unpleasantness. Yet, before setting out, I resolved—on a sudden and without a word

to anybody—to let the unsought meeting serve, if
it might, a purpose I should not otherwise have
contemplated.

Our schoolboy son, then reaching the stage when plans
for a career begin to be discussed, had indulged for many
years in the game of imaginary countries. A not uncommon pastime; but he had carried it on with increasing momentum for more than a decade, directing
into it all he learned or read. Ten original inhabitants
had become as many hundreds, and their history and
geography had been so much elaborated that, from their
early situation in a couple of attics, they threatened, by
way of provinces and colonies, to submerge our entire
house and garden. Of late, however, the game had increasingly transferred itself to paper by way of typescript,
maps and diagrams. John Buchan, I told myself, was a
man of wide experience and noted for his imagination.
Moreover, he had sons of his own. Just possibly this
odd encounter might provide me with a chance to ask
for his opinion. If not, no harm would be done and
nobody need know. So, before starting, I rolled up a
wad of specimen pages chosen at random, and carried
them unobtrusively with me.

I arrived a couple of minutes before time. But he was
before me—in both senses. There he sat under the clock
in the lounge on a sort of sofa covered with red velvet.
Rather, he was disposed there in a posture of the most
admirable relaxation, his head leaning against the high
back of the seat, his eyes closed.

I had sometimes wondered how he managed to get
through his many and varied undertakings. Member of
Parliament, partner in a busy publishing firm, prolific
author in several kinds, speaker, member of committees
and—with all the calls of a successful public man—lover
of country things, fisherman, climber, long-distance

walker, reader, father of a family, laird of a farming
estate : how did he compass it all ? He had, as I then but
vaguely knew, suffered from illness. He looked a frail
being here before me, unconscious as yet of my presence.
I found, however, at least part answer to my question.
He is always the first, I reflected, at any rendezvous. He
uses the extra minutes to rest every nerve and muscle.
At this moment his mind is emptied of everything except
the brief opportunity for repose or meditation.

The picture I had carried away from his public appearances was of a man spare, even meagre ; precise, even
prim ; compressed in manner and movement. His
speech, somewhat clipped and—to a critical Scottish ear—
synthetic, had confirmed this impression. A cautious
correctness had seemed in him to be personified. Here,
at close quarters and in a light at once more intimate
and more exposed, he gained immeasurably. His face
was revealed as "fine-drawn"—to use one of his own
favourite terms of description [1]—in lines of energy
and fatigue, sensibility and asceticism, recklessness and
reserve : fastidious lines composing a delicate harmony of
contradictions which lost very much with distance.
The scar from an accident in childhood drew attention
to the strikingly noble contours of his head. The long,
queer nose, questing and sagacious as a terrier's, was in
odd contrast with the lean, scholarly cheeks and with the
mouth narrowed as by concentration or the hint of pain
subdued. A peculiar countenance, subtle, in no respect
trivial.

It is to be lamented that no portrait of him was
ever painted that conveyed the elusive quality of
his features. He was, moreover, indifferently served
by the camera, being apt, one may think, to assume

[1] He liked double-barrelled words, and one could easily make a list of
those he most favoured. " Four-square " would have a high place in it.

a set expression under the eye of the lens. Yet better no portrait than one by a modish or merely official painter. Violet Markham, I have heard, once said that he made her think of an El Greco portrait. That was well observed, the better for not being obvious. But it could have been made only at a near view and when the subject was off his guard. As I stood looking at him, revising my impressions and gathering courage, I remember hoping that his eyes, when they opened, would not regard me with coldness or reproach.

Here is the place to make a confession. From time to time I had heard it suggested that this man was something of a careerist : worthy, of course, and admirable, but with something of what the term might imply of distaste. Those who made the suggestion—usually fellow-Scots of less luxuriant attainment than his—had not the smallest personal acquaintance with him. It was perhaps natural that they should see in him the typical, never wholly sympathetic hero of the "success story." Such a verdict has little weight, but it was not for me wholly contradicted by his public appearances. Add to this that his tastes in men and books had seemed to be as contrary to mine as were his politics. True, he had shown us both courtesy and signal kindness. But unbiassed judgement does not always accompany proper gratitude in the uneasy commerce between wealthy success and needy obscurity. If poor as against rich people have some disadvantages, their liberalities are less liable to misunderstanding. In that moment, however, I was divested of all prejudice. Here he was, a man of my own generation and country, all unknowing under my regard. I had been interested; I became disposed to friendliness without reservations. At the same time I was also conscious to an acute degree that we should presently be talking together—of what ?

The clock struck one. His eyes opened and saw me. He sprang up smiling, without a hint of lassitude, to make me welcome. On the instant he was the perfect host, with no apparent thought outside the existence of his guest whom he immediately set at ease.

> John always shames me. He has dire diseases and at times much suffering; but he always looks as well fed, as spruce and smiling as a robust ploughman on a Sunday morning.

It was an old friend, F. S. Oliver,[1] who wrote this in a letter to Susan Buchan in the autumn of 1932. When I read it, only the other day, I already knew how things had been with my host that same spring. Several doctors had shaken their heads after trying their hands on him without avail. An operation had failed of good effect. His malady was not, as I had then thought, a thing of the past, nor was it merely a menace. It must have been full of annoyance to one who loved hard bodily exercise and loathed fads of regimen. Yet at the time I could not have guessed at anything of the sort.[2]

I should not, myself, have likened him to a country ploughman. His appearance was too scholarly or legal for that, and he was too thin and far too quick. He was "a short-tailed horse."[3] But there was a freshness, an equanimity: *spruce* was a happy word. Above all, a most complete, self-forgetful readiness about him bestowed pleasure, gave confidence, conveyed a sense of well-being. For the "human dynamo" (I had heard

---

[1] For a sketch of F. S. Oliver see *Memory Hold-the-Door*.

[2] I doubt if ever better informed people could have guessed. "Also my health needs a little attention," Lord Bessborough read in a letter from him received on the day his death was announced.

[3] As Professor Plesch, one of his London physicians, put it to him, "There are two kinds of horses, short-tailed and long-tailed. The short-tailed are the most difficult to make plump, because they are specially annoyed by flies and are therefore active and restless. You are a short-tailed horse."

him so described), for the piece of finely regulated mechanism, I was prepared. Not for this unintimidating, gay alacrity, nor for this warmth of companionable charm.

"Everything at home sprang into cheerful new life the moment my father entered the front door." That was said to me not long ago by one of his sons. By then I had heard that he was never known to be cross or upset by family interruptions while at work, never too busy to join in home games or theatricals (he loved dressing up, was a fine actor, and good at raising a laugh) or to smooth out domestic problems with unruffled good-humour. Even that day in Jermyn Street I could well have believed such things. He might be a short-tailed horse, but the phrase "equable, alert and gay" applied, I should think, with less felicity to Scott (for whom he used it) or to Shakespeare (for whom Walter Raleigh coined it) than to John Buchan himself. Equability seemed to dwell at the heart of the gaiety which emanated from him. This gaiety, one felt, could become neither boisterous nor bitter, could neither exceed decorum nor run dry. It played like a fountain artfully controlled to create a reliable verge of greenness round its margin. One could not imagine the man becoming under any circumstances jumpy or glum, short of temper or in-ordinate of mirth. He was no breaker of bounds. But, at close quarters for the first time, I could detect no lack of spontaneity. What, I wondered, was his secret? How far did this temperate climate of his derive from nature, how far from manipulation or the will to exclude?

We sat down on opposite sides of a table for two, reserved for us by the farthest wall of the restaurant and, with smooth, unwasteful gestures, he ordered our meal. We drank, I remember, a glass of sherry, but nothing else. Then, giving me a glance at once keen and confidential, he asked if I knew any of the people in a party surrounding a larger table some way off.

I knew them slightly, I told him, naming the host and hostess, a couple noted in London for their entertainment and encouragement of artistic talent. On first coming to London, many years earlier, I had dined at their house. But I doubted if they would be likely to recognise me. "Do you want to speak to them?" he enquired. "No, but do you?" He shook his head, grinning like a mischievous schoolboy. "I can't be bothered," he said. "Too Bohemian for me."

This evidence of a capacity for indiscretion in speech gave me another surprise. I had thought he would have shown more caution. But his reserves, as I was to discover, were not of that order, and his forthright expression of likes and dislikes had not seldom got him into trouble.

His next remark astonished me in a different way.

"Is it to be business or pleasure first?" he asked, looking across at me with an expression of extreme, if also purposeful, kindliness.

Now it's coming, I told myself. To cover some degree of embarrassment I produced my roll of typescript and diagrams. "I thought," said I, "that I'd take this chance of asking your advice about my son, John. He has been producing this kind of thing for many years in his spare time. He's about fourteen now, and he's bent on getting to one of the Universities if he can do it by scholarship, as, of course, he'll have to do."

Then came the greatest surprise of all.

"It's to talk about John that I've asked you to come to-day," he said, taking the sheets from me and examining them with swift intentness. "Yes," he continued, as he turned them over, "I did the same sort of thing myself,

but not for so long. And I didn't carry it nearly so far."
He handed them back. Tucking them away again I
waited, not without anxiety, for him to proceed.

"I have a great favour to ask of you," he said, "and
from what I guess of you, you'll perhaps find it difficult
to grant. I want you to let me be a kind of godfather to
John. I've thought a good deal about the most useful and
pleasant thing a man like myself can do with his experience,
and it has seemed to me that few things can be better than
to give a hand to the younger ones who may most need it."

I had no reply ready. He filled the gap by speaking
about my husband's books and mine. He expressed regret
that these should, as he correctly surmised, have brought
"small pecuniary reward." "I have quite a number of
adopted godchildren," he said, "and I find great satisfaction in the relationship. What I want you to understand and, if you can, accept, is just this. If John at any
time should need a pair of boots, or help or advice of any
kind, you'll write and tell me so that I'll know what to
do. If you can bring yourself to agree, you can't think
how it will please me. First, of course, he and I must get
to know each other. Has he ever had tea on the Terrace?
May I write and ask him to come there one day soon?"

So far as I am able after the lapse of time I have given
his exact words. In particular I remember the boots,
which raised in my agitated mind the vision of seeing my
son off to college in a brand new pair. I knew that I
should never ask John Buchan for boots. But the suggestion made his offer both clear and homely. I say I have
tried to give his exact words. I cannot hope to convey the
friendly simplicity and the sincere, gentle energy with
which he spoke them. He did everything to make it
seem that I, not he, was the donor. He made it not merely
impossible to refuse but easy and natural to accept.

Seeing, however, that I found it difficult to thank him

adequately, he brushed the whole thing aside as settled and went on to talk of other things. Speaking himself of his own sons, of professions for young men, of conditions present and to come, he led me to tell him of my son's character, of his schools and so forth.

Contemporary writers and their books came up for an exchange of opinion.

What surprised me here was the confiding recklessness of his comments. He stated his personal preferences and distastes with entire lack of caution. After all, I was a stranger. But he was as careless and as little on the defensive as if he were talking with a tried friend. It may have been, in part at least, this quality which enabled him to get so easily on terms with young people. His reserves—and he had absolute reserves—were not due to policy. His conversation was uncalculating. There was in him a strong spring of youthful imprudence. To me this came not only as a surprise but as a relief, because I am nervous in the company of the over-careful talker.

Equally refreshing and unexpected was his attitude towards women in general. "Most completely happy" (his own words) in his marriage, his liking and sympathy went out to women of all sorts and ages. His approach was without effusion, as without shyness or suspicion. A traditionalist in so many respects, he was yet a champion of the modern girl, delighting in her independences, even in her defiances, frowning neither upon her sometimes extravagant make-up nor upon her occasions for wearing trousers. As among the goddesses, his preference was for Artemis.

I venture to think that with regard to women, as in some other respects, he displayed his Scottish nurture. The Scot, while he delegates—like the Englishman— the entire domestic province to women, does so more commonly as an appreciative equal. He also maintains a keener interest in the domestic province and in the effect which centuries of intrinsically feminine activities have had upon the woman's outlook. He is accordingly more given to exploring the mind of any chance woman companion with inquisitive friendliness, and is himself more open to corresponding inquisition. Further, where women display abilities that are extra to domesticity he is readier with recognition and encouragement. This may be a fancy of mine, but if I tried to maintain it as a fact I should find a good example in John Buchan. Talking there in Jermyn Street, he questioned me in the friendliest yet most pertinent manner about the conduct of my household, about how and when I made time for writing and reading, and he seemed to be genuinely interested in such problems.

Taken on broader lines, his habit was one of insatiable curiosity and eager welcome in any individual contact. Ready to proclaim his own predilections, he wasted neither time nor thought upon his dislikes beyond stating them. I think that his enemies, if he had any, must have been people who never met him personally. Not witty, he had the sort of embracing humour that is easily shared. Fastidious, he was not in the smallest degree sensitive on his own account, and I doubt if in all his life he ever administered a snub. His wife has told me how, again and again, a hostile visitor, after a single conversation, left him as a firm friend. His vanities and foibles lay in the region of romance. Arrogance belonged with him as little as protective shyness.

To take only one example. In the event of harsh or belittling criticism of any of his books—and he often met with both, in private and in public, together with a condescension that would have galled many writers—his invariable habit was to smile, to brush aside, without resentment to forget. "Tushery," or "shockers," he could call many of his adventure stories, finding in them "the most restful and delightful thing in the world to write . . . when having a rest," and recommending a like practice to friends who were convalescent after an illness. In some of his fiction he seriously tried to explore the mysteries of time and space and the mutability of things, which he came increasingly to feel. From *The Path of the King* onward, disappointment was expressed by many readers and reviewers over his forsaking the highways of adventure for more wistful excursions. With his biographies and histories he took long time and the utmost trouble. But "more and more I find I write to please myself and a few friends," he has said, and he left it at that.

As we talked in Jermyn Street, he told me that he avoided literary parties and literary cliques, finding them a bore and a waste of time. He wearied, he said, when the conversation turned, as it so often did, upon ways of publishers, amounts of royalties and advances, sales, reviews, and the rest of the business gossip where writers gather. I know now that he talked for hours with delight about the use of words and the technique of composition to friends like T. E. Lawrence (whom he tenderly honoured and not uncritically loved), or about the work of Virginia Woolf,[1] which he warmly admired. He had evolved his own strict practice in punctuation and the balance of sentences, upon which he would willingly descant. All his life he was an assiduous reader within limits early set by his needs and tastes. Byways attracted him—for example, books on hawking. He made considerable efforts to maintain and increase his familiarity with the Greek and Roman classics. Of history and philosophy he never tired. But he was as

[1] Virginia Woolf was a long-standing friend of Susan Buchan, who had from her the last letter she sent through the post.

little attracted by much of the analytic and psychological methods of modern fiction as by modern literary "shop." "The truth is, the pathological is too easy," he says somewhere. He was interested in living persons and in dead persons who had lived, in things done or narrated and in the manner of doing and narrating. Keenly attentive to springs of action, as he might discover these for himself in life or in history, he was sceptical of interpretations made by novelists for effect in their art. In particular, to dwell upon the morbid, the pathological or the vicious was, for him, to see life out of focus.

From notes made in his youth and from observations in his autobiography, I find that he had read rapidly and widely in French and Russian fiction, setting himself to master French for this purpose, as he had also mastered Icelandic sufficiently to read the Sagas while still in his teens. But he had decided that the views upon humanity embodied in the great novels of the Continent were outside his orbit, perhaps also uncongenial to his "fastidious" thought and "scrupulous" mind. Like Vernon Milburne, in a story in *The Dancing Floor*, "if he could not have exactitude and perfection in his knowledge he preferred to remain ignorant." Like Milburne, too, he found it imperative "to husband the energies of his mind." Detesting waste, he had eliminated what he regarded as "morbid introspection" as a dominating factor in life. This did not prevent him from reading the most modern text-books of psychology with attention and respect.

At the risk of repetition, the distinction must be emphasised between his living and his literary approaches. In grappling with abnormal conditions, when these occurred in contacts with real men and women, he was both curious and sympathetic. But he wished to relate and diagnose them for himself out of his considered convictions. He was impatient and suspicious of analysis by a third party made for the uses of fiction. His own vein of speculation concerning obsessed or possessed characters, which he developed in his later stories, was profoundly embedded in religious and moral convictions. Action was his prime interest, and men in action his absorbing study—most of all, men in heroic action. It was not for nothing that he depicted himself as Leithen, the "philistine lawyer," whose "finicking" detachment refused any but his own summing up of any given set of circumstances. It is equally significant that Leithen should, in the end, give his life in pursuit of a chivalrous idea and to save a friend.

The attitude demands limitations of the strictest sort. John Buchan became early aware of his defects and capacities, as an athlete is aware when he discards everything that may hamper or impede him.

During our luncheon, while he talked with light freedom of his prejudices and his leanings, at the same time seeking frankly to discover mine, a thought troubled me. Was he, I wondered, in some sort governed by fear? Had he sacrificed or thrust out of sight, because of some nervous disgust, certain aspects of behaviour lest they should disturb his competent clarity? Did his avowed preference for the traditional, the clear-cut, the happy and efficient and brave, savour too much of anxiety or of refusal? His attitude, for all its equanimity, was not without a suggestion of pathos.

This facile conjecture of the moment has not been borne out by anything I have since learned of him. Nor does it gain support from expert analysis. When he had been repeatedly ill, baffling physicians and surgeons, John Buchan was persuaded to visit a world-famous Continental psychiatrist, a man noted for tracing such physical ailments as duodenal ulcers to psychic disorders in the patient. He submitted himself to examination and was long closeted with the specialist. The verdict? "Never in my experience have I met anybody less frustrated or less crippled by inhibitions. He is free from neuroses. His trouble must be wholly of physical origin."

Out of my own later and different knowledge of him I believe this to be true. In John Buchan's lifelong, dual activity there was no confusion, no impoverishing conflict, but rather a recreative interplay between realism and romance, between fact and fancy, between the business and the dream. Words he used in describing Lord Mansfield would apply appropriately to himself. "His was a nature born to success, and free from the little roughnesses which impede; a soul self-contained, clear-sighted, dispassionate and patient."

But there was more to it than that. He recognised the essential strangeness, the tragedy, the pathos in things. But he submitted all ultimate questions to the ruling of the Christian faith, which he accepted absolutely. It was no more than the truth that was spoken of him by Kenneth de Courcy when he said, "He was a supremely honest Christian gentleman, whose faith was simple, unshakable and inspired." [1]

It was consoling to reflect that he was not without his foibles. Upon first visiting Elsfield I was interested by the many and various pictures. My immediate impression that these had been treasured and, in some degree, collected by the late master of the house was confirmed when Lady Tweedsmuir told me how, upon their first coming there, he had prepared for her guidance a catalogue scheme, which included not merely every picture and print, but showed precisely where each was to hang. This, she said, was a characteristic undertaking. A proportion of the pictures, as might have been expected,

[1] First printed in a *Memorandum of Information on Foreign Affairs*. Later reprinted as *A Memorial Tribute*.

were personal to herself and her family. Others were illustrative or reminiscent of the more immediate family life of Elsfield and its children. But the ones which most interested me were those that spoke most personally and eloquently of John Buchan's own choice. They were portraits of his heroes in history, his friends in life and—notably—of men belonging to the noble and ancient house of Buchan.

Here, in their antique bravery of attire or in the panoply of old wars, were the Earls of Caithness, and their younger brothers who had borne the patronymic of Buchan down the generations for close upon five centuries. Here was that John Stuart Buchan who in his day (*c.* 1380–*c.* 1450) became High Constable of France, helped to beat the English at Baugé, and died on the field of Verneuil. A more modern scion of the same family, in broadcloth,[1] the portrait copied from a Raeburn at John Buchan's commission, looked down benevolently from an illumined frame in the place of ancestral honour over the dining-room sideboard.

Now I do not forget what Erasmus said about us. I know that in Scotland all of us who bear (as very many do) a name having associations with heroic deeds or dignities, are used to claim kinship with the most distinguished branch discoverable of that name. As John Buchan remarks in his sketch of Lord Ardwall, "We in the north are very conscious of our history, it dwells with us almost like a living memory; . . . that is why we are such ardent genealogists; we love to find some tangible link between the past and the present." The blood tie may be thin. It may have been made on the wrong side of the blanket. It may be susceptible of proof or merely due to the susceptibility of fancy. No matter

---

[1] David, eleventh Earl (1742-1829), famed for his harmless eccentricities and his patronage of literary men. He died without issue.

so that it ministers to the romantic *snobisme* of a small and clannish country with a history of hardship and battle. Absurd? Perhaps; but not, I think, contemptible in its naïve desire to partake, however remotely, in valorous blood and in a tradition of magnificence that was rarely joined with worldly wealth.

But at Elsfield I was so indiscreet as to enquire if there was any relationship between the Aberdeenshire Buchans and the Buchans of the Border and, if so, where it might be traced. From what I could gather in reply I was obliged to conclude that, if such indeed exists, it is too fine-spun to be made plain.

Had it been less exiguous, the claim would have been made with admirable propriety, one thinks, in John Buchan's *History of the Royal Scots Fusiliers*. This regiment was largely commanded and lieutenanted of old by the noble Buchans of Auchmacoy, and his own much loved younger brother, Alastair, was killed at Vimy Ridge as a company commander.[1] True, the then Prince of Wales, as Colonel-in-Chief, refers in his brief preface to the author's "old family connections with the regiment." But the author himself prefers to remain silent. He was "himself never much interested in the tracing of pedigrees," his sister has informed me, and I well believe this. He was not given to absurdities, and there is some degree of absurdity in troubling to trace a pedigree that needs to be traced. His essential modesty and humour preferred to seize upon the identity of a seventeenth-century Scots Fusilier, John Burnet of Barns (from Tweedside), as the narrator in his early, most autobiographical novel of that name.

Yet here were the portraits, assembled with loving care, for survey, for salutation, for esteem, for sanction, by the

[1] "A most charming and gallant young officer," wrote Winston Churchill, "simple, conscientious, and much loved by his comrades."

head of a house worthily founded by his own unaided
energy. And here, in John Buchan's books, was his
book-plate bearing the sunflower emblem of the Buchans
of Auchmacoy, their coat of arms, and their motto,
Non Inferiora Secutus.[1]

I have no doubt that in all this, for John Buchan as
for Alexander the Great, the value and the operative force
lay not in fact but in the incomputable power of fancy.
"Some would call this a romantic fancy," writes T. R.
Glover, when reminding us how Alexander the Great
formed himself in the belief that he was a lineal descendant
of Achilles : "but," he adds, "it means something real to
a man to have a hero's blood in his veins." Nor was the
boyish fantasy of sharing in a hero's blood enough for the
conqueror of his world. The sober historian, Arrian,
has reported of Alexander's mysterious withdrawal, at
the height of his fame, to the remote temple at Siwa,
whence he emerged with "some dim notion that he was
somehow descended from Ammon," a god of Egypt.
"He was indeed romantic, they say," is Dr. Glover's wise
comment.

So it was with John Buchan. He was indeed
romantic, in the same mode as Alexander, generating
action continually from romance. Romance was at the
source of his activity and of his suavity ; romance and
religion : heroes and the gods. That *pietas* by which he
was throughout informed and directed, derived from
both.

He would not, I venture to say, have denied it, nor that
all his life he retained something of the schoolboy who
harbours under his conformities a splendid, chivalrous

[1] Since writing this passage I have read in *Memory Hold-the-Door* that
there was " a missing link in the chain," and that the descent had not more
than " a high probability," so that John Buchan sums it up by saying :
". . . the children accepted it as proven fact, and rejoiced that through
Auchmacoy we could count kin back to the days of William the Lion."

dream. But it was a dream that flowered in deeds. "Do you mean John Buchan?" exclaimed an unknown Canadian soldier to me the other day when, talking to him by chance in a railway carriage, I had asked what he thought of the late Governor-General of the Dominion. "Ah, we shall never see another like *him*!"

That tribute, from the outside, given with a lighted face, was wholly spontaneous. But it chimes with the considered verdict of an intimate acquaintance of thirty-five years' standing through a variety of circumstance. "There was no more chivalrous man in public life in our time," Violet Markham has said. In all that time she could recall "no harsh or unfair word," and in her retrospective view he was "without vanity."

To return—only once more—to Jermyn Street and to his godfatherly proposition, a particular consequence asks to be recorded.

It may not have been irksome for one so kindly disposed to carry out his self-appointed part in remembering birthdays and festivals, in sending lively descriptive notes upon public occasions which might amuse a youthful friend who could not observe procedures or ceremonials for himself. Again, it may well have made exactions that were not lightly discharged. I know only that discharged they were, with every sign of pleasure.

The specific test occurred later in circumstances that need be no more than indicated here.

The godson-by-adoption had taken upon himself to indulge in some youthful coat-trailing. Trifling as irrelevant, the indiscretion might easily have been ignored. But it was unhappily so timed as to imperil the scholastic sequence upon which he had set his heart and earned the right to count. It ruffled opinion in operative quarters and created alarm and despondency in the home. I, at least, could foresee damaging possibilities out of all proportion to the fault committed.

Lord Tweedsmuir was then nearing the end of his term of office in Canada. He was an anxious, burdened man, labouring under responsibilities which his health barely fitted him to sustain. So fully absorbed was he that we had none of us heard from him for a longish time, and we were far from resenting a silence so comprehensible. I was, further, aware that this particular instance of verbal flaunting, though he might excuse it on the grounds of youth, would not be to his mind. Still, I remembered his request and his promise. Such a problem as new boots was insignificant beside the gossamer, yet, as I saw it, crucial difficulty which confronted us. A mother will venture where a father may not. I wrote to consult the Governor-General.

I scarcely dared to hope for a reply; even less for one that might remedy a situation so delicate and so distant. I saw how plausibly, how pardonably the rejoinder, should it come, would consist merely of amused or deprecating commiseration.

But, with the least possible delay, John Buchan's answer came. He was more than sympathetic. He was helpful. With mirthful tact he had found a legitimate solution. Adroitly and without offence the prospect was cleared. Possibly my fears had been exaggerated. Possibly, if left to chance, the prospect would have cleared of itself. But he did not leave it to chance. He went to considerable pains to make sure.

To-day the whole affair looks as unimportant to me as then it must have looked to him. I record it here because I have since discovered that such actions were of the fabric of his daily life, and because in their multiplicity they have gone largely unrecorded. If John Buchan had not noble blood in his veins—and, for all I know, he had

—his pulses were supplied in the manner proper to great nobles. His conscience was tender, his performance exemplary, his scutcheon without stain. As another friend has said of him, a friend who knew him far better than I, he was "a verray parfyt knight."

Janet Adam Smith [1] writes of coming up to Elsfield on a Sunday:

"Climbing up to Elsfield on a Sunday afternoon—up the road from Marston, or through the fields from the Ferry—one acquired a new perspective. There, looking back, was Oxford; but there also was the line of hills behind Godstow; there, a blue smudge on the horizon, was Wychwood; and there, to the north, that surprising, untamed, earthy stretch of Otmoor whose character John Buchan caught so exactly in *Midwinter*. And what one found in Elsfield Manor itself was true to this view from its approaches. Oxford was there; and a wider Oxford than one had sometimes supposed from one's usual undergraduate round. Senior members of the University would be just as likely to drop in as undergraduates, coming up the hill on foot, or by car, or pushing a bicycle (though in the days I recall it would be undergraduates who rode in cars). I remember the Vice-Chancellor appearing once—could it have been in knee-breeches?—certainly in some dignified and ceremonious dress. And the undergraduates themselves—young men and women who had met John Buchan in the University clubs in which he took so active a part, or who had come up because some parent or elder knew him, or who had simply been brought by a friend to that most hospitable

[1] Now Mrs. Michael Roberts, daughter of the late Sir George Adam Smith, Principal of Aberdeen University.

house—were a more diverse group than would be met at most Oxford tea-parties.

Yet Oxford was only a part of the company, and the other guests would fall into no neat categories. In that room where you might meet, in one afternoon, a Cabinet Minister, a young man lately back from the Arctic, and an administrator on leave from India, you were made conscious of the world outside, not as something opposed to Oxford, but including it, and expanding beyond it. There was a sudden sense of possibilities; Oxford, it was clear, was a good place to start from, the best place to start from, but there was no limit to where the road might then take you. If not to a Persian *khan* or a Norwegian *saeter* (and I am sure that one of the reasons for the great appeal of John Buchan's novels to the young is in their sense of possibilities, the feeling that anything may be round the corner), at any rate to some job that would exact your full interest and energy, to some holiday that would yield more stimulating joys than simple rest or recreation.

However diverse the guests in age, outlook and occupation, there was little division between them. Conversation round the tea-table (with your host pressing you to spread butter thickly on the gingerbread; the only way to eat gingerbread) was general, and John Buchan paid us all the compliment of taking us seriously. One of the delights of a University is finding one's conversational feet; trying out ideas and ways of expressing them that might not be tolerated in the critical family circle. John Buchan never restricted conversation, but he reminded us implicitly that words are, after all, serious tools. I think there must be many besides myself who first consciously learned in that house to be responsible about our ideas. If you expressed an opinion, it was assumed that you meant it, and that you could back it up; not that it was a clever thing to say. If you expressed a wish—say, about your future career—it would be just as well if you had really thought about it, and were not just airing a stray notion that sounded good, for John Buchan would be sizing up your hopes and chances. 'Let's see, I might write to X about it'; or 'Wouldn't it be a good thing for you to talk to Y?' And in due course you would hear about his answer from X, or get an introduction to Y. Seniors frequently make offers of help; few fulfil their promises so promptly and practically as John Buchan did, and there must have been many third and fourth year undergraduates who walked away from Elsfield with their careers stretching rather more solidly before them than they could have hoped without his help."

CHAPTER XI

JOHN BUCHAN AT ELSFIELD

BY A. L. ROWSE

WHEN John Buchan died, the Editor of *The Times* told me that never had they received so many tributes to a public figure, sheaves of them pouring in from men of all walks and conditions of life—only a tithe of which could be published. That already gives us some indication of the man himself; it tells us two things. It is testimony to the extraordinary range and variety of his contacts and friendships with people. But it also shows that these contacts were not merely formal; John Buchan belonged to the rare class of public figure who comes across to people as a friend, with whom they feel a personal bond, and in whom they feel a reciprocal care for them and their concerns.

To a degree that was remarkable and that singled him out among the public men of his time. I suppose there was no one in his generation—and few at any time—who made a real contact, not merely a nodding acquaintance, with so many people.

I can testify from my own experience. When he was on his last leave from Canada and already ill—within a year of his death—I was ill in London of the same duodenal complaint of which he was a victim, and he found time amid all the innumerable claims on him and in his own illness to write me encouraging letters in his own hand. Hundreds of people have had similar experiences of his kindness and thought of them. I appreciated it much then—how much more now; perhaps only a busy author,

174

with writing of all kinds on his hands, knows so well what it means.

No doubt he suffered something, paid some price in energy and concentration of achievement for his readiness and willingness, his constant services to all and sundry. What he gained in stature was unmistakable; what others gained from him immeasurable. He gave himself away, right and left, with no thought for his own strength, with an inner generosity of spirit that was more than generosity, like the man in the fable, *L'Homme à la Cervelle d'Or.*

With that there went—and perhaps from it came— the extraordinary catholicism of his sympathy. A strong Tory himself, his instinctive conservatism rooted in his sense of history—though that did not mean that he was not a progressive—his sympathies and indeed affections were readily extended in every direction politically. In fact, I believe it was a special recommendation with him that one was on the other side. I remember well the particular affection and regard in which he held, and always spoke of, Maxton, then much in the public eye as leader of the I.L.P. and a notable figure in Parliament. With one young neophyte of the Left, ardent, impatient, fanatical, touchy, he was patience and courtesy itself.

Alas, with what can one reward his kindness now? Nothing—except to cherish the memory of the man he was: that quick, spare, gallant figure, with the grave face and frosty Northern eyes that could yet sparkle with liveliness and good-humour, with his old-fashioned Scots courtesy and birdlike quickness of movement, walking cap in hand and in loose-fitting tweeds along the lanes and up the hill from Marston to his home on the brow of Elsfield overlooking Oxford; or walking on the terrace in the green shades of a summer evening, looking down upon Otmoor and, in the gathered blue of distance, his beloved

Cotswolds; or again, sitting on a low chair in a corner of the library at Elsfield, the firelight leaping up and gleaming in the ranks of books, himself the heart and soul of the talk.

The foundation of his life, I realise now, was the principle of Christian love. He really loved people. And everything, apart from his gifts—though they derived strength from it—sprang from that. There was the secret spring of the two qualities that were so marked in him: the limitless, the unsleeping sense of duty, the breadth and catholicism of his sympathy. As to duty, his devotion to it was obvious in every sphere of his life. He was very stern with himself in his work; always beforehand with his engagements (like Trollope), never failing to perform what he had promised—in that so unlike the ways of authors in general. He was a good deal of a stoic—except that, to balance that strain in him, no one had a greater natural gift for the enjoyment of life. But only someone who knows the physical anguish and pain that goes along with that illness from which he suffered, knows what such devotion to work and duty must have cost.

Perhaps I may say something of him as a writer, though it is a great disadvantage not to know the Scottish background, the society, the tradition out of which he sprang and against which his work must be regarded. But I appreciate all the more the importance of that background, what he owed to it in his work, the very inspiration that came from his native region, the memories and associations that went back to his childhood there, since a writer, to be any good, must have roots. His were vigorous and idiosyncratic, at once hardy and nourishing to the life of the imagination; there were the beginnings in the manse in Fife looking out upon the Forth; the long summer holidays in the Border country, that was

Sir Walter Scott's own country too, the beloved Tweed-side. The memory of those hills and streams is never far away in his writings, and it may be said that his best books are either inspired by them or somewhere carry their authentic signature. When he came to sum up his own work in *Memory Hold-the-Door*, he wrote : "The woods and beaches (of Fife) were always foreign places, in which I was at best a sojourner. But the Border hills were my own possession, a countryside in which my roots went deep. . . . The dying shepherd asked not for the conventional Heaven, but for 'Bourhope at a reasonable rent,' and, if Paradise be a renewal of what was happy and innocent in our earthly days, mine will be some such golden afternoon within sight and sound of Tweed."

One can see something of what he owed to that distinctive background and the life of its people. For a writer, it was a great advantage to have been born a son of the Manse; he knew what it was to be poor, to work hard, to share the life of the people; at the same time, the standards that he imbibed from childhood were the educated standards of ministry and gentlefolk. It meant, as with Kilvert or Crabbe—to take writers from different English environments—that all doors were open to him, the ways of life of all classes. There was, too, the very freshness and vividness of the Border country itself, the sense of the soil and its life, the love of its solitary spaces, above all for him the historic memories and associations with which it is crowded; nor should one forget the importance attached to intellect and the things of the mind—in a way that Scots are apt to feel more keenly than English people—to appreciate learning, scholarship, intellect as such. There you have a further strain in him, the tradition of Adam Smith, Lockhart, Caird, and of so many generations of Scots coming up to Balliol. He once told me that he should have come up to

Balliol in the usual way if it had not been for his intense admiration in his undergraduate days at Glasgow for Walter Pater as a writer. And it was out of that romantic devotion that he chose to come up to Brasenose. (By the time he came up Pater had died.)

But how right the young John Buchan was to follow his instinct! There is a tendency to-day, in letters as well as in life, to make a cult of what is intrinsically uninteresting, to disclaim admiration for what is exceptional or remarkable, to cultivate the colourless and feeble. It is really a form of inverted snobbery; for of course the uninteresting is less worthy of attention than the interesting, the standardised than the exceptional. Not to see that is, quite simply, a denial of quality or even, in a way, of virtue.

John Buchan had no such inclination. He was a romantic and he had the simplicity of heart of the country-man: two qualities insufficiently regarded in the literary fashions of our time. But they are both important in his make-up as a writer.

I conceive that he started very much as a follower of, and inspired by, Robert Louis Stevenson. There could be no better school for a beginner. For Stevenson was a wonderful craftsman and Buchan had a mastery of words —an initial gift which greater writers have sometimes been without and which some writers who make a noise nevertheless never achieve. His romantic temperament, a spirit naturally gallant and courageous, his preference for the life of action, admiring the heroic and stirring deeds, responded to Stevenson, and one sees the influence on his early stories—among his best. Buchan has told us how potent that influence was over the young men of his generation, especially at the Universities in Scotland. R. L. S. was "at once Scottish and cosmopolitan, artist and adventurer, scholar and gipsy. Above all he was a true companion. He took us by the hand and shared in all our avocations. It was a profound and overmastering influence."

But it was one that Buchan himself grew out of. In time "Stevenson seemed to me to have altogether too much artifice about him, and I felt a suspicion of pose behind his optimism and masculinity." And that helps to define a point for us about Buchan's own work: he was an admirable stylist. His own style was the reverse of artificial or affected; it was vigorous and natural, athletic and spare, running beautifully clear like one of his own Border streams, with an occasional rare and coloured pebble in it to arrest the attention, some infrequent word that was yet authentic, coming out of the life of the land and the language of its people. He had a most discriminating use of words, deliberate, sensitive, scholarly. He was, by nature and inclination, a scholarly writer, having both a classical education, with its accompanying training in the use of words, and a strong and imaginative historical feeling. In consequence he wrote—to use an old-fashioned phrase, which he would not reject—like a scholar and a gentleman; would that more people did to-day! Since style is one of the most preservative elements in literature, his best books will continue to be read so long as we care for good standards in letters.

Of his novels I am not really qualified to speak; but it is obvious that to his gifts we must add—what again is something not very common—the sheer faculty of telling a story. John Buchan was a Tusitala in his own right. He loved the story for its own sake—an accent perhaps insufficiently regarded at the moment, which is yet a lasting thing and will see out the more temporary moods of literary fashion. He certainly understood suspense, the art of excitement, the thrilling quality of his master, Stevenson, in such stories as *The Thirty-Nine*

Steps; that he was a master of atmosphere may be seen from a story like "The Grove of Ashtaroth" (one of his best) in *The Moon Endureth*. In his autobiography he tells us how from early days he told himself stories, or rather stories told themselves in his head; in that one sees the born story-teller—it reminds one of what Trollope says of himself in his *Autobiography*.

I think John Buchan kept a clear distinction in his mind—such as the literary public has not sufficiently appreciated, hence some mis-estimate of his work—between his lighter efforts, his thrillers and tales of adventure, and his more serious permanent work, whether in fiction, *belles lettres* or in the field which came to weigh most in his ultimate output, historical biography. I remember him telling me one day that he wrote his novels at dictation speed; but that he never could write more than fifteen hundred words a day at serious history. That from one of the quickest of workers tells us some-thing: that he took biography as serious history, devoted himself to it with all the energy and application of his mind, working hard at his sources, making himself into a professional historian—but a professional who could write: there is the difference. And here in this field, in my opinion, is to be found his most lasting work.

That coincides with his own judgment; and usually an author knows best about his own books. He tells us, in his autobiography, of his *Montrose, Sir Walter Scott, Cromwell* and *Augustus*: "All these four books were, indeed, in a sense a confession of faith, for they enabled me to define my own creed on many matters of doctrine and practice, and thereby cleared my mind. They were laborious affairs compared to my facile novels, but they were also a relaxation, for they gave me a background into which I could escape from contemporary futilities, a watch-tower from which I had a long prospect, and could see modern problems in juster proportions. That is the supreme value of history."

Above all, there is the Life of Scott. Good judges have held that this is the best of all Buchan's books. There he had a magnificent subject, to which all his impulses, his very heart-strings, responded. "It is a book which I was bound one day or other to write, for I have had the fortune to be born and bred under the shadow of that great tradition." There was the noble background of Scott's country, Edinburgh—the most striking, the most sharply-etched, the most idiosyncratic town in this island, with its fugitive and mingled sharpness and sweetness, like the cold showers and rare lights of a Northern spring ; there were the shared experiences of beloved Tweedside : "Above all, Scott had that kindest bequest of the good fairies at his cradle, a tradition, bone of his bone, a free life lived among clear waters and green hills as in the innocency of the world. . . . The world opened to him as a wide wind-blown country, with a prospect of twenty miles past the triple peaks of Eildon to the line of Cheviot, the homely fragrance and bustle of a moorland farm, the old keep of Smailholm as a background, and a motley of figures out of an earlier age. . . . He had mingled intimately with every class and condition of men, he had enough educa-tion to broaden his outlook but not enough to dim it ; he was familiar alike with city and moorland, with the sown and the desert, and he escaped the pedantry of both the class-room and the drawing-room ; above all, he had the good fortune to stand at the meeting-place of two worlds, and to have it in him to be their chief inter-preter." From the country that gave him birth to the man himself : there was the poetry, the peopled imagina-tion, the human nobility of Sir Walter, one of the grandest and most magnanimous men that ever lived—besides being a great genius. John Buchan devoted to him a life worthy of the greatest, the most Shakespearean, of Scots. It is a superb biography, a beautiful book.

Of his historical biographies, *Montrose* and *Cromwell* have special claims: *Montrose*, because Buchan had a lifelong devotion to that most gallant and romantic figure out of the Scottish past, and, more, because he had an inner sympathy with him and his point of view. It is true, and perhaps unavoidable, that he sees the history of that time, with all its unhappy confusion and inextricable politics, through the eyes of Montrose. But he gives a just estimate of the character of Montrose's great opponent, Argyll, and, as in all these books, he has a firm hold of the personalities of the historical figures, whether his sympathies are with them or not. This book must be regarded as his chief contribution to historical research, in the strict sense of the term; it is written wholly from original sources and he had various additions and corrections of his own to offer in writing it. Here, too, he had a wonderful subject which he had made very much his own. He had an intimate knowledge of the country-side over which Montrose fought, all those astonishing marches and counter-marches in and out the Highlands, the Homeric battles—the whole story has a Greek flavour, as of an early heroic age. He had an intimate knowledge of the literature, and even of the pamphlet literature, of the seventeenth century; he collected the traditions and stories, what there was of verbal tradition. It all goes to make a masterly historical biography.

The Life of Cromwell is not less, though it necessarily covers a less original track, a more well-trodden field. It is an even more splendid subject, a large canvas crowded with fascinating figures, and Buchan made of it a very fine book. It sprang out of his deep and abiding interest in the seventeenth century, which he had made his own chosen period of history, where he was most at home.

He read, conscientiously and critically, all the sources and authorities; he visited, as an historian should, the places and studied the battlefields. He had a very good understanding of military history. (An historian friend of mine, who fought in the last war, told me that Buchan's account of trench-warfare in his *History of the Great War* was both vivid and very true to the fact.) But he brought something more to his study of Cromwell—his own gifts of mind.

Here we see the breadth of his sympathies at their most advantageous, enabling him to thread his way with fairness and understanding through the maze of sects and sectaries, the parties and factions and cliques. There is an essential justice of mind—the proper attribute of the historian, though not all possess it—in his treatment of the men on both sides, Cromwell and Charles, Laud and Strafford, Ireton and Vane, of these men whose fate it was in life to bring each other down. With Cromwell himself, that extraordinary man, Buchan had an inner sympathy that makes him at last clear to one. I believe that his view of Cromwell—that character so open to controversy, the subject of so much debate—is essentially right. Then there is the firm composition of the book, well conceived and built up, the sense of scene, the practised rendering of action, the unsleeping gift of phrase. Of Cromwell's religion, for example: "He has been called a religious genius, but on his genius it is not easy to be dogmatic; like Bunyan's Much-afraid, when he went through the River none could understand what he said." On the constitutional dilemma of the great Protector's government, its inner contradiction: "He was to be a prince, but a prince who must remain standing, since he had no throne."

I remember meeting Buchan on his way back to Elsfield the afternoon he came down into Oxford to send off the manuscript of *Cromwell*. (He did all his writing in his own hand; hence the high standard he always maintained.) It was early summer, June over the Oxfordshire countryside, the long grass lush in the water-meadows, the elms of Marston in their full panoply of foliage. He was feeling a little sad, he said, at parting with someone with whom he had lived for two years now. Not a word about the immense labour and effort that had gone into it; he took all that for granted; it was very like him.

The truth is that he lived most willingly in the realm of the historical imagination. How naturally it came to him may be seen in a delicious essay, "Thoughts on a Distant Prospect of Oxford," full of feeling for the place and its thronging memories; it is printed in that most agreeable volume of essays, in which the sense of history illumines the study of literature, *Homilies and Recreations*.

Of his classical biographies, *Julius Caesar* and *Augustus* —the latter his last big work—I am not able to speak. But they have this quality of authenticity, that they go back for their inspiration to his youthful interest in Roman history, to the ambition of his undergraduate days to paint a portrait of Augustus. "I had already done a good deal of work on the subject," he wrote lightly—amid all the distractions and the calls on his time of being a Governor-General—"and my first two winters in Canada gave me leisure to re-read the Latin and Greek texts." "I have rarely found more enjoyment in a task," he adds, "for I was going over again carefully the ground which I had scampered across in my youth." What spirit, what boyishness, what verve!—and this from a man in highest office and often in pain.

It testifies, too, to the extraordinary width of his reading and culture; a man of a type all too rare in public life to-day. For he was a great reading man. "Reading has

always filled so large a part of my life," he says disarm-
ingly—as if there were not a score of other interests and
avocations : fishing, bird-watching, walking; the Empire
—first South Africa, then Canada; publishing, Reuter's,
serving on the University Chest at Oxford; becoming a
Member of Parliament, Governor-General of Canada.
And this in addition to being one of the most prolific
authors of his time. Yet—reading filled a large part of
his life all the same. You will get some idea of his powers
in this direction—and there went along with it a most
retentive and concrete memory—from an essay on Scott
in *Homilies and Recreations*. He tells of how during his
serious illness after an operation in 1917 he read through a
dozen of the Waverley Novels, the Valois and D'Artagnan
cycles of Dumas, then Victor Hugo's *Notre Dame* and the
immense *Les Misérables*, almost a library in itself, ending
up with half a dozen of Balzac; and this in order to
consider how Scott stood the test. He quite clearly had
a good deal of Sir Walter's amazing powers of work.
How he contrived to get through all the reading and
writing he did, let alone everything else he accomplished,
beats me ; though I do not forget the ceaseless watchful-
ness and care, the aid and help, direct and indirect, of his
wife : a rare comradeship in life, in work and public
service.

When in those days one went up to Elsfield, when he
was there, one always found him abreast of contemporary
reading as of affairs, interested in all that was being written
and thought. Alas, being young, one took so much for
granted ! It is only now that one knows how remarkable
that was, the gift of such vivid sympathies, the passionate
enjoyment of everything good life has to offer. There
was such generosity of spirit in it : he was by nature an
admirer, an encourager of others' work ; he had nothing
of the denigrator about him : I never heard him utter

depreciatory words of anyone—a rare attitude in literary circles. But then he did not move in literary circles; he was by nature a man of action, who happened to have the gifts of a writer. I well remember how he won me by his warm appreciation of "Q"'s novels and stories— then as now under-estimated; and, for a young Labour man, his friendly admiration for the ability (and industry) of some of the leading writers of the Left, even though he did not agree with them.

And now, when one thinks of Elsfield, something rare has gone from the familiar landscape. Everything there reminds one of him; the way up the hill, the little bridge and culvert at the foot, the road winding between the elms and ash trees, the elder I once saw in blossom-time gleaming like a ball of snow in the frozen moonlight, while a great parachute-flare slowly descended over Otmoor, lighting up its spaces with the strange light of another world. There is the little church, hipped up on its platform, with its bell-cote at the west end overlooking the road; then around the bend to the tall house with its eighteenth-century core, and something Scottish about its rigid vertical lines—that ever-hospitable house with its friendly welcome for the young. On Sunday afternoons in those days there was always a crowd and much good talk. Out of a kindly thought for my shyness, I used to be asked on quieter occasions, when there was just the inner circle of the family, a few guests, and all the gracious domesticity and firelit charm which those two, John and Susan Buchan, gathered naturally around them. Evening wore on; the firelight leaped on the hearth and made a comfortable glow in that square shelved room with its cargo of books. Now it is autumn and the trees outside are turning lemon and gold and brown; the mellow evening light comes across the green spaces of Otmoor and in at the western windows. Or it is winter and there is a winter stillness outside—darkness in the trees, a little snow-light upon the slopes, the village street moonlit as in Arnold's poem. At the door one takes leave of that friendly house, which will not soon be forgotten in English letters; it is time to go downhill once more, back to the spires and colleges waiting down there in the night. As one recalls that so familiar routine, the village on the brow, that well-loved house, time slips away and one is there again, the circle, that is now broken, rounded and complete once more.

CHAPTER XII

SOME MORE OF OUR FRIENDS

BESIDES the undergraduates, we were visited by John's friends who were Fellows of All Souls. W. P. Ker, Leo Amery, Willy Bridgeman and Dougie Malcolm would walk out to Elsfield on a Saturday or Sunday to see us. W. P. Ker was a scholar whose silences were more eloquent than most people's words. Someone said of him that he had a face like an intelligent brick wall. We attended his lectures at All Souls when he was Professor of Poetry. This was an entrancing experience as the lectures, besides being full of eruditon and charm, were also full of surprises. I remember that one of them ended rather suddenly, as if the lecturer had got tired of it, with the words, "But this may be all nonsense and I may have been wasting your time."

Our friendship with the Amerys dated from our early married life in London. It was always a red-letter day for us when they came singly or as a couple to see us. John's and Leo's taste ran on much the same lines. They both enjoyed mountaineering and reading the classics, and John would read Leo's essays to us as a special treat. Willy Bridgeman's ironic detachment and gift of phrase made him delightful company. I remember John once asked him what was his opinion of the dons of one of the most august of the Oxford colleges. "If you ask me, I think they are a stingy and irreligious lot," came the swift reply.

We dined often at All Souls with the Pembers, and had the good fortune to see much of H. A. L. Fisher and his wife when he was Warden of New College. We also had many contacts in the country; the G. N. Clarks lived at Marston, and G. N. Clark wrote a history of Elsfield with my husband's collaboration. We also went much to Kiddington Hall, which belongs to the Gaskells. It is a Queen Anne house tucked into a fold of hills, with a lake and garden like the setting of a Walter de la Mare story. John dedicated *Midwinter* to Dorothy Gaskell. She embodied to him so much of the peace and beauty of the English countryside.[1]

We went often to Cornbury Park in Wychwood forest, which in the spring is carpeted with flowers. Our host, Vernon Watney, was as dry of speech as his wife, Lady Margaret, was racy and amusing. Their hospitality at Cornbury made it a centre of warmth and pleasantness to everyone who came there. Mr. Watney approved of our interest in birds, but was extremely sceptical when we told him we had seen a Golden Oriole at Elsfield. His disbelief was open, and his greeting to me ever afterwards was always followed by the query, "And how is the Golden Oriole to-day?" Wychwood forest and Cornbury come into John's historical novel *Midwinter*. The scene of *The Blanket of the Dark* is also laid in Oxfordshire. One incident he placed at Minster Lovell, where we often picnicked in the ruins of the old house by the swift waters of the Windrush.

The Alan Camerons lived near us in a little house in Old Headington. I was much interested in helping to start Oxford's settlement at Risca in South Wales, in the desperate years of unemployment in the coal industry. Alan was chairman of our committee, and an abler chairman it would have been hard to find. Alan's wife,

[1] When we settled at Elsfield John was delighted again to meet his friend of Oxford days, Edgar Evetts. Edgar and his wife were then living at Base Court, Tackley, and Kathleen Evetts and I became warm friends.

Elizabeth Bowen, and I quickly became friends, and some
of the happiest afternoons and evenings of my life were
spent in the little sitting-room in the Camerons' house,
where we smoked endless cigarettes and discussed books
and people. John was a great admirer of Elizabeth's
writing and thought "The Cat Jumps" one of the best
of modern short stories.

Our friends meant a very great deal to us both. In the
previous chapters of this book some of John's friends
wrote of him, and it seems fitting that I should write of
others. Hilda Grenfell, my first cousin, has since our early
youth been my closest friend, and John, who had known
her in South Africa as a child, adopted her when we
married as a sort of extra sister. After she married Arthur
Grenfell they lived at Roehampton House and we went
there constantly. One of the last of the lovely enter-
tainments of the pre-1914 world that I remember was
given there. The graceful eighteenth-century rooms
seemed to enjoy being lit up and full of people. Hilda
in a long white dress and tall diamond tiara looked like
a princess in a story-book. Just before the war, when the
shadow of strife was deepening over Europe, Arthur's
affairs became very much involved, and John spent all
his spare time and strength in helping him to get them
straightened out. For Arthur he always had a great
admiration, and he dearly loved Hilda, and admired her
courage and humorous acceptance of all the ups and
downs of fortune.

Violet Markham had been John's friend before he and
I ever met, and she remained always one of the people
we most loved and admired. He liked her vitality and
richness of mind, and her sudden explosive violence of statement, as well as her generosity and immense kindness.
Whenever he met her they talked of philosophy, history,

politics and books for hours on end. When we lived in London we often dined with her in her small and perfect house in Gower Street, and when we came to live at Elsfield she constantly visited us. We also stayed with her at Tapton House, just outside Chesterfield. This house, which overlooked the town, standing in a little park, Violet had kept as a perfect Victorian period piece, having softened its sternness by adding some charming furniture and chintzes of her own choosing. Any house in which Violet lives is stamped with her own personality. John and she knew each other so well that they plunged at once into that best kind of talk which is only possible after long years of friendship. He wrote to her often, asking her opinion and advice on many subjects. If she had died before him, I know he would have missed her sorely, as I know how much now she misses his friendship. She wrote of him after his death : [1]

"John Buchan, a Lowland Scot, had that mixture of serenity which springs from contact, during long generations, with the soil, combined with the sunny nature often to be found among the Scots of the Border. And with that gaiety and humour went no less the sense of those tears that touch the heart of mortal men and of reverence for the august powers which spin the web of mortal life. *Pietas*: that word lay at the root of John Buchan's personal life as son, as brother, as husband, as father. No man had the sense more profound of the value or the dignity of human relationships and the claim they make on the best that man or woman can bring to the task of living. The home life at Elsfield was a sanctuary for others besides his family. The salt and savour of existence was to be found round that hearth in the book-lined library with the large double writing-table—mute but eloquent witness of the

[1] From *The Times*, February 14th, 1940.

daily life and work of a husband and wife bound to one
another by ties so rare and so beautiful as those of 'John
and Susie.' Susie to whom it is anguish for some of her
friends to think of in this hour.

Quip and jest; things grave, things gay, would come
under review as the talk slid east, west, north and
south, and the host, like Ariel, could at a word transform
them into something 'rich and strange.' Sometimes he
would read aloud, or sometimes quote from that
prodigious memory in which was garnered a whole
harvest of treasure from the poets. Equally gifted as
a story-teller, his tales, especially in the Scotch vernacular,
would keep a room alight with laughter. He was too
real and too vivid not to have his dislikes as well as his
likes, but in the long thirty-five years of our friendship—
years on which no cloud or speck of dust ever rested—I
cannot remember a harsh or unfair word spoken by him
of anyone."

John has written at length of T. E. Lawrence in *Memory
Hold-the-Door*. I can only add a small footnote of my
own. I only saw him four or five times in my life. I have
just put down what I can remember of my brief glimpses
of him.

I was dressing for dinner some time in the spring of 1919
when my husband came in and told me that Lionel
Curtis [1] had arrived, bringing Lawrence with him.
"Lionel asks that no one shall mention Arabia or the war
to him," he added. After the usual flutters of a hostess
upon whom distinguished visitors descend like angels
unaware (a few moments before a meal), I came into the
library with a beating heart. (Two cousins of mine,
Maurice and Maudie Glyn, were staying with us, both

[1] Fellow of All Souls, author of the *Problems of the Commonwealth*,
etc., etc.

people of tact and charm, who well understood and appreciated the interest of meeting Lawrence.) Lawrence sat next to me at dinner. I was tongue-tied from shyness, first because I had heard that he did not like the society of women, secondly because the subjects of Arabia and the war persisted in cropping up in my mind, in that unfortunate way which forbidden topics always do. Lawrence was then at All Souls. He was silent keeping his eyes veiled by heavy lids, but occasionally opening them widely and disconcertingly and letting me look into their deep porcelain-blue. I thought that they were of the most wonderful colour and depth that I had ever seen in a human head.

The evening was no doubt a wonderful one, but it left me with a lurking hope that I should never have to go through such another again.

Next time Lawrence came to see us a rather amusing incident took place. Harold Baker [1] was staying at Elsfield for a week-end, and my husband had in his possession one of the original copies of *The Seven Pillars*. He was under no embargo against showing it to anyone, but it was understood that Lawrence disliked the matter referred to, and was not anxious for people to read it. Harold (that most discreet of men) asked to be allowed to glance at it, and there seemed no reason to refuse this reasonable request under the seal of secrecy. We went off to church and he had settled down to read it in our library, when Lawrence, in the uniform of an Air Force mechanic, walked in suddenly. Harold, with admirable presence of mind, draped the *Spectator* over the book, then rose, and casually laid both paper and book down in a dark corner of our library near the book-shelves.

When we returned from church the two men were conversing happily together. Lawrence had altered since

[1] Warden of Winchester College, 1936-1946.

the first time I saw him. He looked happier and somehow "loosened up." I vanished discreetly from the room, leaving him to talk to the two members of the preferred sex, while I sought out my two small boys, and explained to them that Colonel Lawrence had had a price put on his head by the Turks, was an extremely famous man, and that if they were allowed to shake hands with him they mustn't bother him, but must take a quiet look at him in order to remember him all their lives.

Unfortunately these motherly admonitions were at once forgotten, as they had caught sight of Lawrence's high-speed motor-bicycle (the predecessor, I think, of "Boanerges") outside our front door, and they were so earnestly examining every detail of it, that they gave no more than a casual glance at the slight blue-clad figure who stood beside it for a moment before he mounted and rode rapidly away.

The next time he came, our newly arrived, ancient and not very intelligent butler remarked on our return from a walk that an Aircraftman called Shaw had called, and that he had said we were "not at home and he didn't know when we should be," his manner conveying that he did not consider Air Force privates had any right to bother people. We stared at him in exasperation, and my husband told him whom he had sent away. I warned him never to make such a mistake again. Lawrence returned later in the day, to be let in by the still bewildered butler into the library.

The next time I saw him he was in the uniform of the Tank Corps. He came in with his usual unexpectedness and informality, and had luncheon with my husband, myself and my daughter Alice, and stayed on for a while afterwards. I have seldom passed a more charming two hours. We gossiped a great deal about mutual friends. He had become easy and friendly and was altogether delightful. I ought to remember all sorts of interesting things he said; as it is, I can only recall that he said of someone that "she was so frenziedly tidy that you could not put down a parcel in her drawing-room without throwing out the whole rigid pattern of the room. I hate tidiness like that," he added.

The last time I saw him was a few weeks before his death. No one could have been more charming than he was that last time, though at moments he relapsed into a kind of sadness. He seemed somehow older than when I had last seen him, lines had deepened on his forehead and around his mouth, but he looked as always, both hard and fit. My youngest son, Alastair, was in bed fighting a bad cold. Lawrence went in to see him. They had a very short but interesting talk. (Alastair has, I am glad to say, written down his impressions of it.)

I happened to mention that day (rather shamefacedly, I must admit) that I had bought two copies of his translation of the *Odyssey* as a speculation! A look of horror came into Lawrence's eyes. "How could you do such a foolish thing?" he said. "You have wasted your money. How *could* you let her do it?" he said, turning to my husband.

A few days later John received a letter enclosing an envelope upon which was inscribed Lawrence's signature and a Greek quotation. "Please give this to Mrs. Buchan," he wrote, "to stick in one copy of the *Odyssey*. It might help the sale of the book some day."

My impression of Lawrence that day was that he was happy on the whole. He described his household arrangements; his fuel of rhododendron twigs, his pots of jam on the shelf. We stood, as always, on the doorstep to see him ride away. A few weeks later we read of his accident in the paper, and we heard of his death on a Sunday morning at Cliveden. There was nothing to be said. We were all struck dumb by the tragic waste of it.

The F. S. Olivers played such an important part in their friends' lives, and they meant so much to us, that no book about John would be complete without a mention of them.

Fred was one of the handsomest men I have ever seen, but handsome in an elder fashion. The osseous structure of his face was curiously like that of his admired Alexander Hamilton. He had the kind of head which would have been admirably suited to a peruke, or to his own hair worn long and powdered and tied with a ribbon.

That was Fred *en grande tenue*, but he could also look exactly like a Border shepherd. Fred in old tweeds with a crook striding over the hills could have been paralleled by a hundred shepherds between the Cheviots and Galloway.

When I first knew Fred I thought he looked much more like a lawyer than a business man. But he reminded me that he was a shopkeeper several times, until this fact became fixed in my mind. He alluded to his firm Debenham & Freebody's shop as the Emporium, and I always wondered as I passed their counters heaped with ladies' gloves and artificial flowers how much he was interested in the more frivolous aspects of the business. As I made my purchases I used to amuse myself by fancying Fred sitting spinning the larger policies of this vast concern in some remote upstairs office.

Those of us who had the privilege of being counted as friends by the Fred Olivers behaved a little like the members of a secret society. Our passwords were Checkendon, Hereford Gardens, Kenry and Edgerston, and we asked each other a little jealously, "Have you been there lately ?" We sometimes lowered our voices in alien company, for, in the depths of our selfish hearts, we did not wish to share our privilege of being admitted as members of Fred's circle with many other people.

Between being hospitably and kindly entertained by Fred, and being accepted by him as a friend, there was a great but invisible gulf. Fred only accepted you if you had certain qualities that he considered indispensable in friendship. He preferred those human beings who never overstressed anything, were sensitive to atmosphere, and above all who made the right remarks at the right moment. He once remarked about someone that "she was never in the way." That was, from him, a great meed of praise. But the quality of not being in the way alone did not suffice. There must be intelligence as well, and responsiveness, and some kind of subtlety of mind, and above all a sense of humour, kept well in check, but still very much there.

Fred had none of the usual snobberies of the world, and would not have got out of his chair or walked across a room to meet anyone, however famous, had he suspected that they did not possess the qualities for which he sought. It goes without saying that he abhorred sentimentality and slushiness of mind. But if he disliked anything more than these two defects, it was pretentiousness in any form. He derived a mocking amusement from the airs and graces of the would-be intellectuals who thought they were impressing their smiling host, while he led them like a will-o'-the-wisp over the bogs of their folly and ignorance. To the humble and stupid he was invariably kind, drawing them out and making them feel clever and interesting.

To talk to Fred was one of the most stimulating things in life. I have seldom played tennis, but I imagine that it was like a game played over the net by an amateur with a professional. The weaker party must keep all his faculties at a stretch, watch every movement of the professional, and run all over his side of the court, perspiring profusely, while his adversary hardly seems to move at all, as he sends devastating volleys over the net. He talked, and the ball came straight at you, and the chances were that you failed to return it, but if you did so no one was more delighted than he was. He had that love of conversation which is heightened by good wine and the mellow glow of a polished table, and a sense of leisure after the labours of the day. To spoil your palate by cocktails, gobble your food, and rush out to a party, seemed to him so uncivilised as not to be worth comment. Wherever he was, he led the conversation in the direction in which he wanted it to go. I have never met anyone else who achieved this so unobtrusively, and with such consummate skill. He never did anything so crude as to change a subject that bored him. He simply froze out the uncongenial topic. Somehow no one felt they wanted to go on talking about it any more, and however much it might have interested them beforehand, it just joined the stale and unprofitable things of the world.

Fred's *bons mots* were repeated with delight by his friends, but *bons mots* are evanescent things at the best. I think he aimed more at creating an atmosphere in which conversation could flourish than at verbal triumphs. He could say very neat and effective things, as, for instance, when asked his opinion of a statesman, he replied, "He's that most lovable of all things, an incompetent Scotsman."

I first heard of the Olivers when I was engaged to be married. We were reading our letters of congratulation, and oh! what a sameness there was about them. Suddenly John exclaimed, "Here's a letter from Fred Oliver." I read the letter and knew that the man who wrote it must be cast in an exceptional mould. It was written from a sanatorium, for Fred had even then been attacked by lung trouble.

Several years passed before I met the Olivers. We dined with them at their house in Kensington Square. I well remember that evening, and the light winds which played on us. (The windows were always kept open to give Fred the maximum amount of air.) I remember also the airy brilliance of the conversation. I myself talked more that evening at the Olivers' dinner-table, I think, than I ever did again, and I have no doubt that I made many rash statements. But Fred was indulgent of my youthful follies, and his sincere liking for my husband probably carried the day, for I was accepted as a friend, and that evening had many amusing and memorable successors.

Owing to Fred's health, which made him tire easily, the Olivers never went out a great deal or entered much into the duller and more crowded social life of London. Fred's mind tired easily as well as his body, and if people wanted to see him he waited for them to do so. And they always came, and if he liked them (but not unless he did) they came again. He enjoyed the company of soldiers, who valued his advice, as did politicians, writers and artists.

The Olivers left Kensington Square and acquired 8 Hereford Gardens, and their circular dinner-table, made of polished acacia wood, was soon surrounded by their chosen friends.

Many of my recollections of Fred are of the First World War years, when we met a great deal and pooled our anxieties and hopes. Debenham & Freebody were doing great things in clothing the Army, and Fred, who was over age for the war, was working hard at the civilian end on Army clothing problems. Katy was head of a V.A.D. detachment, and later of the Red Cross Depot for parcels sent to prisoners of war. We met and shared rationed meals, and I always came home from dining with the Olivers with a feeling that some few of the valuable spiritual and intellectual things of the world were still in existence.

In 1915 Fred wrote his brilliant pamphlet *Ordeal by Battle*, which caused some controversy and had a great deal to do with the bringing in of conscription.

After the war ended (—that sentence brings its own sadness now! All through the years from 1914 to 1918 those three words "after the war" meant to us a renewal of the peaceful and, on the whole, sane world we had known before) the Olivers sold Checkendon, and Fred returned to his beloved Borders—to Edgerston, near Jedburgh in Roxburghshire. I shall never forget my first sight of Edgerston. It stands on a shelf of hill overlooking countless round, hummocky hills covered with silvery bent. It was adorned by the most beautiful garden I know anywhere, planned out under Katy's masterly guidance. The large Charles Furse pictures which had hung on the walls of 8 Hereford Gardens made one feel at home. Edgerston is a charming house with a wide shallow staircase winding up from the hall to a long upper landing. It has tall windows which give a magnificent sense of space and light. Fred had his usual upstairs library, a long room from which you could see the hills huddling into the far distance. I am a poor hill-climber, but I always love those hills; one can walk all over them without being crushed by a sense of alien immensity.

I remember many delightful visits there. One especially stands out in my memory. Charles Whibley [1] was also there. He was in one of his most combative moods and his mordant humour delighted us all. He declaimed against many of our friends, and tried to throw down all our idols. When I attempted to protest he clearly thought me both foolish and sentimental. "You like ——, and were married by the Bishop of —— ; there's no hope for

---

[1] Charles Whibley, author of "Musings without Method" in *Blackwood's Magazine*; *A Book of Scoundrels*; *Studies in Frankness*; and many other books.

you; in fact, you like far too many people," he added. Charles Whibley suffered from an excruciating form of neuralgia. His head was tied up in a black silk handkerchief, which was surmounted by a knot, the ends of which stood up straight like a rabbit's ears. He looked like a pirate who was addicted to literature, not to the high seas. When he talked about books his judgments were mellow and delightful.

The politician nowadays is rather at a discount. His fellow-countrymen are apt to hold him cheap. Fred never did so, and often said with emphasis that it was unfair to decry those who were willing to take their share in the government of the country, or to serve for years in Parliament with little hope of reward, and he set himself to vindicate the politician in his book in three parts called *The Endless Adventure*. He takes as the illustration of his thesis the life of Sir Robert Walpole, his long years as Prime Minister, and his masterly achievements in maintaining the prestige of England, while preventing her from involving herself in war. These three volumes are well worth study for their unforgettable turns of phrase and penetrating judgments. The research involved in writing them left him amused and happy in his later years, when illness was pressing him hard and he could only see for short times those people who came to his house, eager to see Edgerston and the garden, and to secure a few words with their urbane host.

Fred was a Borderer, and he had that sense of history and love of romance and poetry which is deep-rooted in all the people of that countryside. He had that gaiety of mind which belongs rather to the Borders, perhaps, than to other parts of Scotland. He had little sympathy with Calvinism, and I have often heard him maintain that most of the gaiety and charm of the older Scotland vanished when John Knox superimposed an unnatural gravity and Puritanism on the land. I have also heard all the Scotsmen round the table agreeing with him about this!

He had the Borderer's interest in sheep, and farmed on quite a big scale. Once I went for a long drive with him, and he punctuated the conversation about friends and politics with keenly observant remarks about his woolly dependants, who lifted up their faces to look at us when the car passed by.

I don't think that the consciousness of death was ever very far away from him. "I lie awake at night and hear the worms in the churchyard (at Checkendon) sharpening their claws for me," he wrote to my husband. But he never seemed to fear death. About two years before he died we were walking beside one of the rushing streams near Edgerston, and he said, "I thought the Angel of Death was coming for me many times this winter." "Life will be a much duller thing for us all when you are not there," I replied. He looked surprised and asked what I meant by that. I tried to tell him what his friendship and companionship had meant to his friends. I didn't do it well, and he looked amused, but a little touched.

But alas! illness was taking a heavier toll of his strength, and we saw him only rarely, and for short half-hours. He had bought Kenry House at Kingston, an attractive mansion with a terraced garden, but he returned more and more often to the Borders, seeking the solace of the garden and the hills of his own country.

My last sight of him was in the second year that we were at Holyrood. Katy had been staying there with us, and she and I returned to Edgerston together. I went upstairs to visit Fred. He pointed to a little writing-desk which I had given him; he had put his manuscript inside it, he said. His wit was still there, and he made me laugh several times though I was more in the mood for tears, for I knew that I should never see that kindest of friends and best of companions in this world again.

Fred was a *revenant* from the eighteenth century. He had all the intellectual courage, scepticism, wit and hard-headedness of that period. The yearning *schwärmerei* of the nineteenth century, masking its love of material gain, made no appeal to him. He liked shape and form in everything. These lines describe his tastes and preferences :

> A bin of wine, a spice of wit,
> A house with lawns enclosing it,
> A river running by the door,
> A nightingale in the sycamore.

Folly collapsed in his presence, pricked like a bubble with his pointed wit. He kept his urbanity, a just balance of mind, in a time which was keyed up to nightmare pitch. To talk to Fred after the war was to remind oneself that at any rate the world had once been sane.

The Chinese have, among their other excellent qualities, a calm and courageous attitude towards death. I have read that it is customary for the merchants and gentlemen of China to have prepared for them a robe in the mode of the Ming period, and draped in this exquisite garment they are laid to rest. The man who knows he is going to die invites his friends into his garden, where they discuss hour after hour the correct cut of the sleeves.

Had this been an Anglo-Saxon custom, I can well imagine that Fred would have gravely considered the shape of a surcoat or the correct fashion of a sprigged waistcoat, for he should undoubtedly have gone to Heaven in the dress of an eighteenth-century gentleman.

Noel Skelton I can never think of without a pang of regret that he is no longer here to laugh with, or to make ironic comments on the state of the world.

He had a massive commanding presence, deep-set blue eyes, an aquiline nose, and a very pleasant voice, salted by a Scottish flavour. When I first met him he seemed almost too good to be true—the hero of a Disraeli novel come to life. He was young and impressive-looking, a convinced and earnest Conservative, successfully mounting the first steps of the political ladder.

We all went to a meeting in Selkirk where, emphasising his points by beating his clenched right hand upon the open palm of his left, he announced that a United Kingdom should be the heart of a United Empire. He also uttered other unimpeachable Conservative sentiments. I was astonished when, on returning to Broadmeadows Cottage for supper, he completely dropped the manner of the earnest young politician and spent the remainder of the evening telling us Scots stories. I laughed a great deal, for Noel was the best of mimics and never over-stressed his points.

I did not see him again for some years. When we did meet he had become stouter and had jettisoned all his earlier gravity. He loved his food and was especially fond of Tiptree jam. I have seen a jar of the famous "Little Scarlet Strawberry" in front of him on the table empty itself in the twinkling of an eye. There is something very lovable about people who enjoy good food and enliven a meal with jokes.

Since Noel's death his friends have felt a smarting sense of loss. The world without the sauce of Noel's wit is like a dish of cold veal. Had I enjoyed the benefits of a classical education I should have on the tip of my pen just the right words tersely to describe that wit of his. As it is, I can only say with Anglo-Saxon circumlocution that his descriptions of people and their behaviour cut clean into the consciousness of his hearers. Or, to vary the metaphor, they were like the pins which transfix rare butterflies, leaving the impaled insects static and lifelike. But his summings up of points of character had so much fun and fancy in them that those who were mocked could not fail to smile (if ruefully) at his epitaph on their living selves.

"He showed more performance than promise" was his comment upon the maiden speech of a slick young orator in the House of Commons. Noel once detected me in the act of going to a lecture in Oxford by a psychologist on the subject of "nervous children." This amused him greatly, and after some derisive laughter he remarked, "I should have thought that 'fierce children' and 'nervous parents' were more in the picture."

One of his most refreshing characteristics was his violence of statement. "Of course, my dear, everything is going to the dogs," he would say if one pressed upon his notice the weaknesses of the Government and Party which he served. An old lady timidly asked him if he did not think the Labour Government which had recently relinquished power had been alarmingly extravagant? He replied, "No more than a Conservative or indeed any other kind—all Governments are hopeless about money." If he sometimes jettisoned accuracy for the sake of making his hearers laugh, who can find it in their heart to blame him? He deeply offended my eldest son, Johnnie, a lover of wild nature and open spaces, by telling him that he hoped to see an England covered by smallholdings, with each smallholder living in a separate little red house. In fact, Noel's conversation must have given continuous pain to those who take everything *au pied de la lettre*. But to those who regard conversation rather as a wild adventure than a pedestrian plodding among facts, Noel's talk was a perennial delight. He once found in the hall at Elsfield an anti-litter notice I was proposing to put up in the village. He promptly handed it to some undergraduates who were leaving the house after tea in a much overcrowded car, remarking, "If you have a spill and are all killed, you will make a lot of litter," and he added impressively, "Remember that a littered landscape is a shame to England" (quoting the slogan on the anti-litter board).

One of Noel's most amusing achievements was his breaking up of what he foresaw would be a very dull dinner-party followed by a long spell of boredom. A glance round the room showed him that the evening did not hold out much promise of entertainment. As he sat down to dinner he noticed that his neighbour had a slight cold. He remarked to her how dangerous it was to go out in the evening if one was not in the best of health. He turned to the lady on his other side, remarking, "I am afraid you have caught a bad cold too!" and he painted an even darker picture to her of the dangers of catching 'flu. He worked upon their feelings so skilfully that both ladies left for home immediately after dinner, and the whole party broke up in alarm and confusion.

Noel had a special dislike for anyone who was *affairé* or busybodyish, and his boredom with men and women who could talk and think of nothing but public affairs was very great. "She may do good, I don't say she doesn't, but she has completely destroyed her own atmosphere," he remarked of a well-known female philanthropist.

When he disliked people he made no bones about it, and did not deal in those would-be charitable half-truths in which weaker minds are apt to take refuge. "He's a bore and crook and a fool," he would say, looking round the table in a challenging manner, often adding, "But I like him very much; in fact he's a great friend of mine." I don't doubt that the said "bore, crook and fool" passed many pleasant hours in Noel's company, and when down on his luck had received many kindnesses from him.

Noel was an excellent writer. He wrote little, and he wrote laboriously, but the result was most vigorous and luminous prose.

When Noel entered the House of Commons as Member for Perth he joined the group of younger Conservatives who were often only so in name. From the Ladies' Gallery I have looked down to see him hunched up on one of the benches, brooding in ironic amusement while speaker after speaker rambled on, tying themselves up in endless and meaningless repetition, "for all the world," as he remarked, "as if they were a butler telling a ghost story to the cook!"

Noel was the complete Parliamentarian, and he would never have been happy out of the House of Commons. Now and then he would get very tired of its trivialities, and talk about retiring to a chicken farm in Scotland. Upon which Walter Elliot observed drily that if Noel had a chicken farm he would have one pen for the "Ayes" and another pen for the "Noes"!

Of Noel's years of hard work for the Conservative Party and for the Government in which he was Under-Secretary for Scotland, many other people are more qualified to write than myself. All I can add to what they would have to say is, that he contributed something to the Mother of Parliaments that I hope she may never lack, a carelessness about personal rewards, an unequalled sense of the comedy of pompous official things, and a love of humanity in every shape and form. All this went with a flair amounting to genius for finding out people of all conditions of life who possessed the gift of being funny or interesting, but above all of being funny. I think perhaps Noel's epitaph might be that he preferred, in a world of mass-production and mass-movements, quality in all things rather than quantity.

He once said to me about a mutual friend, "She takes

life too seriously. It's a mistake; the only thing that's the matter with life is that it's so short." Alas! his own term extended no further than early middle age.

Most families have had a dog who was their companion in their happiest hours, so I make no apology for including a short account of Spider.

When Spider was given to my daughter as a puppy he perhaps in a sense deserved his name. His legs shot out in every direction when we lifted him off the floor, but he lacked the purposeful activity of his namesake. As he grew older he resembled nothing so much as a lamb bought in a toyshop, and facetious visitors urged us to try a wheeled stand for him, painted green!

We all thought him at first a dog of colourless and indeterminate character, and half regretted that we had not acquired a grimmer specimen of the canine breed. We little foresaw the tyranny to which we were all to bow our heads.

The year that Alice was given Spider we went to Ardura. Spider grew up and matured rapidly in those attractive surroundings.

I can remember many mornings when I sat at a writing-table looking out of a window. Just outside, a tangled fuchsia bush climbed luxuriantly up the side of a white-washed porch. The flowers hung in brilliant clusters like large tassels, and bees buzzed round them, sometimes disappearing completely as they sucked the honey from the flowers. Nowhere have I ever seen such fuchsias as in Mull. They grow with an abandon and a vigour unknown elsewhere. The ground sloped down from the house to the river Lussa, where, rain or shine (mostly rain!), the male members of my family were to be found fishing. Beyond the Lussa, heather and bracken-covered slopes merged into a distant view of mountains. Just dis-

John Buchan, 1934.

tinguishable from the window was an active white blot running to and fro as if weaving an invisible pattern. This was Spider at the age-old terrier's sport of hunting rabbits.

By the time we returned to Elsfield the house was beginning to revolve around him. The next year we went to Benmore, and he daily thumped Anna with his forepaw so insistently and commandingly that she meekly left the room and mounted a flight of stairs to fetch him a morsel of the brand of chocolate to which he was much addicted.

When visitors asked in tones of slight surprise to what breed (if any) Spider belonged, we replied proudly that he was a Jack Russell terrier, a blend of Sealyham and Wire-hair. He stood erect upon four long legs, but had a great deal of the clumsy Sealyham charm. His head was that of a wire-haired terrier, and his stumpy tail and stout fleecy body were from his Sealyham ancestry. Anyway, he was deeply endearing and attractive, and we let it be seen that we didn't care a pin what his pedigree had been.

One of my boys when small said that he had a "rocking-horse run." He rocked fore and aft when he cantered on his straight legs, so much too long for his body. His black-and-white face was not admired in Mull; in fact, our old ghillie, Ronald, disliked his coming out in a boat with us. "There's something unlucky about a dog with half a face," he said; but Spider was by that time far too well established as a tyrant for any of us to take heed to such remarks. He wanted to come in the boat, and so he came; that was all there was to it. He always greatly enjoyed a drive in the car, doing a sort of chamois "stunt" all over us, and standing heavily on any convenient part of our anatomy, while he poked his head out of the wondow, "making his face all windy," as Alastair said on first seeing Spider's wisps of hair and snuff-coloured ears flying in the breeze. His tail, rhythmically wagging, brushed the faces of the long-suffering persons nearest the window on whose knees he stood, in spite of their protests.

Spider had a very sweet temper, but was capable of holding resentment. He must at some time before he came to us have been kicked by someone, for he shrank away from any chance touch of a shoe. Even a bare foot approaching him frightened him very much. If any one of us was so forgetful as to stretch a foot out in his direction, or if we swept him off the best place on the sofa when a visitor came, he would sit on the floor (or upon a chair) gazing coldly into space. I have often been summoned out of the room three or four times in a morning, and on returning found Spider still gazing resentfully before him. He also "registered" love, boredom, disappointment with the skill and punctuality of a film star.

He was an ardent lover of the chase, and although he was never known to catch even the youngest and smallest rabbit, he never gave up trying to do so. He loved illicit expeditions into the woods. Someone would say at tea-time: "Where's Spider?" and a search would be made for him. When he was nowhere to be found we all knew that the call of the wild had come upon him. Then, usually about dinner-time, into the library (or the nursery) would crawl an object which would drag itself sea-lion-like along the carpet, one paw uplifted, simply oozing apologies. His fleece would be clotted with yellow sand and mud, and the fur flattened round his eyes would give them a strange glaring appearance. Except to the eyes of love he was completely unrecognisable. He would submit miserably to the unavoidable bath which, administered with severe ejaculations of "Bad boy!" and "Wicked dog!" from the irate washer (usually the master of the house), we always hoped would cure him of hunting, but it never did.

Spider hated us to go away and always gave us wonderful welcomes when we returned. I fear his manners at meals were far from correct. He would gobble down his allotted food and then, as the boys called it, "aeroplane" in order to be given some of ours. Aeroplaning consisted of leaping about two feet in the air to attract attention, and we used to see with helpless amusement our guests' shocked faces at his appalling behaviour. "Our dogs," they were wont to remark severely, "stay in the stables" or (alternatively) "their baskets during meal-time." Neither, I imagine, did their well-trained animals sit on sofas or appropriate the best chairs. We admitted to each other that Spider's manners were rather those of a pampered pet than a well-behaved dog, but to outsiders it was a point of honour not to show any surprise at Spider's behaviour. I cannot regret any of it, and every one of my readers who has had a spoilt and beloved dog will sympathise with us.

Spider lives on in the pages of *Castle Gay* under the name of "Woolworth," and will always be a household word in our family. He belongs to the days of my children's youth, and happy memories of picnics, holidays and quiet evenings by the fire.

CHAPTER XIII

AMERICAN INTERLUDE

IN the autumn of 1934, one day when John came home from London, he told me that he had been invited to go to New York to open the Harkness Library at Columbia University. "How would you like to go to New York for ten days?" he said. There seemed to be no reason why we should not go, and every reason why we should.

We sailed on the *Olympic* (I think it was her last voyage) and came slowly up the Hudson River in a fog. After talking to a great many journalists we went up to see if the fog had lifted. Our breath was taken away by what we saw. Night had fallen and what appeared to be the sky, looked like grey velvet in which someone had pricked row upon row of tiny holes through which shone points of coloured light.

We stayed at Columbia University with Principal Murray Butler and his wife. They welcomed us with generous kindness and hospitality. The telephone rang incessantly and John was asked many questions by all the newspapers. We were photographed, fêted and entertained.

The days passed in a flash and we met many interesting people. John spoke at the Pilgrims' Dinner, and the opening of the Harkness Library was a dignified and interesting ceremony. We also went to plays and films, and I shopped for Christmas presents for my family in the glittering shops piled high with attractive objects.

We also spent a day on Long Island with the Julian Peabodys. We had not met before, but they were lovers of John's books from whom he had received letters from time to time. We had seldom met people with whom we were so quickly happy. They were a great contrast as a couple; Julian was a tall man with a grave face and humorous eyes. Titine (*née* Hitchcock) was small, blonde, and sparkling with fun and vitality. We had long talks about books and she gave me some American books to take back with me, and I promised to send her some English ones when I got home.

On my return I sent them off and was puzzled by receiving no acknowledgment of them. Then I heard that both the Peabodys had been drowned on a ship which sank on the way to South America. John and I felt an abiding sharp sense of loss.

The Murray Butlers gave a dinner-party for us, where we met many charming people. John sat next to a woman who had an arrestingly beautiful face, whose profile was worthy of being incised on a Greek coin. I was told that she was a writer and that her name was Alice Duer Miller. I talked to her after dinner and we made friends at once— a friendship which ended only with her death.

On the evening that we met at the Murray Butlers' Alice Miller said urgently to me, "Alexander Woollcott and I want you to go and see Edward Sheldon.[1] He is the writer of *Romance* and other plays. He sees very few people, but he would like you both to go and see him." A day or two later we were whirled up in a lift to his apartment. We were a little intimidated by the shrouded and recumbent figure which lay in the middle of the room, for Edward Sheldon was blind and totally paralysed. But all shyness was instantly dissolved by the greeting we received in a vibrant and beautiful voice. Edward Sheldon asked John a great many questions and we gave him, I remember, a long list of Scottish books. In

[1] Died April 1st, 1946.

that room we felt we were privileged to be with a human being who had endless resources of fortitude, nobility of outlook, joined with such a fine and distinguished intellect. His influence was widely felt; actors came and acted their parts to him and went away helped by his advice; writers of plays and poems read him their work. To a wide public he was known as a playwright, his play *Romance* having had many long runs.

John was extremely happy those ten days at Columbia University; he responded to the stimulus in the air and to the sparkle of excitement which New York gives to her visitors, and he was endlessly interested in and amused by the American way of life. He had long talks with Principal Murray Butler on many subjects, and we left their house where we had been so happy one evening when the buildings of New York again were outlined by tiny lights.

We embarked on the *Berengaria*, to find that Hugh Walpole, the J. B. Priestleys and Beverley Nichols were also on board. Hugh Walpole was ill and stayed in his cabin, so the Priestleys, Beverley Nichols and we sat round his bed beguiling the hours by conversation.

I remember Hugh saying to John, "Do you realise that if this ship goes down to-night four of Great Britain's best-selling writers will be lost, and that all the non-best-selling writers will probably have a party to celebrate the event?" John looked surprised and a little mystified, and I shivered, as this remark was underlined rather unpleasantly by the way in which the *Berengaria* was behaving. She rolled and pitched with increasing violence. We had run into a big storm soon after leaving New York, and had woken up after some uneasy sleep, to find our cabin ankle-deep in water and the vases which held the flowers which had been showered on us when we left a mass of splintered glass, and our suitcases seemed to be fighting amongst themselves on the floor. The gale went on for several days and the chairs made strange mad rushes across the floor of the saloon, which caused the passengers to avoid it at all costs. With real detachment of mind we continued to sit by Hugh's bedside and to talk about books and people while the ship's timbers creaked and groaned and the seas roared outside. Then the gale subsided and we arrived safely at Southampton, where William met us.

CHAPTER XIV

CANADA

I

THE year 1935 started uneventfully for us. John had just completed a book about King George V under the title of *The King's Grace*, and he was also writing a story called *The House of the Four Winds*.

Alice and Brian were in Edinburgh, Johnnie had gone into the Colonial Service in Uganda and we missed him horribly, William was at New College and Alastair still at Eton. We were both very busy, and life was interesting, and except for the disquieting rumours from Europe we had no reason to expect that life would not go on much the same as before.

One day in the early months of 1935 the King sent for John and told him of his wish to appoint him to succeed Lord Bessborough as Governor-General of Canada, and that both parties in Canada were in favour of this appointment. John had always been enormously interested in Canada, and after our first short visit there we had gained many Canadian friends and correspondents. Since his South African days with Lord Milner, he had always viewed the British Commonwealth as a whole, and had seen his country and policies and problems in the light of something much greater than the British Isles.

In representing the King in Canada he felt that he was being offered a position which had immensely interesting potentialities and great responsibilities, and he accepted the honour which had been so gracefully bestowed upon him.

Tweedsmuir Village.

The late spring and summer of 1935 passed in a whirl. I can remember nothing about it save that it was a confusion of preparations for departure to Canada, and an endless answering of letters which poured in by every post. But if I had an arduous task, John had a much heavier one, as he was involved in so much public work and was chairman of so many committees. Years afterwards Mrs. Killick [1] told me that she and John had worked in their little office at St. Stephen's House for nearly ten or more hours a day, and that she frequently had to take work home to finish off at night.

We said a final farewell to our family, except Alastair, who went with us, and sailed on October 25th. We had a rough crossing and were delayed by fog at the mouth of the St. Lawrence, but on November 2nd we glided in smooth water between the shores of that famous river. We gazed at the venerable Laurentian Mountains, said to be the oldest geological formation in the world. This claim has also seemed to me a true one, though I know less than nothing of the science of geology, as there is something so exquisitely timeless in their aspect, and their outlines have the precision and charm of a cameo.

On that day in early November they stood shaded by the afternoon light into soft blues and mauves behind a biscuit-coloured foreground.

We steamed into Quebec at sunset. The line of the Citadel, and all the pinnacles and towers of the town, stood etched black against a sky of brilliant scarlet and orange—and the ships' sirens hooted in unison.

(A hundred and seventy-six years before, General James Wolfe's silent army of British soldiers rowed with muffled oars, before their perilous climb up the Rock to fight one of the most decisive battles of the world.)

[1] See Chapter XVI, page 279.

We drove up the Rock in darkness behind our escort, with the sound of horses' hooves and jingling harness in our ears. Romance seemed to come to us that evening with arms outstretched.

John was sworn in as Governor-General by Mr. Justice Rinfret, senior Puisne Judge of the Supreme Court. The whole ceremony had that quiet dignity which characterises Canadian official occasions.

We went when the ceremony was over to the private cars attached to the train. They were extremely comfortable and pleasantly furnished, and our suite of rooms somehow managed to convey a feeling of home, even when the train to which we were attached rolled and rocketed over the difficult Canadian permanent ways.

The next day our Comptroller, Lieutenant-Colonel Eric Mackenzie, knowing that we were a family of bird-lovers, had arranged a very pleasant afternoon's expedition for us near Cap Tourmente to see the snow-geese.

We drove through the town of Quebec to the shores of the St. Lawrence. The snow-geese were driven towards us, their wings making a noise like people clapping at a concert. They wheeled in orderly formations in a sort of aerial quadrille. They were snow-white, all but the tips of their wings, and seen against the vivid blue of the hills the other side of the St. Lawrence one compared them inevitably to a Japanese print.

Some of the snow-geese had had their wings clipped and were used as decoys. They stood about in the grass paying little attention to us, or indeed to the geese that swooped over their heads. They continued to feed in thoroughly sensible and bourgeois manner.

No one who saw it could ever forget this marvellous spectacle of bird life where ten thousand snow-geese were in the air at once.

The following day we went to Ottawa and drove

through the streets lined with people, and we arrived at Government House with the warmth of our welcome having brought a glow to our hearts.

We settled down in Government House on November 4th, 1935, and started to make our life there. Government House manages to retain a feeling of dignity and homeliness which is remarkable as it is lived in by a Vice-Regal family for five years, and each Governor-General's wife puts her fleeting imprint on it in the matter of curtains and sofa-covers. The little park which surrounds the house and gardens is varied and charming, and is peopled by coal-black squirrels which run about, their tails looking like black exclamation marks.

After we arrived in Canada the whole Empire was plunged into mourning by the death of King George the Fifth. This meant for us the cancellation of social activities, and the Court mourning lasted for a year. The King had always shown a great kindness and friendliness to my husband, who felt his death as a great personal loss, and Canada mourned her dead Sovereign deeply and sincerely.

While we were living so quietly we worked at gaining a greater knowledge of Canada and we each devoted a bit of the day to our writing. John was busy over his biography of *Augustus* and I was able to finish my first novel.[1]

I shall not attempt to describe each year in detail, and alas it is not possible to write about the people we met, or all the varied things we did, during our years in Canada. I will merely make some attempt to describe the places we lived in, and some of those we visited.

Ottawa, of course, comes first, as we spent so much more time there than anywhere else in Canada, the Governor-General having to be there while the Dominion

[1] *The Scent of Water*, by Susan Buchan.

Parliament is in session. The Parliament Buildings at Ottawa stand on a bluff and the city extends along the Ottawa River, which is wide and flows swiftly along. The town is set in beautiful surroundings of hills and woods, and those who are country-minded can get quickly out of it for walks and picnics. Canada's capital city has many foreign legations, and during the parliamentary session is the home of members of Parliament and their families from all over Canada. John delighted in talking to them and hearing all they had to say, and he went down to the East Block of the Parliament Building once a week in the morning, where any of the M.P.s who wished to do so could come and talk to him. Apart from the people who used to come to lunch, tea and dinner at Government House, John used to see one person daily after tea, and I could hear the murmur of their long conversations as my sitting-room was next to his room.

He had a very happy relationship with the Prime Minister, Mr. Mackenzie King. We had known him a long time before we went to Canada, and he was most kind in inviting us to go up to one of his houses near Ottawa, at Kingsmere, to have tea and a walk over his grounds.

So many recollections crowd back into my mind when I think of Ottawa. Long drives into the country, expeditions with Mrs. Hughson to find those attractive but elusive Canadian spring flowers which are adepts in concealing themselves under the lee of boulders or drifts of dead leaves. The Northern Lights which always made me think of transparent Shetland shawls quivering in the sky. Two old crows which sat on a tree just outside my bedroom window at Ottawa and in harsh voices announced the coming of spring, and the little chickadees who came with the turn of the year chanting their call of chick-a-dee, and the sparrows whom no snow could defeat, voraciously devouring the crumbs I threw to them outside my window. The exquisite light towards evening when the snow from silvery-white merges into pale grey, and the sky is shot with mauve and green; and in the daytime the sun which shines on a winter's day from a turquoise sky casting shadows of the blue of the Madonna's robe on to the snow.

We were extremely fortunate in our staff and on the whole suffered little from those disharmonies which trouble a set of people rather fortuitously brought together to live under the same roof.

Lady Byng [1] in her autobiography has paid a tribute to our senior Canadian A.D.C., Willis O'Connor. He was appointed by her husband, Field-Marshal Lord Byng, just after the last war. I should like to add my tribute to hers. I can't imagine what we should have done without Willis. His charm, good-humour and wit made ife happier for all those he met. He had an encyclopedic knowledge of his fellow-countrymen. He saved us from many of those little unintentional mistakes made by Governor-Generals and their staffs. Whenever we went on tour he was welcomed everywhere with acclamation, and we listened eagerly to all he had to tell us of the country and the people. He went with us both to all sorts of functions. He and I sometimes went out together to Women's Institute meetings in Ontario. I had been a W.I. member for many years, and the members of Canadian Institutes, realising this, asked me to their meetings. It is no exaggeration to say that Willis was the life and soul ot the party. I remember once looking round to see where he was, as I thought perhaps that we should go home, only to find him and one of the members gravely discussing the best way of cooking a ham.

His wife, pretty and chic, helped me in countless ways.

[1] *Up the Stream of Life,* by Viscountess Byng of Vimy.

She is an exquisite needlewoman and ran a work-party I had for sending clothes to the women on the Prairies through the bad years of drought. This later became a work-party for clothes for the United Kingdom, and when I left Canada they continued to make clothes which they sent me all through the war for people in the bombed areas. The clothes were marvels of ingenuity, made often from odd bits of stuff, and so pretty and so smart that all who looked at them desired at once to possess and wear them.

It is no exaggeration to say that the morale of the people in the places devastated by bombing was raised by the clothes which came not only from Ottawa but from all over Canada, to be worn by those who had lost their homes and all their possessions. Canadian women do this work with great imagination, chic and finish. I remember a woman in Stepney saying to me with tears rolling down her cheeks, "Oh, Canada is good to us."

Our staff was joined later by two other Canadians, Edson Sherwood and Dunne Lantier. Edson comes from the Maritimes, and possesses great distinction and charm, and Dunne had a most attractive French Canadian gaiety as well as keenness about his job.

Michael Adeane, David Walker and Patrick Campbell Preston have happily come through the war. Our other three A.D.C.s are dead. John Boyle was killed commanding a battalion of the Royal Scots Fusiliers on the Anzio beach-head. He fell when bringing in a wounded man. He much enjoyed all the outdoor life in Canada and was an excellent and enthusiastic skier. He remained with us for over a year and when he went back to England was much regretted by the many friends he had made. Gordon Rivers-Smith, fair, blue-eyed and slim, had that matchless efficiency in his work which is characteristic of a naval officer. Always good tempered and kind, he saw what needed to be done and did whatever was necessary without fuss. After an outstanding war record he died in 1946 as a Lieutenant-Commander, having contracted a fatal illness on active service. Robin Scott was also in the Navy. He was tall and slight, and his dark eyes held more than a glint of irony. When Robin arrived in Ottawa, John was quick to see the quality of his mind and character. He always enjoyed talking to Robin and hearing his opinions about many things. Robin was devoted to mathematics, and in the evenings when I was devouring a detective story, and John was either reading or playing Patience, Robin would amuse himself by doing abstruse mathematical puzzles.

In the spring of 1939, when we were in Victoria staying with the Eric Hambers,[1] Robin and Willis had birthdays on the same day. We sat for a long time at dinner while the evening light coloured the Olympic Mountains across the straits.

John rose after dinner and made a little speech. He first said grateful and affectionate things to Willis, then he turned to Robin and spoke of the brilliant career which he foresaw for him in the Navy. The Pacific ceaselessly pounded the island coast, and we could not guess that Robin would lie fathom deep in another ocean before two years were past, when he fought his destroyer *Greyhound* all day, till she sank in the waters of the Mediterranean.

My two ladies-in-waiting, Beatrice Spencer-Smith (now Lady Graham) and Joan Pape (Mrs. George Pape), who succeeded her, were also a great help to us, and the companionship they gave me was a perpetual stimulus and amusement. They both loved Canada and entered into the life there with the utmost zest, making friends wherever they went. Our Comptroller, Eric Mackenzie,

[1] Lieutenant-Governor of British Columbia.

managed the affairs of the household with the greatest possible success.

The Governor-General of Canada lives at Quebec for some time each year. Quebec is a town which commands wide prospects of river and mountain. It has enchanting narrow streets, and the flat-fronted houses with green-painted shutters always reminded me of provincial France. The Citadel was once the officers' quarters of a British regiment and some of the rooms have barrel-vaulted ceilings which was part of Vauban's fortress design. There is an intimate cosiness about the house, as all the rooms are snug and small. You approach it by a steep hill and several hairpin bends, and as the car moves through the gateway of the barrack square the sentries salute. We were on very friendly terms with the *Vingt-Deuxième Régiment* who were guarding the Citadel when we were there, and who distinguished themselves so greatly afterwards in the Italian fighting.

My bedroom looked out on to a square surrounded by low walls, and each morning a band played light and cheerful music for an hour or so. Outside the windows was a line of willow trees which made curtains of pointed green leaves between us and the outside world. From the other side of the house you see the swiftly flowing St. Lawrence, and on the hill opposite the town of Lévis with its many churches, seminaries and convents set in gardens and trees. The view from the terrace shows the widening of the river, and the mountains take on every variety of colour as the light changes. The drives round Quebec are lovely, and I have seen fields of wild iris brilliant against a pale green background. The Island of Orleans was our favourite drive, and we often visited its old churches or spent afternoons at Mrs. Porteous's house and explored her garden, which goes down in terraces to the St. Lawrence.

Lady Tweedsmuir at Government House.

French Canadians have a great respect for tradition and there is an enchanting mixture of old and new in the Province of Quebec. Montreal has all the modernity of a busy North American city, while in the city of Quebec, and the surrounding country, lingers the grace of old France. In Quebec the ear is caressed by delightful sounds. Bells ring at all hours from the churches and convents. At dead of night you are awakened by an insistent ringing which summons the nuns to prayer. At the same moment you may hear the ships on the river hooting, and you go to sleep again comforted by the feeling that nuns are praying and that sailors are at their work.

On a summer evening the light is a deep and intense blue, like the colour of dark blue glass. On the river the ferry plies to and fro to Lévis, whose lights spangle the dark hill opposite, and those from the ferries break up the dark river round them into quivering arcs of gold. This always reminded me of glittering golden combs being drawn through dark hair.

The French Canadians always showed us great cordiality and kindness, and my husband, having all the Scottish *penchant* towards anything French, absorbed every detail of French Canadian culture and entered into their industrial and agricultural life with the utmost keenness. He also studied their speech and delighted in learning the ancient words they used which date from the days of King Louis XIV. He sat writing in the Citadel for hours, often in a corner of the terrace where he drew inspiration from the beauty of the scene around him.

President Roosevelt visited us there for a day, and John and he each gave a broadcast from the terrace in front of the Château Frontenac Hotel. He stayed for luncheon and tea, and in between times John and he and the Prime Minister talked to each other. In spite of the rather uncertain weather Quebec was thronged with people that day. The President charmed us both. He had that so rare gift in being interested in the person he was talking to and in getting the best out of them in conversation. My husband and he made friends, a friendship which was continued by correspondence and sealed by our visit to Washington.

II

We first went to the Maritime Provinces in June 1937 and enjoyed their beauty to the full. We saw enchanting glimpses from the train window of white and grey houses surrounded by lilacs—lilacs such as I had never imagined, as they grew with a luxuriance which one never sees in England and were marvels of massed colour and scent. The towns have much charm with their dignified Georgian public buildings. We met numbers of interesting people and saw many diverse activities and ate every variety of delicious fish. John went later to Prince Edward Island, where, alas, I did not accompany him. He has paid a tribute to the Islanders in his speech at Charlottetown under the name of *Island Magic*.[1]

Ontario was our most permanent home. We continued to be struck dumb by her variety of scenery, her fertile agricultural land, and the dainty charm of the countryside in the Niagara peninsula. John set himself to learn about her mines, which were rapidly developing whilst we were there. Technical questions interested him profoundly and he loved to master as much of them as was possible. He talked often and long to the members of the Department of Mines and Resources, listening with absorbed interest to all they said to him.

[1] *Canadian Occasions*, p. 29.

In his speech at the Canadian Institute of Mining and
Metallurgy Dinner at Ottawa [1] in March 1936 he said:

> In the few months I have been here I have had the privilege
> of seeing something of two mining areas—the gold and copper
> mines in Northern Ontario, and the Asbestos mines of Thetford,
> in the Eastern Townships. I hope during my time in this country
> to see a great deal more; and that will mean pretty extensive
> travelling, for you have mineral wealth everywhere from the
> Great Lakes to the Arctic ocean, from the Prairies in the West to
> the Atlantic coast. The great Laurentian Shield, which at one
> time was thought to be a useless no-man's land, now proves to
> be the roof of a gigantic treasure-house. . . . It is a gift from
> Providence which has come unexpectedly out of the void, and
> of which we have only just begun to scrape the edges.

We saw the Prairies in all seasons of the year: we saw
them when the snow was melting and the red dogwood
stood in patches of black earth; we saw them in the first
flush of spring; then when the burnished ears of corn
rippled in the wind for countless miles; and again after the
harvest, when the corn-stooks dotted the great plains like
endless lines of chessmen.

We first saw the southern Prairies in the tragic days
when a long drought had made the land into a desert.
We went down to Alsask in southern Saskatchewan to
see the Alec Frasers, as John and he were at school together
in Scotland. The whole countryside appeared to be
blowing away and there were drifts of grey dust over
everything. Huge thistles grew and maleficent little
gophers peeped out of their holes. The only feature of
the place that was not depressing was the fortitude and
optimism of the people. I enquired of some of the
women what I could do for them, and they asked me to
send them books. With John's constant help and encouragement I started what was called the Lady
Tweedsmuir Prairie Library Scheme, and with generous

[1] *Ibid.*, pp. 204-205.

help from Canadians, from England and from the Carnegie Trustees in New York, I managed to send out forty thousand books from Government House. Her Majesty Queen Mary sent me a great many books which were specially appreciated both in Canadian households and in the Prairie schools.

I gained the friendship of many of the Prairie farmers' wives and other women who lived in remote places. They wrote me delightful letters saying which of the books they had most enjoyed, and telling me of all the difficulties and pleasures of their lives. My admiration for the rural women of Canada deepened all the years that I was there. I am glad to say that this friendship has continued through the years of war. I still receive many letters from the Canadian West. All his life John received endless books and he gave me many of them for the Prairie Libraries.

We visited the West again in happier days when better times had come. We went to the picturesque Calgary Stampede and watched the many-coloured crowd of Indians, Mounties and Cowboys as it moved and shifted round the track where rodeo, broncho-busting and "chuck waggon" races were in full swing. Towards evening we sat and watched an open-air cabaret show. A storm gathered in the sky and thunder growled and rumbled in the distance. At the end of the entertainment the curtains parted and we saw riding across the back of the stage in single file on magnificent horses about twenty Indians dressed in beautifully embroidered white garments. They progressed in complete silence and it was all over in a trice. They were like lovely ghosts and gave one a pang of the heart. The Indians we had seen in their Reservations are often dressed, the men in shabby shirts and dirty flannel trousers, the women in declining woollen jumpers and old skirts. Their Reservations are apt to look like Heath Robinson drawings, as everything is off the straight and the doors hang crazily on one hinge. This brief glimpse at the Calgary Stampede showed us what they looked like at their best.[1]

British Columbia lies between the barrier of the Rockies and the Pacific coast and has a completely different atmosphere to the rest of Canada. It holds enchantment and mystery in its forests, lakes and rivers, and John felt a great longing to go off exploring its more distant parts. But we had our job to do, and we spent some very pleasant times seeing the city of Vancouver, where he took a special interest in the City Archives so admirably looked after by Major Matthews. We sailed from Vancouver's lovely harbour in a battleship to stay with Mr. Eric Hamber and his charming wife. Government House, Victoria, stands in enchanting gardens where quails and partridges run about all the time. From my bedroom window I could see the Olympic Mountains surmounted by their splendid glaciers. They are divided from Victoria by a strip of sea, and often a band of mist lies on the water above which they rise in all their sculptured beauty. Vancouver Island has everything that makes life pleasant. The scenery is exquisite; nearly everyone grows flowers and there is an abundance of fruit. Life moves there a little more slowly than in the rest of Canada, and the English lark sings there, which is perhaps symbolic. The great forests of Douglas firs, sometimes over two hundred feet high, are magical with their red stems and dark foliage through which a fine dust sifts, producing a perpetual twilight.

The Lieutenant-Governor had a yacht, and on those trips which we went with him and his wife John got a great deal of most exciting and delightful fishing. The yacht steamed along among the islands revealing glimpses of trees and

[1] In this war, as in the last one, the Indians fought with outstanding gallantry and dash in the Canadian Army.

little valleys, and sometimes one caught a glimpse of a house or garden. These islands seemed to float lightly on the waters of the Pacific, serene and remote from the world.

Our tours included much speaking in public. In his first year John spoke on "Brevity in Speaking." This was a favourite theme of his. He always maintained that there was no subject which could not be dealt with in a twenty-minute or at the most a half-hour speech if you kept to the point and knew how to express yourself. He also spoke on "Literature and Law," "On what Constitutes an Educated Man," on such other subjects as Social Service, Patriotism, and Peace, and sometimes he talked about his friends, T. E. Lawrence, Lord Balfour, and others. Some of his speeches were reprinted in 1940 under the title of *Canadian Occasions*.

With the Universities in Canada John had much to do. He delivered addresses to them and received honorary degrees. As Visitor to McGill he saw much of the Governors and Professors of that University and they sought his advice on many matters. He was interested in every detail of their work and loved to meet and talk to their students.

We had many happy visits to Canadian cities, and our programme usually included some University function. It is difficult to get into the life of a city when you are a Governor-General, but my husband's wide knowledge of Canadian conditions, and his eager interest in all phases of Canadian life, made him penetrate more deeply into the lives of the townspeople than many official visitors have done.

In March 1937 we paid a visit to Washington. We started by going through a blizzard in Vermont, but when we arrived at Washington the sun was shining and there were flowers everywhere. We were met at the station by Mr. Cordell Hull and drove to the White House, where the President and Mrs. Roosevelt stood in the dignified porch to greet us. We had very little time to talk to our hosts, but were again fascinated by the President's charm and courage. John and he had a great deal in common. They talked to each other like old friends, wasting no time on the preliminaries of acquaintanceship. Both were good talkers and both good listeners. We had an unforgettable afternoon when we went to Mount Vernon, George Washington's country house. The President took us on his yacht, and we moved slowly along the Potomac River till we reached the landing-stage below the house.

John laid a wreath upon Washington's unpretentious tomb, and then we walked up the hill, where a large crowd had gathered. The President sat in his car, while Mrs. Roosevelt, John and I went into the house. The rooms at Mount Vernon are full of graceful furniture. They seemed to me to cry out to be lived in by a family, rather than be tramped through by daily crowds of sightseers. As it stands, overlooking the river and surrounded by its pleasant gardens, it looks like a fragment of eighteenth-century England with the added richness of Southern colouring.

We also went to Arlington, the house of the Confederate General Robert E. Lee. I have seldom seen John so happy. He examined everything in the house and asked innumerable questions, and deepened my interest by telling me again the details of the life of the soldier he so greatly admired. Mrs. Roosevelt and I visited the Folger Museum to see the Shakespeare treasures. She was busy all the time, but we managed to talk together a little. She left on my mind an impression of dignity and ability. It is not surprising that she has made for herself a unique place in the estimation of the world. The visit passed all too quickly. I longed to buy some of the little flowering trees which stood outside the florists' shops in Washington, but was persuaded not to do so by Joan Pape, who very wisely reminded me that they would all die on the way back to Ottawa.

We had always been very fortunate in having many friends in the United States, to which my husband has paid a warm tribute in his chapter "My America" in *Memory Hold-the-Door*. Apart from the President's visit (the first visit ever paid to a Governor-General of Canada by the President of the United States of America), we had many distinguished Americans to stay with us. Mr. and Mrs. Cordell Hull, Alice Duer Miller, Alexander Woollcott, Ferris Greenslet and other writers. Ruth Draper also came, and many other artists and musicians, as well as representatives from the political and financial world. We used to arrange that they should meet Canadians with like interests, to the mutual satisfaction of both parties.

III

Sir Shuldham Redfern, who has helped me so greatly in writing this chapter, has acted as Secretary to two Governors-General. His outstanding ability and powers of hard work proved an invaluable help to my husband, and they were very good friends. He and I worked together on many things, and I was always much struck by his grasp of all public and international questions. Ruth Redfern made Rideau Cottage, which stands in the park of Government House, a very welcoming and pleasant place for all to go to. Shuldham never knew John till a few months before we all sailed for Canada, so

that the following picture he gives of him is of special
interest :

"Lord Tweedsmuir possessed many qualifications which
were particularly acceptable to the people of Canada.
He was a famous and popular author whose books were
widely read both in Canada and the United States. He
himself was often surprised at the number of people he
met who had read all his books.

He was born and bred in Scotland and this made an
instant appeal in Canada, where large Scottish elements of
the population were not only influential on account of the
very considerable part they had played in the development
of the country, but were also intensely proud of their
origin. The adaptability of the Scottish character, its
shrewd common sense and its quiet humour, seemed to
be admirable qualities for a Governor-General. He was
a 'son of the Manse,' a most welcome qualification in a
country in which the Scottish Church has played a con-
spicuous part in the spiritual life of the people.

He had throughout his public life been associated with
Universities, and his continued interest in education
appealed to a wide section of the people of Canada.
As an historian, and particularly as a military historian,
he was well known, and his knowledge of Canadian
history before he ever set foot in the country was more
profound than that of many who had spent their lives in
Canada. He was an accomplished speaker and was thus
able to satisfy to some extent the craving for the spoken
word which is so marked a feature of the American
continent.

Equipped with this dazzling array of attainments, he
entered upon his new duties with an almost boyish zest
and with a new and refreshing conception of the duties of
a Governor-General. He realised that one of the main

problems on which every Government set the greatest store was the problem of Canadian unity. Every administration had used this as a bedrock for its policy, knowing well that failure to maintain cohesion among the many diverse racial elements would speedily result in disaster. This was a problem to which the Governor-General could apply himself without any risk of departing from the narrow limits of his constitutional position. Lord Tweedsmuir lost no time in taking advantage of the unique opportunities which presented themselves to him of trying to integrate the many and conflicting views which gave rise to latent animosities throughout the country. He formed the opinion that the ignorance of Canadians of their own country was a major factor in these divergencies. Those who lived in Eastern Canada knew little and understood less of the difficulties which beset the Prairie farmers. The great chain of the Rocky Mountains was not only a physical barrier; it was also an obstacle to the interchange of knowledge between the West Coast and the rest of the country. But the greatest differences of all existed between the Canadians of French origin, strongly imbued with the Roman Catholic faith, who formed a third of the total population, and their fellow-citizens elsewhere. To whatever extent the Governor-General could remedy this state of affairs, he would be making a permanent contribution towards the stability of a territory as vast in its dimensions as it was immature in its political evolution.

Lord Tweedsmuir's quick grasp of local problems, his enthusiasm for travel, his accessibility to all and sundry, his powers of expression, all fitted him to an extraordinary degree for the task which he set himself of telling Canadians in one part of the country about Canadians in other parts. It was a task which he much enjoyed. The richness and spaciousness of the Canadian scene appealed strongly to his romantic spirit. The unexplored resources and the physical frontiers of the great expanses of the North stimulated his love of adventure. The bright texture of the many races which made up the fabric of the Canadian nation found a ready response in his profound knowledge of their history. He travelled incessantly in all parts of the Dominion, and wherever he went his interest in everything he saw and everyone he met enriched his storehouse of knowledge, which was reinforced by a remarkable memory. But he willingly and at all times poured out the contents of this storehouse. His was not the mind of a savant which sought information for its own inflation. His rich knowledge of men and affairs was abundantly available to all.

He was a voracious reader and this had a direct bearing on his writing, for he maintained that the mind of a writer was like a tank. It had to be filled before it could be emptied. But he read everything on which he could lay his hands. It may well be imagined that anyone in Canada who wrote a book sent a complimentary copy to the Governor-General—as one author to another. All of these he read, and often wrote personal letters of commendation to the authors. Most of his spare time he occupied with reading and he was never known to have an idle moment. He was thus entirely self-contained, and no member of the Governor-General's staff was ever confronted with the problem of finding some means to keep His Excellency occupied. He took no interest in the administrative details of his Government House and was content to leave the staff to do their own staff work without interference. On the other hand, he never allowed his staff to come between him and the people of Canada. His staff had to act as a bridge rather than a barrier.

The ceremonial duties of his high office he performed

with meticulous precision. Many of them were irksome and tiring, but he appreciated the symbolism for which they stood and he never permitted any deviation from the dignified ritual inseparable from the role of the King's Representative.

His habits were precise and conventional. He worked with bewildering speed and he was always ahead of his work. He had a voluminous correspondence, but he answered every letter immediately on its receipt and dealt with the mass of official correspondence, despatches and State documents that daily confronted him as if they were all of immediate urgency. The word 'Urgent' was never used on any document put before the Governor-General. It would have been unnecessary as he gave immediate attention to everything. He could easily have dealt with ten times the volume of official correspondence that he received.

He prepared all his own speeches and had them typed to his dictation, not in order to refresh his memory but to provide an accurate record for the press. In practice he spoke without reference to the text and without a note of any kind. His speeches were models of clear thinking expressed with a conciseness and lucidity which compelled widespread admiration. He had the gift of sensing the atmosphere and making a speech exactly appropriate to his audience. He was fully aware of the dangers which beset an unwary Governor-General, but he himself coined the phrase that a Governor-General must confine himself to 'Governor-Generalities.' He was able, however, to make the most banal platitude sound as if it were a novelty. If there was ever the slightest risk of any of his speeches giving rise to controversy, he invariably referred the text beforehand to the Prime Minister and never hesitated to accept such amendments as were suggested.

He met an incredible number of people in all walks of life and was able to make everyone feel at ease in his presence. In his judgment of men he was in the first place uncritical almost to the point of simplicity. The later discovery of inferior qualities was usually balanced by his appreciation of good qualities. He never spoke ill of anyone.

The King and Queen paid a visit to Canada in 1939. The presence of the Sovereign in Canada gave rise to many questions of constitutional significance so far as the position of the Governor-General was concerned. In the solution of these problems Lord Tweedsmuir's personal modesty was a factor of considerable importance, with the result that, so far from being diminished, the position of the Governor-Generalship was in the long run enhanced by Their Majesties' visit.

The outbreak of war found Canada with a united front. Racial, political and religious differences were submerged by the immediate recognition of a threat to Canada's safety. The decision to come in on the side of Britain was as unanimous as it was independent. The efforts which the Governor-General had made to integrate the various parts of Canada were abundantly and dramatically justified. But it was clear that the outcome of the war would be in jeopardy if the United States remained aloof. The Governor-General had numerous American friends and he found many opportunities for strengthening the ties of friendship between Canada and the United States.

Lord Tweedsmuir would probably have desired no better epitaph than a recognition of his assistance in strengthening the bonds of friendship between the United States on the one hand and Canada and Great Britain on the other.

The war had not developed beyond the preliminary skirmishings when he died in February 1940.

'Few can ever have gone wearier to the grave; none with less fear.'"

Shuldham also contributes an account of a journey in 1937 to the Arctic.

"Ever since Lord Tweedsmuir first arrived in Canada, it had been one of his most cherished ambitions to visit the North Country. That vast inaccessible region that stretches across the whole width of Canada and pushes northward into the little known and inhospitable tracts of the Arctic made a special appeal to his adventurous spirit. Towards the end of 1936 it was decided to visit the area of the Mackenzie River and to travel by rail, river and air and by any other means of transport that might be available. The start was timed to coincide with the departure of one of the Hudson's Bay Company's River services, and the Governor and Directors of that ancient and historic Company of 'Gentlemen Adventurers' invited the Governor-General to be their guest.

The party was a small one which included my wife and myself, and an Aide-de-Camp, Lieutenant Gordon Rivers-Smith, R.N. The other passengers consisted of Colonel Reid and Mr. Bonnycastle of the Hudson's Bay Company, Inspector Martin of the Royal Canadian Mounted Police, the Reverend George Macdonald, Dr. Thomas Wood, a distinguished musician and writer, Mr. Guy Rhoades of the Canadian Press and Miss Margaret Bourke White, a well-known American press photographer. In addition there were various officials, missionaries and traders who took advantage of the steamer service to return to their lonely posts. It was a gay and friendly party, very much after the Governor-

General's own heart, and everyone was soon under the kindly influence of his enthusiasm and informality.

Edmonton is the gateway to the Canadian North-West, and Lord Tweedsmuir left there on the evening of July 20th, 1937, by the leisurely little railway that threads its way for 200 miles through a tangle of fir-weed, golden-rod and flaming wild flowers.

Waterways on the Clearwater is the 'end of steel' and the beginning of the river service, and it was reached the following morning. The Governor-General took the opportunity of visiting the Abasand Oil Field, where it was said that by extracting oil from the sand there would be enough to supply the world for a hundred years. Lord Tweedsmuir and his fellow-passengers were seen off in the evening by Lady Tweedsmuir, who had come as far as this. As the water was low, they left in a barge to join the *Athabasca River*, a stern-wheeler that looked like a cross between a Nile steamer and a Henley houseboat. She sailed in the evening into a soft and lingering sunset, and, as Lord Tweedsmuir himself described it, the river 'was like an elongated lake in a rather over-wooded English park.'

Lord Tweedsmuir discovered that one of the most peaceful forms of voyaging is to sit in the prow of a barge pushed by a river steamer, and here he spent a restful day as the strange craft threaded its way through the narrow channel of the stream and towards evening emerged into that wide expanse of shallow water known as Lake Athabasca.

A short stop was made at Fort Chipewyan, an agreeable place with historic memories, for it was from here that Sir Alexander Mackenzie started on his journeys to the Arctic and the Pacific. On the following day the steamer reached Fort Fitzgerald, where the rapids, named 'The Casette,' 'The Pelican,' 'The Mountain' and 'The Rapids of the Drowned,' form an effective barrier to further navigation. Here the Governor-General and his fellow-passengers disembarked and drove the sixteen bumpy miles to Fort Smith in a series of antiquated cars, of which the Governor-General's was the newest—it had only done 72,000 miles. It was during this drive that the famous mosquitoes of the North Country first appeared, and they put up a devastating performance. The cheerful inhabitants of Fort Smith gave a small reception for the Governor-General, and then he visited the Roman Catholic Hospital and many of the local gardens, where the extra hours of northern sunlight produced delphiniums fifteen feet high. In the evening the Governor-General's party boarded the stern-wheeler *Distributor*, which was gaily 'dressed' for the occasion and was to be his home for the next ten days. After a day of leisurely travel interrupted at intervals by the incongruous whirr of a passing mail-carrying aeroplane, the steamer entered the western end of the Great Slave Lake and succeeded in reaching the entrance to the Mackenzie River just before a violent storm arose which might have delayed the boat for several days.

July 25th was a Sunday, and Dr. Macdonald held a service on board which was of the type calculated to make an instant appeal. It was short, there was no sermon and there was no collection. The singing, however, fell somewhat below the highest standards. Here is a note about it from the diary of a member of Lord Tweedsmuir's staff: 'The start of one of the hymns was a failure. We all began on a different note, in a different key and in a different tune. The result was indescribable. It was like a party of roysterers far-gone in their cups putting the final touches to a hilarious sing-song. At the end of the first verse it petered out in a melancholy burble of in-ebriated disharmony. We then all took deep breaths and began again. This time the result was superb and we finished the course in fine style.'

The steamer stopped at every sign of habitation and at all the old Hudson's Bay posts—Fort Resolution, Hay River, Fort Providence, Fort Simpson, Fort Wrigley, Fort Norman, Fort Good Hope, Arctic Red River and Fort McPherson. Although these little centres, which are fairly evenly spaced along the solemn majestic path of the great river, closely resemble one another in many respects, yet each has its distinctive features. Lord Tweedsmuir went ashore at all of them and met all the inhabitants.

At Fort Providence there was a crowd of gaily attired school-children looked after by a dozen or so Grey Nuns. They assembled in a hall and, accompanied by a wheezy harmonium, sang a doleful little song. After an awkward pause and a shifting of feet Miss Bourke White, the press photographer, arrived with a battery of equipment and there was a series of blinding flashes, which, of course, delighted the children. Fort Simpson is perhaps the most elaborate of these old trading posts and the most typical; the stockade has been replaced by neat white palings, and over the entrance to each compound of the Hudson's Bay Company is the historic legend which survives from more heroic days, 'Incorporated 2nd May, 1670.' There is also invariably a Royal Canadian Mounted Police barracks, a Roman Catholic or mission church, a wireless station, a school, a few houses belonging to traders or trappers, and the simple houses of the Indians. Immediately beyond these modest clearings lies the bush. Everyone everywhere turned out to meet the Governor-General: policemen in their scarlet uniforms, Hudson's Bay Company officials, bearded priests, missionaries, nuns, traders, Indians and their serious-looking children. Lord Tweedsmuir spoke to them all.

There was something Irish about Fort Simpson—the

kindliness of the people, the faint nostalgic smell of burning turf, the spick-and-span police barracks, the one antiquated motor-car, the potatoes growing all round the church, the vivid green grass and the cool, swift waters of the river.

Fort Norman was reached on July 28th, and there was a stop of thirty-six hours to enable the boilers of the vessel to be washed. Here, at the junction of the Great Bear River, the first tinge of Arctic weather was noticeable. Lord Tweedsmuir spent an afternoon climbing the face of Bear Mountain, a rocky crag which proved too much for most members of the party, two of whom were stranded half-way up when the crumbling limestone gave way. The Governor-General reached the top without apparent difficulty and was delighted to find there the homely grass-of-Parnassus among strange plants like *Labrador Tea*, the Indian *Paint Bowl* and odd lilies and orchids.

The next day, after passing through a narrow channel appropriately named the Ramparts, and calling at Fort Good Hope, the ship reached the Arctic Circle. A ritual similar to that of Crossing the Line was prepared by some of the passengers; Santa Claus, accompanied by Bard and Medicine Man, came aboard and the Governor-General was admitted to the Sanctuary of the Arctic, with the Eskimo blessing, 'May you have warmth in your igloo, oil in your lamp and peace in your heart.' The last day of July was warm and summery and the ship called at Arctic Red River. The following morning the Governor-General was aroused by the barking of dogs tethered along the bank at Fort McPherson, a small and pleasant settlement on the Peel River. Here, unlike other such posts, there was no Roman Catholic mission. The Anglican authorities had it all their own way. The explanation was that old Mr. Firth, aged eighty-four and doyen of Hudson's Bay employees, had always refused to give credit to Roman Catholics. As was discovered and practised by many Elizabethan adventurers, a little commercial bullying is worth any amount of sectarian propaganda.

The same evening the ship reached its farthest point north at Aklavik in the dreary mud-flats of the delta of the Mackenzie River.

A large concourse of officials, traders, nursing sisters and nuns came on board to greet the Governor-General and they were led by the Lord Bishop of the Diocese, who signed himself 'Archibald the Arctic.' Two days were spent at Aklavik, and the Governor-General visited everyone there and opened the new Anglican Hospital. The weather was bad, with a cold north wind and constant rain.

Up to this point Lord Tweedsmuir had been the guest of the Hudson's Bay Company, who had made the most complete and admirable arrangements for the journey. The rest of the trip, including the return journey to Edmonton, was made in aircraft provided by the Royal Canadian Air Force. It had been Lord Tweedsmuir's intention to fly to Herschel Island, but it was cut off by bad weather, and so he flew instead to Tukto-Yaktuk, an Eskimo settlement on the shore of the Arctic Ocean, Lord Tweedsmuir felt almost at home in this Far Northern outpost, for in the thin layer of soil which covers the ice he found blaeberries and cranberries. On the way back to Aklavik he flew over Richard Island at the mouth of the river and saw the herd of reindeer which had been brought from Alaska after a trek lasting three years, in order to encourage the Eskimo to be a herdsman as well as a hunter.

The northern fog thickened and the pilot lost his way over the pock-marked delta. It was only through the

Governor-General's own skill at map-reading that after some delay the aircraft got back to Aklavik and landed safely in appalling weather conditions.

The return journey began on August 4th, and although the flight started in tolerable weather, rain and mist compelled the pilot to fly a few feet over the surface of the river.

In the afternoon the plane was forced down at Fort Norman, where storms held up further progress for twenty-four hours. Never had this small outpost seen such activity. Six aeroplanes and twenty-six visitors, including the Governor-General and two Bishops, descended on it at the same time. Mrs. Skinner, the wife of the Manager of the Hudson's Bay store, was, however, undaunted, and cheerfully provided hospitality for all. The Governor-General here made a diversion and flew to the western end of Great Bear Lake to visit the famous El Dorado radium mine. He remained there two days and made a series of flights far out into the Barren land to the upper reaches of the Coppermine River and to Coronation Gulf. He had the unusual experience of flying over the Arctic Ocean up to the edge of the pack ice.

From Great Bear Lake he flew south to Fort Rae and the rich gold-bearing district round Yellowknife. From there he flew back to Edmonton after spending a night on the way at Fort Smith. Altogether the Governor-General had covered about 2000 miles by boat and well over 3000 by air.

It had been a memorable journey. The Governor-General was able to meet many people living hard lonely lives in numerous small isolated communities scattered over a vast area. He had demonstrated to them, and in fact to all the people of Canada, that the Crown and the Crown's representatives are not just the ornamental symbols of a fading tradition but living realities and just as personal to those who live and work in distant places as to those who are in daily contact with the King in London or with the Governor-General in Ottawa. The journey was one more example of Lord Tweedsmuir's policy of integrating the many and diverse people of the Dominion and making them realise that they were all the citizens of one great nation and of one great Empire, and above all it drew attention to the tremendous future possibilities of Northern Canada. But this long and strenuous journey was a severe strain on the Governor-General's health. His stern sense of duty to the people of Canada would not have permitted him to curtail it or seek the soft and easy path, nor would he omit a single item from the itinerary of a tour into the interior of British Columbia which was planned to take place immediately afterwards.

When in future years the Canadian North is swept by a tornado of economic development and the crust of the Cambrian Shield is prised open to reveal the treasures within, there will be many in the valley of the Mackenzie River who will tell their children of the time when, though isolated from the world, they were not forgotten by the King's representative, who took the trouble to go among them and cheer their lonely lives with his kindly smile and abiding interest."

The British Columbia Government named their new National Park "The Tweedsmuir Reserve," [1] and I

[1] Tweedsmuir Park was established by the British Columbia Government as a reserve in March 1936. It is a triangular piece of land, with its southern apex almost touching the Bella Coola River, and with an area of approximately three and a half million acres, or 5400 square miles.

The Park is for the most part a high tableland with an average altitude of between two and three thousand feet. Most of it is a mosaic of noble

wrote an article about our experiences there which
appeared in the *National Geographical Magazine* in April
1938. I quote here from this article.

"On August 15th, 1937, we left Burns Lake on a fine
morning after a week of rain. The party consisted of
the Governor-General, myself, Shuldham Redfern, Ruth
Redfern, two A.D.C.s—Gordon Rivers-Smith and
Patrick Campbell Preston, Alastair, and Joan Pape.

We were also accompanied by Mr. Wells Gray, the
British Columbia Minister of Lands; Mr. Parsons, the
Assistant Commissioner of the British Columbia Police;
and the local Members of Parliament.

Our party was completed by a sparrowhawk, which
we had acquired on the road and named Tertullian

lakes—not muskegs, but limpid sheets of water fed from the snows of the
hills. All the western side is the main chain of the Coast Mountains.

It shows no high summits, nothing more than from eight to nine
thousand feet, but the mountains are most exquisitely configured, and as
a piece of upland architecture it is comparable with the most beautiful parts
of the Alps.

Towards the southern apex the mountains increase in height to nearly
10,000 feet until the great trench of the Bella Coola Valley is reached. Here
in what is called the Mackenzie Valley, where Sir Alexander Mackenzie,
in his famous journey to the Pacific, first entered the Park, is a superb
piece of mountain scenery, and just beyond the south-eastern borders lies
the Rainbow range, which is also a most satisfying bit of mountain
architecture.

The British Columbia Government selected well, for it chose a tract of
country which contains in itself every variety of forest, lake, stream,
plateau, and mountain scenery, and each variety is a perfect specimen of
its kind.

The ranges of western Canada can provide many scenes of savage
grandeur, but none of them, I think, comparable to Tweedsmuir Park for
grace and beauty. There one is conscious of the amenities as well as the
grimness of the wilds.

The Park is still almost untouched by man, but it has already its place
in history. Once it was in the hands of the Coast Indians, but two centuries
ago they seem to have been driven out by the Carrier tribes of the central
plateau. To-day the few Indian encampments are all of Carriers until we
reach the Coast tribes at Bella Coola.

(William for short), dressed in an exquisite costume of speckled brown and blue. He was very young and very peaceful, and preferred sitting upon somebody's hat to any more orthodox form of perch.

The country between Burns Lake and the Park is a charming mixture of wild and settled. We crossed François Lake, which is almost seventy miles long and anywhere else but in Canada would be considered a notable sheet of water.

At various stopping-places we were greeted by bands of school-children, and at François Lake by a party of Babine Indians who made John one of their chiefs, under the title of 'Chief of the Big Mountain.'

At Ootsa Lake we reached the beginning of the Park. There we embarked in boats on our journey to our base camp. Our boat was of the type of the old Hudson's Bay York boat, plus a 'kicker.'

All afternoon we chugged along in a stately procession, John and I in the first boat feeling rather like Antony and Cleopatra. The landscape had a lowland air, except that now and then a snow-topped mountain appeared in a gap, to the delight of John, who, as an old mountaineer, becomes slightly lunatic at the sight of the high snows.

The water was glassily calm, except where, in the Ootsa River, it was broken by small rapids. The spruce and jack pine on the shores, varied by meadows of wild hay, gave one the impression of travelling through the slightly over-wooded park of a great English country house.

There was little sign of life, except broods of young mallards that squattered away from the boats.

Presently we rounded a corner of the river and on a headland saw a little township of tents, and a flag-pole from which fluttered the Governor-General's flag. Below, in the small bay, lay four seaplanes, looking as innocent as a taxi rank in Piccadilly.

I should like to make my readers believe that we lay under the stars, bitten by mosquitoes and black flies, and molested by grizzlies and cougars, but the truth is that our camp, provided by the hospitable British Columbia Government, was the last word in comfort. We slept in sleeping-bags laid on camp beds, and there was always hot water available; but, as usual in a tent, I at once began to lose everything, and spent much of my time ranging my 'Mountie' bag and my 'sausage' for lost articles.

I shall never forget those nights in my tent, when, before sinking into profound slumber, I kept picturing the many miles of mountain, forest and snow-field around me, and thought of Elsfield, like the tigers in the story, 'very wee and far away.'

I used to be awakened by the sound of conversation and wonder irritably why people should sit around my tent so early in the morning, until I realised that water carries sound very far, and that the talk was really coming from distant lodges.

Still, like the Frenchman when he banged on the wall of his hotel bedroom after being kept awake half the night by girlish confidences in the adjoining room, I felt inclined to cry, 'Young ladies! Young ladies! I am afraid of overhearing your secrets of the heart!'

They had honoured me by calling the promontory on which the camp was laid Point Susan, so I really felt a proprietary interest in it.

Each night a huge campfire was built on the headland, and most of us sat around it. The moon was nearly full, and beyond the glow of our fire the lake lay sleeping with its amber capes. It was the hour for good talk, and of that there was no lack.

In our company we had a wealth of experience which it would be hard to beat. There were officers of the British

View of Whitesail Mountains.

Columbia Police who knew every corner of the Province;
air pilots who had surveyed for months in the Northern
Plains and had flown in all weather in most parts of
Canada, including the Arctic North; old-timers who
could speak of the Caribou gold rush seventy years ago;
neighbouring ranchers who entered the country long
before the days of roads and maps; civil servants who
had seen greater change in their lifetime than their fathers
had known in generations.

British Columbia is in a special sense a frontier province.
We were close to the Pacific divide, and a hundred
miles north of us was the height of land beyond which
the streams run to the Arctic. Since it contains every
variety of landscape and economic asset, its people have
wide interests.

Moreover, they are dwellers on the Pacific shore, and
the Province is a window from which Canada looks out
to the confused and uncertain East. There is nothing
parochial about the outlook of British Columbia.

Such campfire talks tended always to turn towards the
frontier of the unknown, for Canada still has a considerable frontier beyond which exact knowledge ceases.

We discussed, I remember, the secrets which still await
discovery. My husband's fancy had been caught by a
certain Rivière de l'Enfer, which is supposed to be somewhere far away in the hinterland of Quebec, and about
which he was always trying to get news.

There was talk, too, of that tongue of forest land which
runs far up into the Northern Plains on the Thelon River.
For long that was only a legend, but now that the Thelon
Game Sanctuary has been established we know something
about it.

It was there that that almost legendary figure, John
Hornby, and his two companions perished a few years
ago. The diary of the last survivor, young Christian,

has now been published—an extraordinary record of endurance and fortitude.

But the talk always drifted to the valley of the South Nahanni River, which is one of the mystery spots in the North.

There used to be a tale of a valley in the Northern Rockies where hot springs produced a kind of tropical vegetation, and where, it was rumoured, strange pre-historic beasts were still alive. This pleasing story has been disproved by Dr. Camsell's flight in 1935.

But the mystery of the South Nahanni remains. The river enters the Liard from the north about one hundred miles above Simpson. A gigantic waterfall makes exploration by boat impossible beyond a certain point.

Our purpose was to explore Tweedsmuir Park from our base camp, for a mere traverse from north to south would have shown us very little of it. So from Point Susan we made daily expeditions by boat, seaplane or pack-horse.

There is no limit to the expeditions to be made in the Park, in most of which the traveller will have to do his own pioneering; but there are three major expeditions.

The first is the water route, which has been given the name of the Great Circle. By canoe or boat it is possible to make an easy circuit nearly two hundred miles in length.

Starting west of Ootsa Lake post office (Ootsa means 'the way around'), the route follows the lake to its head, where the Whitesail River enters. Then come some fourteen miles of river where there are no difficulties except a few log jams.

We are now under the high mountains, the Whitesail Range to the west and the Quanchus Mountains to the east. Whitesail Lake is a magnificent sheet of water which burrows its way into the heart of the hills.

About half-way up on the south shore the traveller

leaves the lake, and after a short and easy portage reaches Eutsuk Lake, which continues for forty miles.

This is one of the most beautiful lakes I have ever seen. On the west it throws out numerous fiords which are fed by the glaciers of the peaks, and it has superb shores of golden sand. One inlet on the south leads to a little lake, Pondosy (named after an early missionary), which is wholly enclosed by the mountains. All around it there is a lacework of other lakes, in most of which no angler has ever cast a fly.

The colour of some of these tarns is unbelievable— every variety of green, from the deepest emerald to the palest jade; every shade of blue, from sapphire through aquamarine to what, in certain lights, is the purest turquoise. The shores are clothed with jack pine, spruce and balsam, above which alpine pastures lead to the rocks and snows.

There are no big glaciers, but a multitude of little stumpy ones in the high corries. The western ends of Whitesail and Eutsuk are only some thirty miles from the salt water of the Gardner Canal.

From the eastern end of Eutsuk a short stretch of river leads to Tetachuck Lake, whence, for some few miles, a boat must be lined down the rapids of Euchu Lake. Tetachuck means 'sick water,' but I saw nothing unwholesome in its limpid depths. A short riffle leads from Euchu to Natalkuz Lake, and then by way of Intata Lake and a lovely stretch of the Ootsa River one returns to Ootsa Lake and the starting-point. That is the chief trip by water.

THE PACK-HORSE ROUTE FOLLOWS AN OLD INDIAN TRAIL

The main route by pack-horse threads the Park from north to south, being the old road of the northern Indians to the salt water and Bella Coola.

It starts from a point on the Ootsa River, crosses Chelaslie River, which enters Euchu Lake, and then, through an easy country of spruce and jack pine, skirts the western end of Entiako Lake until it crosses the divide and enters the upper valley of the Dean River. It passes the Indian village of Ulkatcho, and continues across the Dean to the Tanya Lakes, where it enters the Mackenzie Valley.

To the east lie Anahim Peak and the fantastic summits of the Rainbow Mountains. To the west rises a wonderful peak which the Indians call the Thunder Mountain—the Himalayan Siniolchu in miniature, draped with hanging glaciers and resounding every summer day with icefalls. The Mackenzie Valley trail crosses the pass and enters the Bella Coola trench by way of Burnt Bridge Creek.

All the first part of this trail is easy, but the last part, though perfectly safe, involves some precipitous scrambling. We had baddish weather for the first part, but I shall never forget some of the incidents.

At one place we found a circular hump on the ground where a grizzly had killed a moose and buried it in order to return and devour its prey at leisure—a primitive form of cold storage!

Swimming our saddle-horses across the Ootsa River was a lively business. They were whirled down a long way by the current, their heads just above the grey-green water.

The young man who rode the leading horse was drenched to the skin, but he triumphantly produced a dry packet of cigarettes out of his hat on landing.

It was a wild and lovely picture—the low, cloudy sky, the dark, impenetrable woods, and the horses' heads, like bodiless steeds from the Parthenon frieze, emerging from the cold and angry waters. All along the trail were regiments of tall, dark-blue delphiniums among the fire-weed.

I was not very comfortable, for I was tightly wedged into a Mexican saddle and my horse was of such a pushing disposition that I nicknamed him after a well-known social climber in London.

The last part of the trail offers marvellous prospects. From the higher ground on a clear day the traveller sees in the south Mount Waddington and its brother giants hanging like ghosts in the heavens.

All the fur-bearing animals of the West are plentiful, though the beaver is patchy. Among big game the only lack is the mountain sheep. There are quantities of mule deer and coast deer, goat and moose; the cougar, coming up from the coast, has begun to appear in the woods; the lynx is plentiful; and in the mountains there are large herds of woodland caribou.

Black bears can be found anywhere, and all the higher altitudes are full of grizzlies; indeed, in the southern valleys approaching the Bella Coola the grizzly is, I believe, as plentiful as anywhere in North America, so much so that it is in danger of becoming an actual nuisance.

So far, little hunting has been done in the Park area, and when it is fully established it will, of course, be made a reserve for wild game. In no part of the country, I think, will it be possible for a traveller to see the wild life of Canada in a more varied form or at closer quarters.

On the climbing facilities I reproduce John's views as an old mountaineer. Most of the peaks, as I have said, are not lofty; but all the Whitesail Range is good rock and offers excellent rock climbing.

At the end of our stay at Point Susan the weather broke, and for two days we kicked our heels in the tents. Happily there was excellent company to relieve the tedium. Then one morning it looked as if it were going to clear, and the wireless reports from Bella Coola were favourable.

I had made my first experiment in flying a few days before, and did not like it, for as soon as we rose from the water a horror of vertigo descended upon me and I got no value out of the magical scene. While we were waiting for the weather to clear for the flight back, I felt like someone sitting in a dentist's waiting-room!

The first thing that happened when we started was that something went wrong with the plane and we had to go back to put it right. As soon as we rose, my wretched vertigo returned. I put my scarf against the window to shut out the landscape and absorbed myself in a novel called *And So—Victoria*. A horrid text from the Book of Job came into my mind: 'Thou liftest me up to the wind; thou causest me to ride upon it, and dissolvest my substance.'

For the first three-quarters of an hour flying conditions were good. Then the whole landscape darkened, and the plane began to bump.

I looked up and saw in front of me what appeared to be a mass of twisting grey cotton-wool above a range of forbidding dark mountains. We made straight for these uninviting peaks, and I thought to myself, 'The pilot has misjudged the altitude and we shall certainly crash!'

John, who is air-minded to the pitch of being light-minded, studied the map when he was not asleep. He is always looking for sanctuaries, as if some day he might be forced to be a fugitive from justice, and now he discovered the perfect one.

We looked into a cup on the top of a mountain perhaps 6000 feet high. There was a lake, a half-moon of wild meadow, and behind it another half-moon of forest. It was a perfect situation for a house, and John pointed out that a dwelling there could be provisioned from the air and would be wholly secret, for unless a plane looked directly down upon it its whereabouts could not be discovered.

I am afraid this thought did not comfort me, for I have no wish to dwell on a hilltop. We were in a narrow mountain valley, very high up, and almost brushing the sides, with glaciers all about us on intimate terms.

I could only hold my scarf between me and the window and resolutely keep my eyes on my book.

Presently John touched my arm and pointed downward, and below us I saw what looked like a tarnished silver ribbon lying between crumpled folds of grey-green velvet, and far beyond a gleam of something silvery. 'The sea!' John bawled in my ear.

Our pilot slipped through the clouds into the lower Dean Valley. It was a very remarkable feat to get into a narrow gully and then sideslip down it. We turned left out of the gorge and came out above a great river which looked like green milk. Soon afterwards we reached the salt water, and, oh, blessed relief, taxied along it.

The Bella Coola people had been much worried about us, as they had no sooner sent the radio saying that the weather was fine than the mist began to descend. It was a dangerous flight and a real test of skill, but the pilots were equal to it.

At Bella Coola, strictly speaking, we had left the Reserve, but it will always be the southern entrance to Tweedsmuir Park.

It is very like a Norwegian valley, and many of the settlers are Norwegians who came from Norway by way of the United States.

We drove up the Bella Coola River forty miles to Stuie Lodge, where we had the pleasure of meeting Mr. and Mrs. Don Munday, who were the first to explore Mount Waddington.

The whole valley is full of grizzlies, and much of the talk was about those unpleasing animals. Apparently, when you meet a grizzly the wise thing to do is to stand

255

still, or at the worst to climb a tree. (It is well to remember, however, that while grizzlies cannot climb except as cubs, other bears can.)

It must take some fortitude to stand still and stare a grizzly out of countenance, but if you can do it he usually turns round and walks away.

At Stuie Lodge we met the Prime Minister of British Columbia and the Federal Minister of Defence.

We watched the salmon that had come up from the sea to spawn and die, moving like dark shadows in the clear water below the great peaks. Alastair caught a salmon of twenty-six pounds, with a head like a fish in a pantomime, which I believe is the only one ever taken by a rod from that river.

Presently we said goodbye to Stuie Lodge and drove down the valley, where John had to lay a wreath on a war memorial and attend a celebration by the Bella Coola Indians.

We crossed the river in a dug-out canoe, which threatened to tip over at any moment. John was then made a chief under the title of 'The Man from Above Who Has Come to Help Us,' and the Indians danced the Thunderbird Dance, which their forefathers had danced for Alexander Mackenzie almost 150 years before.

It is the old story of Prometheus, but, though the masks were impressive, the spirit had gone out of it. It is not easy in these days for Indians to be traditional.

Our expedition was now at an end. A comfortable steamer took us to Prince Rupert, and five days in the train took us back to Ottawa.

To those whose heart is in the kind of sport which involves skill and hardihood and loneliness, and who regard wild life as a sacred thing, and will never divulge the shy secrets of the wilds, the Tweedsmuir Park Reserve is like the gift of a fairy godmother.

It is one of the few remaining earthly paradises for the sportsman and lover of nature. It is largely unexplored, and even unmapped.

I hope it will remain remote, though accessible to visitors, and with proper accommodations at a base like Point Susan. I shall always think of it as I saw it, a place exquisite and far away, where life still goes on as in the morning of the world."

When John came back to England for a short visit from Canada in the summer of 1938 he had the question of the King and Queen's visit there much in his mind. To his great joy, Their Majesties accepted the Canadian Government's invitation to come to Canada in the spring of 1939, and on our return to Ottawa we set ourselves strenuously to prepare for their visit. By May 1939 the preparations were completed and we waited for the King and Queen's arrival. War was in the air, the dictators were shouting defiance at the world, and in April Mussolini had entered Albania. Canada held her breath wondering if she should have the promised visit, and marvellously the King and Queen were able to come. They were held up by fog and arrived a little later than we hoped. From the moment that the King and Queen stepped on to the quayside at Quebec they captured all hearts in French Canada. We drove to an improvised station to meet their train on a day when all Ottawa blazed with flags, and were witnesses of the unbounded enthusiasm with which they were welcomed there. Canada was united in a focussed loyalty which drew her together in a way that nothing had ever done before. In the West men, women and children travelled on horseback, in cars and in canoes to see their Sovereigns at wayside stations. The war clouds darkening the sky were temporarily forgotten. Everyone smiled and was happy.

I remember saying to John, "How good happiness is for people," and I quoted a dictum of John Masefield's, "That which makes us happy makes us good."

In Ottawa there were many functions. One evening the King and Queen stood on a high balcony overlooking the Parliament Square and waved to the vast cheering crowds of people below. On another day, after the unveiling of the War Memorial, they became engulfed in a sea of ex-Service men. "Hitler wouldn't dare to do that," one of the men said to me. John had many talks with the King lasting late into the night, and Their Majesties were the kindest and most gracious of guests. At the end of their tour we went down to Halifax by sea on the *Empress of Britain* and in the early morning of June 15th John went off by car with Shuldham to meet the Royal train at the side station, while I waited on the ship for their arrival. We had tea with Their Majesties at Government House, Halifax, and I remember the froth of white flowers and the great branches of apple blossom from the Annapolis Valley, with which the charming old house was filled. We went to see them leave the harbour and stood on a balcony while the wildly cheering crowds watched the *Empress* move slowly away, the King and Queen's figures getting smaller and more distant and then being lost to sight.

The line from *Antony and Cleopatra* came into my mind. I tried to push the thought away, but it kept coming back. "The bright day is done, and we are for the dark." But before the war came down on us we had some happy times.

Johnnie had gone into the Colonial Service in Uganda and in 1934 became dangerously ill with amoebic dysentery. He was able to get back to England, where he spent some time in the Hospital for Tropical Medicine in London. Then he came out to Canada and I journeyed to Halifax to meet him. He was thin and tired-looking and remained so for some time. When his health improved he went into the Hudson's Bay Company and worked at Hudson's Bay House in Winnipeg. In 1938 he was posted to the Hudson's Bay post at Cape Dorset as Assistant Post Manager.

It was an anxious year for us because he was completely out of reach; we could only communicate with him by means of radio messages. John was much better at composing those messages than I was, but even his invention failed him at times, and once he could find nothing to say but that Alastair had just got a bulldog. The nearest wireless station happened to be having radio trouble, and stuttered out for about half an hour the words "Alastair has got" over and over again. All those in the North who had receiving sets listened with breathless interest to hear what Alastair *had* got, and when the words "a bulldog" finally came through they were much amused.

We were allowed to start the Northern broadcasts at Christmas 1938 with a message to Johnnie. John did his broadcast without faltering, but mine was insufficiently prepared and I broke down in the middle, not from emotion, as my listeners supposed, but in having my script in rough notes which did not make smooth reading.

Johnnie's Arctic year was a very happy one. He went great distances by dog team and boat and served behind the counter in the store when the Eskimos came in to make their purchases. Chesley Russell, the Post Manager, and he worked together in complete harmony. John had always been anxious to visit Fort Churchill and he planned a tour with Shuldham by which we could meet the Hudson's Bay boat, the *Nascopie*, and which would include a visit to the Peace River. So in

August 1939 we went off, taking Alastair with us, also Anna and Walter, who were paying us a visit.

We went north from Winnipeg on August the 6th. After passing through the corn-lands, we went into park-like country of green slopes and trees. I remember some wonderful sunsets, and one especially where the sky looked like a stained-glass window with bars of purple behind red clouds. A glassy lake reflected the sky; it was covered with wild duck who, hearing the train coming, fled with their ducklings, making pale jade ridges on the water. After stopping at Le Pas the train rolled and bumped all day on very rough tracks through the country called by the Indians "The country of the Little Sticks." You see thin little trees whose thread-like stems are surmounted by a tuft which looks like pampas grass. Then we went on to the tundras, which are flat and covered with soft grey caribou moss. There are lakes of every size and shape, the colour of sapphires, which arranged themselves in patterns as far as the eye could see. When we reached Fort Churchill we were greeted by a crowd of people, and saw husky dogs with their puppies tied to iron stanchions to keep them from straying all over the place. The *Nascopie*, which was bringing Johnnie back to us, was due to arrive that evening and we waited on the quay breathless with excitement.

The sea was palely luminous and there was a soft glow in the sky. The moon looked like a gold dish, and a red planet hung low in the sky like a jewel. We had imagined, I don't know why, that Johnnie would have a long beard and perhaps be dressed like an Eskimo, but he stepped off the *Nascopie* looking very much his usual self and very much healthier than when we had last seen him.

It was so wonderful to have him back with us, and we all talked at once in the most approved family fashion. John was anxious to hear every detail of Johnnie's Arctic year, and some of his experiences there appear again in *Sick Heart River*. We left Fort Churchill and went back to Le Pas, where John, Walter and Robin flew to Flin Flon Mine. We lunched near Grey Owl's cabin, now empty and deserted, and heard that Jellyroll, his favourite beaver, does not come when she is called, and that his other beavers do just what they like in his cabin.

From there we went on to Edmonton, where we saw the Columbia glacier and had a day on Beaver Lake. It rained as we sat in boats while John, Walter and the boys fished. We saw two moose at the lake-side. They were not shy and took no notice of us, hunting greedily for the water-lily roots at the edge of the lake. They put their heads into the water and lifted them up again while the drops streamed down their long ugly faces. Their clumsy bodies and strangely patterned horns made them look like animals from a much older world.

We went back to Edmonton and did a tour in the Peace River. The landscape is delightfully varied. We sometimes saw smooth green hills on which we looked with delight as they reminded us of the Scottish Border scenery. The mighty Peace River rolls in majestic calm through cornfields and valleys, with a very strong current which hardly disturbs its polished surface. We came on lovely splashes of colour. Spruce trees, their stems the colour of steel, standing in masses of willow-herb and Michaelmas-daisies, the mauve of the daisies contrasting charmingly with the vivid pink of the willow-herb. The Indians call this flower "Fire-Weed" as it grows riotously in Canadian woods where there have been forest fires. (I was to see it later growing on the blackened balconies of houses in London after the blitz.) John was charmed by our visit to an old Hudson's Bay post. It had the mysterious quality of a Walter de la Mare story. It stood between a river and some smooth green hills and was approached by an avenue of trees. The "Fur House" was filled with hay and had long been disused. The buildings were made from axe-hewn timber and were set in a grove of gnarled and twisted Manitoba maples. Three little graves surrounded by white palings stood at the edge of the wood. A rising wind moaned eerily around us. Had John lived to write more about Canada, this lonely and deserted Hudson's Bay post would, I am sure, have found its way into some romance.

This was our last tour and it remains in my mind like an oasis where a traveller may rest before he is engulfed in a storm. John was on the whole well, and to have Anna and Walter, Johnnie and Alastair, with us was pure delight. We had gone far from Europe and had very little news from there, all the country we saw was lovely, and the people were vital and interesting. When we got back to Ottawa the news of the Russo-German Pact struck us like a blow in the face. The sense of impending war was in the air. Lord and Lady Maugham curtailed their visit to us, and Anna and Walter left a fortnight earlier than they had intended to do. The weather was very hot and the days went by slowly. Two small things will always remind me of those anxious hours— the hot scent of phlox, and crickets continuously making a sound like two bits of wire being rubbed together. People came and went looking grave and preoccupied, Robin Scott and David Walker left us to go home, and our hearts were heavy when we said goodbye to them.[1]

In early September 1939, Canada declared war on

[1] Tom Goff came out to us as A.D.C. from England in November 1939. He greatly helped by his charm and cheerfulness to lighten the anxieties of the war. John enjoyed talking to him and discussing books and friends. I also enjoyed his talks, and listened spellbound whilst he played on the beautiful clavichord, made by himself, which he brought with him to Ottawa.

Germany. The whole country came into the war with a clear-eyed unanimity and put all her men and resources behind the Allied cause. Canada's contribution to victory has been so important, unstinted and imaginative as to arouse the sincere respect of her enemies and Allies alike. Johnnie and Alastair joined the Canadian Army and William the R.A.F. in England, and became busy with their training. In December Johnnie went overseas with the First Canadian Division. We were both busy helping as much as we could with all Canada's war activities. John constantly visited regiments and war installations of all sorts. He made many speeches and at Toronto gave one of which parts have been much quoted :

... Our enemies are attacking more than the system of Christian morals on which our civilisation is founded. They are attacking Christianity itself, and they are succeeding. Thirty years ago Europe was nominally a Christian continent. It is no longer so to-day. In Europe, as in the days before the Emperor Constantine, Christianity is in a minority. It is no mere phrase of rhetoric to say that we are witnessing a conflict of Christ and anti-Christ.

We who are nominally Christians have in recent years been growing very cold in our faith. Our great achievements in perfecting the scientific apparatus of life have tended to produce a mood of self-confidence and pride. We have too often become gross materialists in our outlook on life.

I believe that the challenge with which we are faced may restore to us that manly humility in the presence of the Unseen which alone gives power. It may bring us back to God. In that case our victory is assured. The Church of Christ is an anvil which has worn out many hammers. Our opponents may boast of their strength, but they do not realize what they have challenged.

We visited Halifax in January 1940 and saw it under war conditions. John spoke to the Merchant Captains before they set out on convoy. I did not, of course, go with him, but I heard afterwards from someone who had been there how much the beauty and simplicity of his speech had appealed to them, just before they set out on their perilous journey.

John's health had had many ups and downs since we had been in Canada, and I could not blind myself to the fact that it was getting worse. The spells of pain came oftener and were more severe. The doctors did not advise another duodenal operation, but they did all in their power to alleviate his constant discomfort. The Canadian medical profession has a very high reputation for skill, and Dr. Meakins, Dr. Gordon Gunn and Dr. Delaney (at Quebec) were unsparing in their efforts to ameliorate his condition. The end of our five years' term would have come in the normal course of things in the autumn of 1940. It was suggested that we should extend our term. Canadians, we were told, would have liked us to go on being there, and some very warmly praising articles about what John had done while in office appeared in the Canadian papers. But he felt that his health was worsening all the time, and that he could make no other decision.

He knew how sorry he would be to leave Canada, for he felt himself to be, as he always said, "an Honorary Canadian." I don't think that any Governor-General was ever more interested in a country and a people than he was in Canada. There was romance to him in every bit of the Dominion, and his only complaint against Canadians was that they did not sufficiently appreciate the enchantment of their great land. He felt that he could do something as a writer to show some fresh aspects of it to the world. He wrote a book called *The Long Traverse* in which a little boy, by the medium of Indian magic, sees some of the most exciting and heroic episodes of Canadian history. He also wrote *Sick Heart River*, in which Sir Edward Leithen goes out on his last and greatest adventure. It ends with Sir Edward sacrificing a chance of recovery of health and strength in order to bring an Indian tribe, who are slowly dying of anaemia and depression, back to life.

John was also writing his autobiography, which was published after his death under the title of *Memory Hold-the-Door*. He set out not to mention all the people he had met or the things which he had done, but rather to show their reflection upon his own mind. This book does not include any reference to Canada, as he could not write of her whilst he held the office of Governor-General. Books about Canada would have come later, but, alas, he did not live to write them.

During the winter of 1939 he obtained leave to go down to New York, where he was overhauled by Dr. Miller of the Medical Centre, who produced some alleviations for his discomfort. We stayed with the Thomas Lamonts and they were kindness itself to us. If there had been no war and John had been well, it would have been an utterly delightful visit. I spent as much time talking to Edward Sheldon as I could, and came away from seeing him cheered and sustained by his counsel and sympathy.

In the first week in February we spent a few days in Montreal. They were very strenuous for both of us, as there was so much excellent work being done there for the war effort and we wanted to see all of it that we could. We came back to Ottawa, and I remember well how on that afternoon in the train we lingered long over tea, listening to John talk while the blue twilight outside deepened into dusk. On the Monday, being tired, he spent the day in bed reading and writing some notes.

On the Tuesday morning he was found unconscious

in his dressing-room. In the terrible days which followed Alastair and I still hoped that he might get better, the doctors were so skilful and the nurses so devoted in their care. But he never regained consciousness. He was taken to Montreal to the Neurological Hospital and was operated on by Dr. Wilder Penfield, famous throughout the world as a brain surgeon. The kindness and consideration of everyone in the hospital which was shown to myself and to Alastair I can never forget, as we sat sick at heart in the room set apart for us. On February 11th, 1940, the doctors came to tell us that he was dead.

CHAPTER XV

JOHN BUCHAN IN CANADA

By LEONARD BROCKINGTON

JOHN BUCHAN was known at many Canadian firesides and in many lonely places where there were none, long before he came to Canada. He had a retinue of harbingers unique for a Governor-General. For the children of his brain had been his heralds. His books had been his advance agents. Canadians, of course, had often before welcomed to Government House famous soldiers and more or less successful statesmen, but this was the first occasion in the history of the Commonwealth when a man who wrote fascinating stories and lilting verses and exciting history, and could always make an apt, eloquent, and short speech had ever been appointed to "shape the whisper of the throne" in a great Dominion. It is true that people recalled Lord Dufferin whose oratory still echoes along the corridor that runs from Halifax to Vancouver. And many viceroys had left memories that were cherished and deserved to be. But when news came that John Buchan was to speak for his King, thousands of Canadians rejoiced that here was coming a man who already knew and understood plain ordinary men and women and the deep unspoken certainties that join all Britons together. There were enough Canadians bred in the Scottish and Latin tradition to honour any man who knew his humanities. And there were many thousands of vocal Scotsmen openly delighting in the knowledge that yet another manse had sent a poor boy forth unto the world to show what industry and education and courage and character could accomplish in a Commonwealth of opportunity. And almost everyone joined in this delight. For Canada, like the rest of North America, feels a sort of family pride in a man who without wealth or privilege or influence, hews his own path through the forests of the frontier. Here, they thought and said, was a man with a North American story. There was a little disappointment that the hero of the story was coming as a peer and not as a commoner, but the necessity for that was understood. There was a general feeling that he was the choice of both great political parties, and that for once Mr. Mackenzie King and Mr. R. B. Bennett were in complete agreement on a matter of high policy.

All those who wrote poems and made books and painted pictures and sang songs and delivered speeches were certain that a master, who understood the yearning of those who set their prentice hand to creative things, was coming to encourage them and to advance the strength of the intellectual life of their country and his. There was a feeling too, that John Buchan would understand not only the lyrical things that had been written of Canada but also the epic things that were being done in far places, the vision beyond the hilltops, the drama of the frontier, the romance of the past, the colour of the fabric of the present, the strength of the fibre of many races of which a new national pattern was being fashioned. Those who thought seriously of the new Commonwealth and of Canada's national and international destiny in a world already darkened by the gathering clouds no bigger and no smaller than the hands of Hitler and Mussolini, those who longed for and were striving to achieve a permanent solution of Canada's historical racial problem and all who found a proud new hope in the stirring of Canada's growing strength, believed that the Scotsman who like so many of his compatriots had conquered the English, the biographer of the brave who lived and died for a cause that was lost and yet never lost, the chronicler of the Great War, one of the earnest young brotherhood who sought to heal the wounds of South Africa, would have something provocative to contribute to the healthy intellectual and political unrest that was the mark of the new Canada that saluted its new Governor-General.

In short, the choice of him was an exciting national event. The unanimity that welcomed him on his first coming was surpassed only by the universality of the grief that mourned his departure.

All those promises were fulfilled by the scholar, soldier, and man of affairs, who for four memorable years enriched our life and gallantly and unselfishly expended his own. I can still hear his voice speaking the wisdom in his heart and the grace of words upon his lips to many and varied audiences of his new fellow-citizens. I re-read the other day some of those speeches, happily preserved, from the first speech he made as Governor-General Elect at the Canadian Club in London when, in the eyes of those who had gathered to cheer him on his way, he detected what he called "an obituary solemnity" to the closing words of his last speech to his fellow-craftsmen, the bookmen of Canada, when he reminded them of their heritage and "That Time is the true winnower of wheat from chaff and what remains in that winnowing is a possession forever." The titles and the occasions of his Canadian speeches form an epitome of his enthusiasms. He analyses the strength of the Western Mind, the contribution of the Icelander to his new country, the magic of the islands, the heritage of Canada, the glories of Scotland, the service of the State, the *genius loci* that is the spirit of lonely places.[1] He speaks in the presence of Mr. Roosevelt at Quebec, to the Senate at Washington, to Americans and Canadians discussing their mutual problems in friendly conference.

[1] He also spoke on the French language and French culture.

He is alternately a traveller, a historian, a statesman, an author. He talks to engineers, to lawyers, to doctors, to miners, to teachers. On five successive annual occasions he talks to Boy Scouts, for he is forever keeping his friendships with the young in fine repair.

Of his mission he has these things to say :

Let me say at once that I rejoice at the opportunity which has been given me. I have seen the prowess of Canadians in two wars. I have known them in sport, in business and in scholarship. I have seen enough of the beauty of their land to make me long to see more. If in any way, however humble, I can serve Canada and her people, I shall consider that my life has not been wasted.

In a very real sense there are no frontiers left on the physical map. They must be sought in the world of the mind and the spirit.

The courage to construct, the insistence that every man shall be able to stand on his own feet and be the master of his soul— these things mean the defence of true democracy.

It is for us to show a better way, to prove to the world that civilisation has twin foundations, and that, if one of them is law, the other is liberty.

On Canadian problems he has this to say :

But I firmly believe that every problem is soluble, that every difficulty is temporary and remediable. I come to you with fresh eyes and, I hope, an open mind, but I am very certain that no Canadian is prouder of his country than I am, or believes more devoutly in her future.

He uses his native Scotland as a test for this message :

To-day unity is the crying need of the world; unity instead of antagonism; co-operation instead of rivalry. We need a union of classes in Canada, in Britain, in the Empire. We need, if I may venture to say so, in this Dominion of ours, a closer unity where national interests are supreme above local interests. We need, above all, a unity in spirit of the nations of the world, for that is the only pathway to peace.

Of Canada's destiny and duty he has these things to say :

Our sufferings have taught us that no nation is sufficient unto itself, and that our prosperity depends in the long run not upon the failure of our neighbours, but upon their success.

Look back to the years before the Great War. Our first thought about them is that in the retrospect they seem a time of unbelievable ease and prosperity. Yes, but if we probe into our memory we shall find that they were uncomfortable years. The world was arrogant and self-satisfied, but behind all its confidence there was an uneasy sense of impending disaster. The old creeds, both religious and political, were largely in process of dissolution, but we did not realise the fact, and therefore did not look for new foundations. Well, the War, with its abysmal suffering and destruction, did achieve one thing. It revealed us to ourselves. It revealed how thin the crust was between a complex civilisation and primeval anarchy. If I were asked to name any one clear gain from the War—and here I am speaking of our own people— I would say that it was a new humility. We had our pride shattered, and without humility there can be no humanity.

Of the relations between the British Commonwealth and the United States this is the pattern of his prescience :

It is my prayer that, not by any alliance, political or otherwise, but through thinking the same thoughts and pursuing the same purpose, the Republic of the United States and the British Commonwealth may help to restore the shaken liberties of mankind.

I believe—I have always believed—that on a close understanding between the British Commonwealth and the Republic of the United States depends the peace and freedom of the world. I say understanding, not alliance. What matters is that we should think on the same lines, not that we should tie ourselves up in any formal treaty. The instinct to avoid formal commitments, to feel our way cautiously and let facts shape our course, is deep in our common heritage. It is a sound instinct.

These are words spoken to youth :

There has never been an age when youth mattered more, when there were so many questions which only the vitality of youth could solve, when the horizons were so wide for youth to travel to.

They will make friends with anybody and meet everyone on the basis of a common humanity. No, gentlemen, there is nothing wrong with our youth to-day.

I do not care how long a man may live ; in one sense he should never grow old. If we get out of touch with our world we cease to be any use in it, and I have always believed that the best way of keeping abreast of our times is to keep in touch with youth.

Always he stresses the strength of democracy because a foursquare man "abhors social snobbery and in practice takes the sting out of natural disparity between human beings which is the only true leveller." He glories in nations with a tempestuous heroic youth ; he quotes with approval that fine saying of John Ruskin's that "We are rich in our inheritance of honour bequeathed to us to a thousand years of notable history which it should be our daily thirst to increase with splendid avarice." He emphasises that our duty is not only to hold the best but to hand on the light. He concludes a statement of his working philosophy with a paradox :

So I conclude with a paradox which I believe to be true, that democracy will only succeed if it becomes an aristocracy, in the classical sense of the word, where the rule of the Many is also the rule of the Best. I am speaking to young men and women on the threshold of life, and I offer you this maxim. It is the duty of all of you to be aristocrats. Of the aristocrat I know only one adequate definition. He is the man who gives to the world more than he takes from it.

He touched on all these things with a distinction of his own, and for that service amongst many others he will be long remembered. With most of us as we watched him, the wonder grew how he found time to do so much. He once told me when I asked him the secret of his intense labours that if one played neither golf nor bridge many precious hours were released to one's use. I am told that he rigidly and rigorously divided his life into compartments and wrote methodically a thousand words every morning of his Canadian years.

I shall never forget my first meeting with him. I was engaged as counsel on a public inquiry into the grain trade. He knew the history of all preceding inquiries (and there had been many) and the gist of the one in progress. I felt that he took a personal interest in me and my humble business. The truth was that he had an immense intellectual curiosity and a fine ambassadorial technique in all his human relations. For so many others have told me of the breadth of his interest, the depth of his knowledge and the subtle way with which he encouraged those with whom he spoke.

I remember an interesting sidelight on that first meeting with him. I knew that his family had been connected for many years with the town of Peebles. As I talked to him in his railroad car at Winnipeg, I told him how many years ago I had met a Miss Brown from Peebles. She was the cousin of the author of "Rab and His Friends." She mentioned that her chief friend at the time was an old lady still living in that ancient borough—the daughter of Hogg, the Ettrick Shepherd. Our conversation was interrupted by an announcement from one of his aides that an old lady from Peebles, then living in Winnipeg, had at that moment called to see him. When she was a girl she had made the wedding dress of the Governor-General's mother. The courtesy and wistful generosity with which she was received can be well imagined. His aides always smiled with a pleasant understanding at his love of Peebles. They knew it was one of his great loyalties.

It was Darcy Magee, the most eloquent of the Fathers of the Confederation, who once pleaded with his fellow-countrymen to foster every gleam of talent and to encourage the blossoming of every creative force. John Buchan did just that. He was there with praise for every journalist who had written well, for every speaker who had something to say, for every muse that carried the promise of wings. I doubt whether any Government House has witnessed so many quiet talks with so many humble people as did Rideau Hall [1] while he was its benevolent tenant.

He knew Canada not only historically and politically, but even geographically as few Canadians have known it. He fished her streams and wandered in those far places where Rupert Brooke once said the air was almost unbreathed and the traveller felt like the first explorer. He seemed to be able to join together by some subtle alchemy the ancient places of his own land still peopled with the shadows of the famous and echoing with the voices of the great, to the new places of the western frontier where there seemed to be no present memory of the lives and deaths of those who had gone before. He made a brave journey to the Arctic and will long be remembered by the trappers and missionaries and the Royal Canadian Mounted policemen with whom he spoke in equal comradeship.

No one understood the growing national feeling of Canada better than he. I recall the sensation that followed the Governor-General's statement about the loyalties demanded of Canadians. It sounds so simple and acceptable now but it needed saying then. An old Maritime friend of mine told me once that Lord Tweedsmuir in his opinion understood Canada far better than most Canadians did because with the perspective

[1] Rideau Hall is the unofficial name for Government House.

of a historian's eye "he saw it steadily and saw it whole."
This is what he said about Canada's loyalty. His words
are still quoted and will be quoted often in the years to
come by those who believe that the first love of a Canadian
for Canada neither weakens his attachments for the
Commonwealth nor his devotion to the cause of all men.

This was the memorable passage :

> Canada is a sovereign nation and cannot take her attitude
> to the world docilely from Britain, or from the United States,
> or from anybody else. A Canadian's first loyalty is not to the
> British Commonwealth of Nations, but to Canada and to
> Canada's King, and those who deny this are doing, to my mind,
> a great disservice to the Commonwealth. If the Commonwealth,
> in a crisis, is to speak with one voice it will be only because the
> component parts have thought out for themselves their own
> special problems, and made their contribution to the discussion,
> so that a true common factor of policy can be reached. A
> sovereign people must, as part of its sovereign duty, take up its
> attitude to world problems.

No one understood the new Canadians better than he
—the men and women with many pasts—the pasts of
Europe—and one future—the future of Canada. He
touched on North American life at nearly all its points
of contact. He knew the journalistic slang of Time
Magazine and could and did dash off a tin-pan alley
lyric in the style of Hollywood. I remember—as who
of his friends does not—his jazz version of "Oh Mistress
Mine."

I do not think he was ever much interested in sport
except fishing, but I shall not forget his description of
American football with its military formations and its
tactics founded upon a system of cryptic numerals as
"a cross between trench warfare and the higher mathematics." He seemed to many of us to be able to do

what Thomas Huxley says a liberally educated man should be able to do—to forge the anchors and spin the gossamers of the mind.

No one realised more profoundly than he did the real meaning of the Statute of Westminster and the structure of the third British Empire. I believe that he was responsible for the imaginative suggestion that the King be accompanied on his visit to the United States by his Canadian foreign minister, Mr. Mackenzie King. And although these things are perhaps hidden forever in the secret places of far-off pigeon-holes, many of us believed that his was the original idea of the journey of Their Majesties to Canada and the United States just prior to the war when the eyes of the dictators had been lent a terrible aspect and were prying through the portholes of their heads like brass cannons. Certainly he was proud when for hundreds and thousands of Canadian children the portraits on the coins and postage stamps of Canada suddenly resolved themselves into a real King and Queen of the Commonwealth walking in mercy along the highways and byways of the Dominion. I know at least how happy he was that the journey was successful and ended in many loyal meetings.

The bravery of Lord Tweedsmuir's closing days made the deepest impression on his Canadian fellow-citizens. The picture of the gallant gentleman in Rideau Hall still working, still finding time to encourage others, uncomplaining in his suffering, will not fade for many years. As we looked at him we remembered another Scotsman of many misfortunes but "With aye a heart abune them a'".

How often in the darkest days, when the Commonwealth endured as he himself endured, did men regret the silence of the voice that was still. When he died all Canada mourned him and almost everyone felt that a great Canadian had passed from our midst. I found myself repeating the words of one of his friends:

> He does not die who can bequeath
> Some influence to the land he knows
> Who dares, persistent interwreath,
> Love permanent, with the wild hedgerows.
> He does not die but still remains
> Substantiate with his darling plains.

One of the great American newspapers—I believe it was the *New York Times*, wrote that with him "The robes of nobility had become the habits of democracy." The Canadians who lived in London said "Ave" to him as he sailed to the shores of Canada. The Canadian Prime Minister in crying "Vale" as he returned on his last journey to the islands of Britain said that many humble men would mourn in his passing the loss of a great-hearted gentleman who once brought sympathy and humanity to the lonely places of the broad Canadian land.

"On more than one occasion Lord Tweedsmuir expressed the wish that he might be truly called a Canadian. Hundreds of thousands of our citizens who came under the influence of his wise gentleness and his modest courtesy were more than willing to claim him as their own. I am sure he would be proud that his epitaph graven on the hearts of our people should mark the grief of Canada at the loss of her adopted son who knew her ways and loved them."

Canada will always remember John Buchan—*multum amans, multum amatus.*

CHAPTER XVI

SOME CHARACTERISTICS

I HAVE included only a few quotations from my husband's letters in the earlier part of this book. When he was in Canada he dictated all his letters, and as he was free from the small details of life he enjoyed his correspondence and his letters from there consequently lend themselves far more to quotation.

The fact of the matter was, he really hated writing letters when he had to put pen or pencil to paper himself. His handwriting was (as he said) like that of a small and cryptic spider. Few people can read it—I myself can do so but only with great difficulty. Many of his manuscripts were typed by a lady in Bournemouth who always since his early days of writing had done this work for him. His handwriting as a young man was larger and easier to read, so I suppose she became rather gradually accustomed to its increasing smallness and illegibility. When on holiday he would only send postcards, trying with great concentration of mind and hand to write so that the recipients could understand them. There were few things in life which he found laborious and difficult, but writing letters was one of them.

He wrote daily to his mother and to me (when we were separated) and constantly to his children, but though at times he throws out telling phrases and comments, his letters are mostly brief and business-like, dealing with arrangements and family matters.

He dictated a great many letters and all his speeches to Mrs. Lilian Killick, who had been his trusted and valued friend and secretary since his days at Nelson's;

when he left publishing she went to run his office in St. Stephen's House and she came with us to Canada. Mrs. Killick's outstanding capacity for work and her intelligence in carrying out any task she was asked to perform helped him enormously all the many years she worked with him. She has written the following account:

"Lord Tweedsmuir always worked to a time-table, whatever he had on hand, and as a rule this time-table was not only adhered to, but was completed a little beforehand. He was not in the least temperamental in regard to his writings. He could sit down and continue with a novel, or whatever he was engaged on at the moment, wherever he happened to be. Moreover, an interruption did not make him lose his train of thought. This applied not only to his writing, but also to the dictation of a speech or correspondence. He would merely ask for the last words dictated, and continue.

He always dictated speeches, and wrote his novels by hand, for he believed that what had to be listened to should be spoken, and what had to be read should be first written. Before dictating any speech, however, he would note down the main headings or sections into which it was naturally to fall. When the speech had been typed he would learn it by heart. In case of need he had the main headings typed on a small piece of paper when delivering the speech, but very rarely had occasion to refer to it.

In Canada he worked at no less than four books at the same time. He never attempted to put down on paper any story until he had the outlines clear in his head. The characters, however, more or less formed themselves as the story progressed. I have heard him confess that a certain character had got out of hand and become insufferable!

I would not say that he was a business man in the ordinary sense of the word, but he *was* business-like and methodical to a degree. Also the essence of punctuality. I think unpunctuality was one of the few things that really irritated him."

Yes, unpunctuality was certainly one of the things John hated most. The large gold watch given to him by his father's Glasgow congregation needed no extra polishing, as it shone brightly from being constantly taken out of his pocket to be looked at. He went early to catch trains, as he suffered like all the rest of his family from a violent train fever. They never consider that they have properly caught a train unless they have stood about for a long time on a draughty platform.

John also intensely disliked untidiness and muddle. The sound of his stick or umbrella being put with a thump into the umbrella-stand in the hall caused a wave of energy to go through the house. Everything was quickly tidied up, and books were put back in their right places. He liked books to be read and immediately replaced on the library shelves. "Please remember," he would say, "that books are my tools just as a plumber's are his, and if you leave them all over the place I can't find them when I want them."

He loved flowers and did a lot of planning and work in the garden, he even sometimes arranged flowers himself. He arranged them very well, with a slight air of superiority, and Alice and I felt duly inferior. To our delight, however, a lady journalist came to see him, and when he said, "It is I and not my wife and daughter who have done the flowers," she remarked sweetly, "Is there anything that you don't do better than other people?" After that we had only to raise our eyebrows slightly and say "Is there anything?" to have the situation in hand.

Facsimile of page of Montrose.

Those who looked at John's manuscripts are surprised to see how few corrections he made. His stories told themselves in his head and then went straight down on to paper. They came to him all the time, on walks, in the train, or when he rode or fished. On our holidays he worked steadily for some hours each day; and, when he was not actually writing, plots and conversations were thronging in his head all the time.

His historical books were a labour of love, but they, of course, necessitated an enormous amount of reading and research and careful correlating of notes and references which were kept by him in meticulous order and sequence. The most laborious task he ever had to do was the re-writing of *A History of the Great War*. He had written the original history for Nelson's to publish in small red volumes which came out serially during the war. When we first came to Elsfield he undertook the vast and difficult work of rewriting the *History* and incorporating a mass of new facts which had come to light about military operations and the political scene in Europe.

He sat for hours a day at his big writing-desk in the library—and I remember the set look on his face as he worked away there. His task was complicated by the fact that he was going through one of his periodical spells of ill-health. He must have been a joy to his publisher, as he was always in front of his schedule of work, often by about two months, and they never had to wait for a book from him.

His complete power of concentration on the task in hand enabled him always to get through a big programme of work. He carried it so lightly that I am afraid his family did not always respect his privacy as much as they should have done, and the children would run in and out of the library and only receive the gentle rebuke, "Run away now, Daddy's working."

It was a relief to my mind when he built himself an upstairs library at the top of the house—I would permit no one to interrupt him there except myself, and I only went there during his working hours if I had to ask him about some urgent matter.

The morning was his time for work. He always said that the hours between nine-thirty and one o'clock were the best for concentration. He never worked in the evenings, and he often read aloud to us poetry or prose (or a chapter from the book he was writing at the moment). As a family we are great readers aloud and attentive listeners to reading.

In the afternoons at Elsfield he either went off by himself or with one of the boys for a long walk at a swift pace, or took us all out for a slower "prowl" where we botanised and looked at the countryside.

After he got into Parliament he would leave Elsfield on Mondays at midday and do his business and parliamentary work in London, returning by an early train on Fridays. For some years he was a member of the committee of the Oxford University Chest, to which he went from his train on Fridays before returning home. Much as it interested him, he had to give it up as he found it too tiring.

John's writing of stories was pure enjoyment to him. He cared enormously for his craft as a writer, and in his novels of adventure he took pains with details of timing and never strained coincidences too far. He was also careful in leaving no loose ends in those stories which could puzzle the reader with doubts as to how they should be tied up.

His reading public was delightfully varied. Many people read only his novels. Someone once said to me, "I believe your husband does write other books besides shockers, but I have never read them." (Nor shall I, was the unspoken ending to the sentence.)

More serious readers thought of John Buchan as an historian and essayist who occasionally wrote poetry. They regarded his thrillers as a lapse from graver things. All this gave him a lot of amusement. His fan mail, though often tedious in the extreme, represented a cross-section of the community.

He had many comic letters from children. Men and women in hospitals wrote saying that his books had helped them through severe illness and operations. Others said that they were in sorrowful circumstances and that his books had made them forget their troubles.

Then there were innumerable requests for autographs and the demanding type of letter asking why he had not written another Hannay book, or what he was going to do next with his characters. His correspondence was always enormous, as he was chairman of many societies and on endless committees. His work as one of the Trustees of the Pilgrim Trust brought him many requests from people who wanted help for some special project.

But John always maintained that he had an immense capacity for idleness, and he certainly could throw off all care and just enjoy himself.

I am often asked how my husband managed to get through all the tasks he set himself to do, and I can give no answer except that he got down to them and did them with single-hearted purposefulness and concentration. He organised his life, and when he made a working plan he stuck to it.[1]

He could give out a great deal of sympathy, and men and women would ask to see him and seek his advice on very varied and sometimes curious subjects. He was a good listener and was known to take immense trouble in

[1] I have seen it stated time and again that John Buchan wrote his novels in the train. This story has no foundation in fact.

helping other people, a quality which, if it brings much interest into life, also brings a vast amount of work.

He talked with apparent freedom about himself if people asked him questions, but his own confidences never went below the surface. There is a shyness in the Buchan temperament and an honourable sort of pride. They never allow their hearts to be worn on their sleeves.

One subject he never mentioned was money. "Money gives Daddy the creeps," one of his sons remarked to me. I think it did. He had a slight contempt for those to whom money was an end in itself. John Buchan never cost his parents anything after the age of seventeen. He got endless scholarships and University prizes, and at Oxford he began to earn money by writing books and reading for publishers. He worked hard for every penny he got. After *The Thirty-Nine Steps* was published he reached the rank of a best-seller. *Greenmantle* has sold more than a million copies, and many of his books have been translated into various European languages.

He took immense pains in helping other writers, whether they were young and promising or elderly and unsuccessful. He read an enormous number of manuscripts. In later years I persuaded him not to do this. In fact, I played an obstructive part as far as the outer world was concerned, trying (often vainly) to shield him from the many demands which were made upon his time and strength.

John sometimes had to refuse to do things which he would have enjoyed doing. He had to say "no" when asked to write Lord Haig's life and that of his beloved friend Lord Byng. He consoled himself with the knowledge that he had paid a tribute to Lord Haig in *A History of the Great War*, and he paints portraits of them both in *Memory Hold-the-Door*.

His own memory was amazing. Mine has always

been pitiably inadequate, and when we were engaged to be married I asked him how it was that he seemed to remember nearly all that he had read.

John replied that he had formed the habit early in life of making notes of anything which struck him as interesting upon the back flyleaf of any volume he happened to be reading. But although I laboriously tried to follow his example my memory has always remained as bad as his was good. If he glanced at a poem he could repeat it correctly and it never went out of his mind.

Fortunately his mind was a selective one, and though he never failed to produce a telling anecdote in a speech or a relevant fact or figure to contribute to a discussion he did not feel obliged to tell everybody everything all the time.

Geography, like history, made a great appeal to him, and he could master the physical lay-out of a country from maps and books. It has come as a surprise to many people that he could have written *Salute to Adventurers* before he went to Virginia, and *The Courts of the Morning* when he had never visited South America.

Some people, I have been told, spoke of John Buchan as ambitious and in love with success. I can say emphatically that this was not true. Success came to him certainly in full measure, although like most people he had frustrations and disappointments. But he cared far more for getting things done which seemed to him to matter, than for whether he got any credit, and he had a way of fading out when rewards or compliments were handed out after a good job had been done.

He was, as Walter Elliot has said, enormously interested in people and he liked people of all sorts and kinds. He enjoyed a party at Londonderry House or an evening in a shepherd's cottage in Peeblesshire or a village party at Elsfield. He sometimes nourished prejudices about people, but when he met them he always found something likeable about them, and he had a knack of bringing out the best in them. As he grew older he went out less and we had fewer people here at Elsfield, as he needed all his strength to concentrate on his work and to enjoy our family life.

John was born with a very healthy body and he had toughened his muscles by mountain-climbing and walking. He would go up a hillside like lightning and walk nearly every companion on a walk to a standstill. Had he not had the duodenal trouble he would probably have always been a strong man.

He enjoyed the only major operation he ever had. "I like operations," he said; "surgeons do something to you that is some use, medicines are no good." Sometimes I used to ask hopefully what he thought of a new medicine, and he would reply, "Well, it's done me no harm so far, and that's the most one can say of a drug."

The most definite relief from pain that he had in later years came after some weeks at the Ruthin Castle clinic in 1938, where he went on his only leave from Canada. He made great friends with the head of the clinic, Sir Edmund Spriggs. John was extremely happy at Ruthin, he loved the mountain scenery swept by storms of rain, he slept a great deal, ate more than usual, and put on weight. He came out to Canada looking stronger and a little less fine-drawn. He and I had planned for him to go back to Ruthin directly his time in Canada was at an end.

He realised as he went into middle age that he was doomed to bouts of pain and discomfort, and he set about carrying on his work as usual and tried never to let his ill-health be a burden and trouble to other people. Anyone who has suffered from duodenal trouble can measure his achievement.

He put into *Sick Heart River* many of his thoughts about physical pain and weariness. Even I had not realised till I read it (after his death) quite the weight that the constant burden of pain had been to him, although we often talked of his health when we were alone. Once or twice in the last year of his life he said to me, "I am like a Red Indian ; I am in constant pain and don't show it."

I think that Sir Edward Leithen is perhaps the most like John Buchan of any of the characters. I recognise in sentences which he gives to Sir Edward to say and in actions which he makes him perform, some touches of autobiography. But he never put portraits of real people wholesale into his books.

Something would suggest an incident in a story to him—the character of Fish Benjy in *John Macnab* came to him from a casual encounter with a boy who drove a cart at Durness in Ross-shire, and whom John talked to on the seashore while the children were bathing. His own discovery of the joys of a safety razor started a train of thought which launched Dickson McCunn on his career of middle-aged romance in *Huntingtower*. *The Magic Walking-Stick* [1] arose out of a game he used to play with the children.

I was always much interested when some story we had both heard reappeared in one of his writings. Often he would seem to be listening politely, but I had thought his mind was on other things, yet on the printed page I recognised where the germ of the idea had come from.

He was happy in the choice of the names of his books, *The Thirty-Nine Steps*, *Greenmantle*, *The Three Hostages*, *The Dancing Floor*, *Huntingtower*, *The Moon Endureth*, *The Gap in the Curtain*, *A Prince of the Captivity*, to name only a few, are all titles which strike the imagination, and are easily remembered by would-be readers.

[1] Published in 1932.

John never worried about things and hated any of us to go back over the past with meaningless regrets. He glanced briefly at reviews of his books. Sometimes he kept one if it had a criticism of his work which might be helpful; otherwise, good or bad, they went straight into the waste-paper basket, and he never gave them a second thought.

His writing was always in his mind, but it would have been quite possible for someone who met him casually just to think that he was a man who took a keen interest in public affairs and who lived in the country. He was delighted when people liked his books, but always seemed a little surprised about this, and about the large quantities of them which sold all over the world.

The praise he valued most was from the many scholars who wrote to him about his biographies—though he was touched by the ill-spelt and blotted letters he got from children and humble people.

Like all authors, he had his own preferences in his books—*Witch Wood* was, I think, his favourite of his novels, and perhaps the *Greenmantle* trilogy came next, or *The Dancing Floor*, I am not sure. He would re-read his own books sometimes and say, "Well, that really isn't bad." One evening at Ottawa I went into his room. He was so much interested in what he was reading that he didn't hear me come in. I asked him what book he found so absorbing, and he said, "As a matter of fact it's *Greenmantle*, I hadn't read it for years."

Gravestone.

CHAPTER XVII

J. B.

By ALASTAIR BUCHAN

A CHILD rarely sees his father as the world sees him. For me affection was too strong a force to permit much detached study of his character when he was alive. I neither knew nor greatly cared why he was thought a man of uncommon gifts; he was my father and that was sufficient. It is only after six dreary, wandering years, and after hearing other men evaluate him, that I have at last formed my own estimate of his value.

Those who in the future may seek to discover the essential quality of John Buchan's contribution to his age will be misled by accounts of his many activities and even by his own writings, for his importance lay rather in what he was than in what he did. To profound scholarship he disclaimed any pretensions, story-tellers have a limited immortality, and the achievements of proconsuls and administrators are overshadowed by an institutionalist age; but his importance as a human being was not negligible.

The most striking characteristic of his mind was its balance. He had developed to a high degree the virtue which the Greek called Sophrosyné: an inner harmony which "saves the individual from extravagance of thought and word, the arrogance that exaggerates his capacities, and the ambition that overleaps itself." From this spiritual restraint (and restraint it was, for the Scots like the Greeks are an intemperate people) sprang a force so warm and positive that it charged the air around him. This lack of jealousy and anger, springing not from indifference but

T   289

conviction, so pervaded the climate of his mind and of his conversation, that in his company one forgot the cheap jibe and the vindictive comment. Many men, I suppose, envied him his success: he envied other men only for their good health.

Greek also was his conception of the proper nature and aims of the man of full stature. Believing that most human pursuits, whether riding, or governing, or writing, were worthy of study and perfection, he held that the fully adult man should enquire widely and despise little. He himself never forgot that "the mood of the philosopher is wonder." He could be happy in any society where men pursued a calling, and aided by an amazing memory he could discuss anything with any man. He plied miners and aviators, sculptors and cowboys with questions, not from inquisitiveness, but because they were contributors to the sum of human experience, and might, who knows, have pure gold to offer.

Finally, he never abandoned a belief in the intrinsic value of individual character, and the importance of an honest conviction, whatever the attainments of its upholder. The growth and play of character fascinated him, not as a basis for generalisation, but as a study worthy in itself. It made him impatient of a determinist view of history, and distrustful of any political system that forgot human beings whom it dealt with. Further, it led him to deep sympathy with those caught in the toils of a mechanised society, and all who had lost the dignified standing of free men. In so far as his writings are more than pure minstrelsy, which is all he claimed for them, he ranged himself with those who respond to Cobbett, Whitman and Chesterton rather than to Bentham, Alexander Hamilton or Marx. It ended in a love of life and a tenderness that was both Greek and Christian. Only twice in Canada did I see the light go out of his eyes: once when endorsing a death warrant; and when signing Canada's declaration of war.

These were the qualities that made his mind so exciting to his family and to our contemporaries. Our halting and jejune opinions were listened to with respect and given an answer which may have been critical but was never unkind. He never stressed differences in age, nor engendered that sense of defeat and frustration which a comprehensive and mature mind so often inflicts upon the young. If he talked to us of South Africa or the War Cabinet, of Haig or Henry James, one was given the impression that only the blindest accident of space had prevented one's own attendance. By treating even small children as quite grown up, by creating the tacit assumption that his hearer was deeply read and widely travelled, used to men and high policy, he made himself the most enchanting mentor of youth. Even this respect for another's mind was coupled with his perpetual delight in human method; his popularity among plain folk is not surprising to one whom he brought up.

Perhaps the generation who were educated before the First Great War will be the last for some time to achieve that vision of life as unity which seems denied to mine. If that is so, if the Greek ideal is dimmed by a world of scholiasts and specialists, it is something to have known one of the best of a great race whose mere letters, the remembered timbre of whose voice, fills the sails of the mind like a fresh wind from shore.

APPENDIX

JACK STUART-WORTLEY

By JOHN BUCHAN

JACK WORTLEY, when I first met him, reminded me of Basil Blackwood, though in most physical and mental traits they were far apart. He was the same natural adventurer, with a gift for finding himself in odd predicaments and a genius for getting out of them. Both were alike in their sangfroid, their dangerous sense of fun, and their appetite for the new and unexplored. But Basil was the eternal pilgrim whose wanderlust would not be sated till his death, while Jack had a trick of being homesick during all his travels, even when he was greatly enjoying himself and would not have returned if he could. Jack would certainly have settled down in England as a country gentleman, for he had a passion for the little things of home, and would have been as careful of his house, cellar, and gardens as if he had never been a tent-dweller. But for Basil age would not have loosed the bands of Orion.

I first met Jack in 1905, when he was home from the Sudan on leave, but I had heard of him for years before. His fantastic career was the fount of many tales in his family, and when I saw him I understood that they must all be true. He had a square head and a fine forehead, bright, mirthful, blue eyes, a Roman nose, and the rolling gait of a sailor. His upper teeth slightly projected under the eaves of his moustache and gave him a perpetual air of suppressed humour. Even when he was grave there was a hint of comedy waiting very near. Few boys can have ever had a more varied upbringing.

292

He was at Mr. Vaughan's house at Eton, but he was not an apt scholar, and his years there were chiefly remarkable for ingenious practical jokes, which are still a tradition in the school. At seventeen it became clear that he could not stay longer at Eton, and his parents wisely decided to give him the chance of learning discipline in a stiff profession. So at seventeen he was apprenticed to the Merchant Service.

He was a born sailor and for two years was uncommonly happy. He was trained in the old four-masted clippers, and in different vessels learned all there was to be known of the sailing ship, and visited most corners of the globe. He was a typical sailor-man, both in his love of things which were shipshaped and Bristol-fashion, and in his adaptability to strange conditions. Whenever he fell it was on his feet, and wherever he landed he made friends. There is a story that once he found himself penniless in Sydney, having spent all his money, with two weeks to put in before his ship sailed. He knew only two people— the Governor, who was a friend of his father, and a certain barman. The Governor was useless in such a case, so Jack became an assistant bar-tender, and spent a merry and profitable fortnight.

At the outbreak of the South African War he was in England, and, as he had to wait some time before the next stage of his training, he resolved to see a little fighting. He enlisted as a trooper in the Hertford-shire Yeomanry, and served with them till 1901, when he was given a commission in the Scottish Horse. Johannesburg in those days was like Piccadilly Circus; a man met everybody he had ever known if he waited long enough. For a little Jack was in the Criminal Investigation Department there; then he went on trek again, was wounded at Moedville, was twice mentioned in despatches, and was promoted captain in 1902. At that time he had attained the mature age of twenty-two, and was probably the youngest captain in the British Army. . . . I never heard a professional comedian half so funny as Jack could be when he chose. He was quick-tempered and as quick to forgive; eager for a row and any escapade of high spirits, and in every circumstance a purveyor of comedy. I remember one true tale of those Johannesburg days. At a dinner in the Club he said something disrespectful about the head of the Roman Church, and was promptly laid out with a champagne bottle by an irate Catholic Irishman. Next day he was visited in bed by his assailant, who came to apologise. "You must be a fool," said Jack. "If you love the Pope, why do you want to apologise? And if you don't love him, why did you lay me out?"

At the end of the war he was given a commission in the regular Army—in the Scottish Rifles. But he saw very clearly that home soldiering was not for him, so he applied at once to be seconded to the Northern Nigeria Regiment. In West Africa he was on the whole very happy, for his iron health made light of the climate, and he got all the shooting he wanted. He developed great skill as a transport officer, and early in 1903 was chosen to command the transport in the Anglo-French Boundary Commission—a responsible post for a young gentleman in his early twenties. It was an expedition after Jack's own heart, for the Commission made the first journey to Lake Chad since Barth in 1851. He had a remarkable power over natives (which he always attributed to the possession of bright blue eyes), and a genius for handling animals; and his sailor-like bonhomie endeared him to his French colleagues. He came home in the autumn of that year, and, still eager to extend his wanderings, got himself transferred to the 11th Sudanese Regiment and another quarter of Africa.

For the better part of nine years he served in the Nile valley, and did admirable work. My wife once happened to be with Lady Wimborne at Assuan when Jack was going up country, and was struck by the eagerness of every native he met to enter his service. He had the mingled firmness and humaneness which has made the British officer supreme in dealing with African races; and he needed all his powers, for in the wilds of the Upper Sudan he had much solitary responsibility. For long he was in charge of transport in the Bahr-el-Ghazal, and ultimately he became one of the Civil Commissioners. His duties took him everywhere from Khartum to the Lado Enclave and from Kordofan to the Abyssinian frontier. In 1910 he was engaged in a difficult punitive expedition, where insurgents had to be routed out of mountain caves, and received the Order of the Medjidieh for his work.

I saw much of him in those years when he was at home, and we corresponded with some regularity. I noticed that his old boyishness was departing, and that he was beginning to think hard about his future. As he once told his mother, with the shrewdness about himself which was one of his characteristics, he was far too apt to be absorbed in his immediate job and not to think of the next stage; but now the next stage was much in his thoughts. The truth is that he was homesick. He remembered England too clearly and he loved her too warmly to be happy at the prospect of an indefinite exile. When he was on leave he cast longing eyes on the English countryside, and his letters were full of a hankering after a greener land than the African bush. He was also too gregarious to be at ease in those vast solitudes. But he did his work with a cheerful stoicism and found many alleviations in his life. One was the chance of sport, for he had all his father's passion for shooting and something of his skill. Once he shot a giraffe in a forbidden area and was asked for his reasons in writing. Jack gave as his excuse that the beast looked lonely! It was not accepted and he had to pay the fine. He used to read widely in those days, chiefly solid works of history, and now and then he found good company.

In 1912 he came home, fell in love, had himself transferred to the Reserve of Officers, and was married in the autumn of that year. He was as proud as Lucifer, and was determined to make as great a success of his life in England as he had made of his work abroad. But it was no easy task for him to find the proper niche, for his experience and training were a little remote from home requirements. He tried various things without quite finding what he wanted, and his forehead was often corrugated and his eyes puzzled by the perplexities of civilisation. He had the makings of a good business man, for he had strong common sense and could toil like a beaver, and in time he must have found his feet. Yet for all his difficulties the two years before the war were happy, for he exulted in his new possessions, his wife, his children, and a household of his own; and it was pleasant to watch his gusto in entertaining his friends. He had still the sailor air and speech, and wherever he went a salt breeze seemed to attend him.

In the fateful August of 1914 he hurled himself—it is the only word—into the war. He hated the business, for he had outgrown his old love of vagabondage, and wanted nothing so much as a settled life. For soldiering in the ordinary sense he cared little, and he had never done any of the regular infantry training. But that his country should be at war and he should not be in the thick of it was unthinkable, and in the first days of August he presented himself at the War Office and demanded to be used at once.

It was some time before he was engaged in a major action. In the spring of 1916 he joined the South Staffordshires at home as second-in-command of their 2/5th Territorial battalion. He took it to France in November of that year, and presently was given command of the 2/6th battalion of the same regiment. Arras, in April 1917, was the first battle he fought in, and there he was slightly wounded. He was in action at Cambrai in the following November, where his battalion was all but destroyed at Bourlon Wood, 6 officers being left out of 20, and 140 men out of 600. It was a fine performance, in which he showed great gallantry and resolution, and he was congratulated by his divisional general and mentioned in despatches.

The more he saw of the war the less he liked it. He detested the mud and cold, for his years in the tropics had not prepared him for Picardy; he longed to be with his family again; he was too set in his ways and too independent to be happy under ordinary military regime. A man who has been much alone and has all his life had large freedom of action takes ill with the ritual of modern war. But when I saw him for the last time in February 1918 I thought I had never known anyone so unchanged by campaigning. He was enthusiastic about his men, and the deadening life of the trenches seemed in no way to have dulled his eye for the human comedy. I think, too, that he was happier about his future. He had learned competence in his new trade, as he had learned it in his old African jobs, and was on the eve of being given a brigade. He liked the idea of ending the war as a General, and returning to the country life he had dreamed of with a good record of service. Certainly there would have been few more varied records than his to carry forward to the days of peace—war in many fields, travel in every continent, administration of new lands, and such opportunities of sport as have now become only a tradition.

It was not to be. The much-enduring Ulysses was not to come to port in Ithaca. On the morning of 21st March 1918 his battalion was holding the forward zone at Bullecourt, and in the misty dawn it took the shock of the German onslaught. We know how at that dark hour of our fortunes the thin outpost troops stood their ground from Arras to the Oise, and by their sacrifice enabled our armies to fight that great battle against odds which in the long run broke the enemy's power. Jack was of the race that defends forlorn hopes, and his men under his command did not yield. They were overwhelmed, and some time about nine o'clock their leader fell. At first there was hope that he was a prisoner, for there were no witnesses of his death; but when the few survivors of his battalion returned from German captivity it became clear that he had fallen in the first hours of the action.

His end was what he would have sought. He had always a horror of being laid in a trim cemetery under a neat cross. On that grim March morning the guns of both sides made the place where he fell a tormented wilderness, and his body was never recovered. It was like a burial at sea. His grave was the whole earth, as the grave of a dead sailor is the infinite ocean.

INDEX

299